国际经济与贸易专业应用型人才"十二五"规划教材

国家级双语示范课程国际商务单证理论与实务研究成果

Training Tutorial of International

Business Documents (2nd Edition)

国际商务单证
实训教程（第2版）

杨静 主编

清华大学出版社

北京

图书在版编目(CIP)数据

国际商务单证实训教程 / 杨静 主编. —2 版. —北京：清华大学出版社，2015(2021.1重印)
(国际经济与贸易专业应用型人才"十二五"规划教材)
ISBN 978-7-302-40933-5

Ⅰ. ①国… Ⅱ. ①杨… Ⅲ. ①国际商务—票据—高等学校—教材 Ⅳ. ①F740.44

中国版本图书馆 CIP 数据核字(2015)第 166179 号

责任编辑：崔 伟 易银荣
封面设计：常雪影
版式设计：方加青
责任校对：曹 阳
责任印制：杨 艳

出版发行：清华大学出版社
　　　　　网　　　址：http://www.tup.com.cn，http://www.wqbook.com
　　　　　地　　　址：北京清华大学学研大厦 A 座　　　　邮　　编：100084
　　　　　社 总 机：010-62770175　　　　　　　　　　邮　　购：010-62786544
　　　　　投稿与读者服务：010-62776969，c-service@tup.tsinghua.edu.cn
　　　　　质 量 反 馈：010-62772015，zhiliang@tup.tsinghua.edu.cn
　　　　　课 件 下 载：http://www.tup.com.cn，010-62781730

印 装 者：北京富博印刷有限公司
经　　销：全国新华书店
开　　本：185mm×260mm　　　印　张：18.75　　　字　数：410千字
版　　次：2012 年 9 月第 1 版　　2015 年 9 月第 2 版　　印　次：2021 年 1 月第 5 次印刷
定　　价：48.00 元

产品编号：066141-02

编写委员会

主　编：杨　静

副 主 编：刘艳萍

编写成员：(按姓氏笔画)

　　　　刘　婷　苏　琳　鄂筱蔓

前　言

　　本书是为培养涉外经济部门所需的既能熟练掌握外贸专业知识，又能熟练运用专业英语从事进出口业务的复合型人才而专门编写的教材，所选用的外贸单证案例内容全面，具有典型性和普遍性，非常适合双语案例教学。本书可以与《国际商务单证理论与实务双语教程（第2版）》（杨静主编，清华大学出版社出版，ISBN：978-7-302-40927-4）配套使用，旨在帮助学习者在掌握专业知识的基础上熟练运用商务英语，并熟练掌握国际贸易相关条款、惯例和单证制作，从而更好地开展全球贸易。本书可用作高等院校经济管理类学生学习国际贸易实务的辅助教材，也可用作从事国际贸易工作的专业人士的自学参考书。

　　本书训练量和难度适中，全书共46个实训项目，包括交易单证、运输单证、出口单证、进口单证、银行单证和特殊单证的实际操作，其中12个实训项目设有实务思考。本书提供实训项目答案，教师可通过配套学习网站http://www.nclass.org/vc/99464161或http://www.nclass.org/cb/99464161获取。

　　本书的编写得到了广西财经学院外语学院刘艳萍教授和经贸学院鄂筱蔓、苏琳等多位老师以及经贸学院学生的帮助。美国外教Shawn Frazier教授为该书英文校对做了大量工作。另外，编写时参阅了多种国内外相关著作和刊物，在此对相关作者表示衷心感谢！

　　由于编者水平和学识有限，难免存在差错、疏漏，敬请读者不吝指正。

编者

2015年6月

目　　录

信用证的审核

一、操作练习

根据下面的合同审核信用证，撰写改证函。

销售合同

SALES CONTRACT

卖方：	编号：
SELLER：FUJIAN LIGHT ELECTRICAL APPLANCES CO.，LTD.	NO.： HG46821001
52 DEZHENG ROAD SOUTH，FUZHOU，CHINA	日期：
买方：	DATE： APR. 22，2015
BUYER：LONGING FLY CORP.	地点：
AKEDSANTERINK AUTO P. O. BOX 9，FINLAND	SIGNED IN：FUZHOU，CHINA

买卖双方同意以下条款达成交易：

This contract is made by and agreed between the BUYER and SELLER，in accordance with the terms and conditions stipulated below.

1. 商品号 Art No.	2. 品名及规格 Commodity & Specification	3. 数量 Quantity	4. 单价及价格条款 Unit Price & Trade Terms	5. 金额 Amount
				CIF HELSINKI
01	HALOGEN FITTING W 500	9 600 PCS	USD 3.80/PC	USD 36 480.00
	Total:	9 600 PCS		USD 36 480.00

允许＿＿＿＿＿溢短装，由卖方决定

With __10%__ More or less of shipment allowed at the sellers' option

6. 总值：

　　Total Value：US DOLLARS THIRTY-SIX THOUSAND FOUR HUNDRED AND EIGHTY ONLY.

7. 包装：

　　Packing：12PCS IN A CARTON

8. 唛头：

　　Shipping Marks：N/M

9. 装运期及运输方式：

　　Time of Shipment & Means of Transportation：WITHIN 30 DAYS AFTER RECEIPT OF L/C ALLOWING

　　　　　　　　　　　　TRANSSHIPMENT AND PARTIAL SHIPMENT.

10. 装运港及目的地：

　　Port of Loading & Destination：FROM FUZHOU，CHINA TO HELSINKI，FINLAND

11. 保险：

　　Insurance：TO BE EFFECTED BY SELLERS FOR 110% OF FULL INVOICE VALUE COVERING

　　　　　　FPA UP TO HELSINKI.

12. 付款方式：

　　Terms of Payment：BY 100% CONFIRMED IRREVOCABLE LETTER OF CREDIT IN FAVOR OF

（续表）

THE SELLERS TO BE AVAILABLE BY SIGHT DRAFT TO BE OPENED AND TO REACH CHINA BEFORE MAY 1, 2015 AND TO REMAIN VALID FOR NEGOTIATION IN CHINA UNTIL THE 15TH DAYS AFTER THE FORESAID TIME OF SHIPMENT. L/C MUST MENTION THIS CONTRACT NUMBER. L/C ADVISED BY BANK OF CHINA, FUZHOU BRANCH. TLX: 444U4K GZBC CN. ALL BANKING CHARGES OUTSIDE CHINA (THE MAINLAND OF CHINA) ARE FOR ACCOUNT OF THE DRAWEE.

13. 仲裁：

ARBITRATION: ALL DISPUTE ARISING FROM THE EXECUTION OF OR IN CONNECTION WITH THIS CONTRACT SHALL BE SETTLED AMICABLY BY NEGOTIATION. IN CASE OF SETTLEMENT CAN BE REACHED THROUGH NEGOTIATION. THE CASE SHALL THEN BE SUBMITTED CHINA INTERNAITONAL ECONOMIC & TRADE ARBITRATION COMMISSION. IN SHENZHEN (OR IN BEIJING) FOR ARBITRATION IN ACT WITH ITS SURE OF PROCEDURES. THE ARBITRAL AWARD IS FINAL AND BINDING UPON BOTH PARTIES FOR SETTING THE DISPUTES. THE FEE, FOR ARBITRATION SHALL BE BORNE BY THE LOSING PARTY UNLESS OTHERWISE AWARDED.

The Buyer
Y.BAKER

The Seller
张立

ISSUING BANK：METTA BANK LTD.，FINLAND

DOC. CREDIT NO.：REVOCABLE

CREDIT NUMBER：LR79802457

DATE OF ISSUE：150204

EXPIRY：DATE 20150116 PLACE FINLAND

APPLICANT：LONGING FLY CO.

　　　　　AKEDSANTERINK AUTO P. O. BOX 9，FINLAND

BENEFICIARY：FUZHOU LIGHT ELECTRICAL CO.，LTD.

　　　　　52 DEZHENG ROAD SOUTH，FUZHOU，CHINA

AMOUNT：USD 3 648.00 (SAY US DOLLARS THIRTY SIX THOUSAND FOUR HUNDRED AND EIGHT ONLY)

POS./ NEG.TOL.(%)：5/5

AVAILABLE WITH/BY：ANY BANK IN ADVISING COUNTRY BY NEGOTIATION

Draft AT …：DRAFTS AT 20 DAYS' SIGHT FOR

PARTIAL SHIPMENTS：NOT ALLOWED

TRANSSHIPMENT：ALLOWED

LOADING IN CHARGE：FUZHOU

FOR TRANSPORT TO：HELSINKI

SHIPMENT PERIOD：AT THE LATEST MAY 30，2015

DESCRIPT. OF GOODS：9 600 PCS OF HALOGEN FITTING W 500，USD 6.80 PER PC AS PER

SALES CONTRACT HGC46821001 DD APR. 22，2001CIF HESINKI

DOCUMENTS REQUIRED：

　　*COMMERCIAL INVOICE 1 SIGNED ORIGINAL AND 5 COPIES.

　　*PACKING LIST 1 SIGNED ORIGINAL AND 5 COPIES.

　　*FULL SET OF CLEAN ON BOARD MARINE BILLS OF LADING，MADE OUT TO ORDER，MARK "FREIGHT PREPAID" AND NOTIFY APPLICANT (AS INDICATED ABOVE).

　　*GSP CERTIFICATE OF ORIGIN FORM A，CERTIFYING GOODS OF ORIGIN IN CHINA，ISSUED BY COMPETENT AUTHORITIES.

　　*INSURANCE POLICY/CERTIFICATE COVERING ALL RISKS AND WAR RISKS OF PICC. INCLUDING WAREHOUSE TO WAREHOUSE CLAUSE UP TO FINAL DESTINATION AT HELSINIKI，FOR AT LEAST 120 PCT OF CIF-VALUE.

　　*SHIPPING ADVICES MUST BE SENT TO APPLICANT WIHTIN 2 DAYS AFTER SHIPMENT，ADVISING NUMBER OF PACKAGES，GROSS & NET WEIGHT，VESSEL NAME，B/L NO. AND DATE，CONTRACT NO.，VALUE.

PRESENTATION PERIOD: 3 DAYS AFTER ISSUANCE DATE OF SHIPPING DOCUMENT

CONFIRMATION：WITHOUT

INSTRUCTIONS：THE NEGOTIATION BANK MUST FORWARD THE DRAFTS AND ALL DOCUMENTS BY REGISTERED AIRMAIL DIRECT TO US IN TWO CONSECUTIVE LOTS，UPON RECEIPT OF THE DRAFTS AND DOCUMETNS IN ORDER，WE WILL REMIT THE PROCEEDS AS INSTRUCTED BY THE NEGOTIAIONG BANK.

FUZHOU LIGHT ELECTRICAL CO.，LTD.
52 DEZHENG ROAD SOUTH，FUZHOU，CHINA

DATE:

Dear sir：

We are pleasure to receive your L/C No.＿＿＿＿dated＿＿＿against S/C No.＿＿＿. However，we are sorry to find it contains some discrepancies. Please amend the credit as follows：

1. ＿＿＿＿＿＿＿＿＿＿＿＿＿＿＿

2. ＿＿＿＿＿＿＿＿＿＿＿＿＿＿＿

3. ＿＿＿＿＿＿＿＿＿＿＿＿＿＿＿

4. ＿＿＿＿＿＿＿＿＿＿＿＿＿＿＿

5.＿＿＿＿＿＿＿＿＿＿＿＿＿＿＿

Please see to it that the L/C amendment soon so that we may effect shipment within the contracted delivery time. Thanks for your kind cooperation.

Sincerely yours

二、实务思考

1. 某银行电开一份保兑不可撤销信用证，电文中并未声明"以邮寄文本为准"的字样。受益人按照电开信用证的文本已将货物装运，并备好符合信用证要求的单据向当地通知行议付时，当地通知行出示刚收到的开证行寄到的"邮寄文本"，并以电开文本或邮寄文本不符为由拒绝议付，后经议付行与开证行联系，开证行复电亦称"以邮寄文本为准"而拒绝付款。请问：在这种情况下，开证行有无拒付的权力？

2. 中行南宁分行收到加拿大某银行电开信用证一份，金额 200 万美元，购买 10 万吨白糖，目的港为温哥华。信用证有以下条款：①检验证书于货物装运前开立并有开证申请人授权的签字人签字，该签字必须由开证行检验；②货物只能待开证申请人指定船只并由开证行给通知行加押电修改后装运，而该加押电修改必须随同正本单据提交议付。请问：该信用证可否接受？

3. 我方某公司以 CIF 洛杉矶出口美国一批货物。5 月 20 日由洛杉矶开来一份即期不可撤销信用证，金额 50 000 美元，装船期 6 月，开证行为信誉较好的 A 银行。我方中行收到信用证后，于 5 月 22 日通知出口公司，5 月底出口公司获悉进口方因资金问题濒临倒闭。请问：在此情况下我方应如何处理？

实训项目2
签订出口合同

一、操作练习

根据下列资料缮制出口合同，要求格式清楚、条款明确、内容完整。

1. 国外客户资料：

NEO GENERAL TRADING CO.

P.O. BOX 99552，RIYADH 22766，KSA

TEL：00966-1-4659220

FAX：00966-1-4659213

2. 我方出口公司资料：

GUANGZHOU FOREIGN TRADE IMP. & EXP. CORP.

15-18/F.，GUANGDONG FOREIGN ECONOMIC AND TRADE BUILDING

351 TIANHE ROAD GUANGZHOU，CHINA

3. 我方通知行资料：

BANK OF CHINA GUANGZHOU BRANCH

HEAD OFFICE 148 ZHONGSHAN SOUTH ROAD GUANGZHOU

TELEX：34226/34327 BOCJS CN

4. 合同签订时间及地点：Feb. 28，2015 GUANGZHOU，CHINA

5. 我方对押汇银行的要求：可在中国任何银行押汇。

6. 编号要求：合同号从 NEO2001026 起编，发票号从 2001STD001 起编。

7. 装运港：中国广州。

8. 对付款方式的要求：买方应通过一家卖方可以接受的银行于装运月份前 30 天开立并送达卖方不可撤销即期信用证，有效至装运日后 15 天内在中国议付。

9. 交易磋商中客户的最后来函。

NEO GENERAL TRADING CO.

P. O. BOX 99552，RIYADH 22766，KSA　　TEL：00966-1-4659220　　FAX：00966-1-4659213

Feb. 27，2015

Dear Mr. Chang：

We have received your E-Mail of Feb.26，2015.

After the consideration，we have pleasure in confirming the following offer and accepting below：

1. Commodity: canned mushrooms pieces & stems

2. Specifications：24 tins per carton，425 grams net weight each tin，227 grams drain weight each tin

3. Package: exported brown carton，with ROSE brand.

4. Quantity：1 700 cartons，one 20'FT CONTAINER

5. Quality：2001 new Crop product

6. Price：USD7.80/CARTONCFR DAMMAM PORT ON FULL LINER TERMS

7. Payment：L/C AT SIGHT

8. Shipment：Not later than Apr. 30，2015

9. Shipping Marks：ROSE BRAND

178/2001

RIYADH

Please send us your SALES CONTRACT and PROFORMA INVOICE，and we hope both of us may have a wonderful beginning.

Best Regards，

NEO GENERAL TRADING CO.，

Tom Smith

销售合同 SALES CONTRACT			
卖方： SELLER:	编号： NO.:		
	日期： DATE:		
买方： BUYER:	地点： SIGNED IN:		
买卖双方同意以下条款达成交易： This contract is made by and agreed between the BUYER and SELLER，in accordance with the terms and conditions stipulated below.			

1. 品名及规格 Commodity & Specification	2. 数量 Quantity	3. 单价及价格条款 Unit Price & Trade Terms	4. 金额 Amount
Total：			

允许 With		溢短装，由卖方决定 More or less of shipment allowed at the sellers' option
5. 总值 Total Value		
6. 包装 Packing		
7. 唛头 Shipping Marks		
8. 装运期及运输方式 Time of Shipment & means of Transportation		
9. 装运港及目的地 Port of Loading & Destination		
10. 保险 Insurance		
11. 付款方式 Terms of Payment		
12. 备注 Remarks		
The Buyer (signature)		The Seller (signature)

二、计算题

1. 中国粮油进出口公司大连分公司对英出口罐头 10 000 箱，每箱的体积 49cm×32cm×19cm。目的港为英国南安普顿，经香港转船。第一程由中远公司运输，第二程装船后由国外班轮装运，计算从大连至目的港的总运费为多少人民币？（设 1HKD=0.824 8 CNY，已知：查《中运表》罐头为 M8 级。大连至香港基本运费为 22 元人民币，各种附加费 17%，中转费 HKD 40/M；又查《中租船》罐头为 M8 级，香港至南安普顿基本运费为 HKD 23.7，附加费为 13%）

2. 一批出口货 CFRC 2% 为 USD 20 000，现客户来电要求按 CIF 价加 10% 投保海运一切险，设保险费率为 0.9%，我方若同意照办，应向客户补收多少保险费？并求这批货的保险金额。

3. 我出口公司对非洲某客商发盘，供应某商品，价格条件为 CIF 非洲某口岸每吨 USD 1 500；按发票金额 110% 投保一切险和战争险，对方要求改报 FOB 中国口岸。经查中国口岸至非洲某口岸的海洋运输费用为每吨 USD 50，一切险的保险费率为 0.5%，战争险的保险费率为 0.3%。问如维持出口净收入不变，改报 FOB 中国口岸价，应为多少美元？

4. 某进出口公司从美国进口美容器械 2 台，每台 USD 3 000 FOB 纽约，海运运费 USD 2 500，保险费率为 5%，进口关税率 33%，增值税应缴 17%，消费税率 17%。求关税、消费税和增值税各为多少？（若外汇牌价 1 USD=6.395 CNY）

5. 我某进出口公司出口某货物，成交价格 CIF 纽约 1 USD=6.395 CNY，已知运费 ≈RMB 1 500，保费 RMB 50，出口税率 15%。求应征关税税额为多少？

6. 我公司出口商品 200 件，每件毛重 95 KGS，体积 100cm×40cm×25cm，查轮船公司运费表，该商品计费标准为 W/M，等级为 8 级，每运费吨 USD 80，另收港口附加费 10%，直航附加费 15%。问：该批货物共计运费多少？我公司原报 FOB 上海每件 USD 400，客户要求改报 CFR，我公司应报价多少？

7. 某票货物从张家港出口到欧洲费利克斯托，经上海转船。2×20'FCL，上海到费利克斯托的费率 USD 1 850.00/20'，张家港经上海转船，其费率在上海直达费利克斯托的费率基础上加 USD 100.00/20'，另由货币贬值附加费 10%，燃油附加费 5%。问托运人应支付多少运费？

8. 假设某公司出口电缆 1 000 箱，装入一个 20 英尺的集装箱。每箱体积 40cm×20cm×30m，每箱重 17.5 KGS。查货物分级表得知该货属于 10 级货，按 "W/M" 计收运费；海运费的基本费率 USD 1 000/TEU；查附加费率表，得知需收取查燃油附加费 30%。试计算运费。

9. 某进出口公司从美国进口硫酸镁 5 000 吨，进口申报价 FOB 旧金山 USD 32 500，海运运费每吨 USD 10，保险费率 3%，其适用的基准汇率 USD 100=CNY 639.5。经查，硫酸镁的最惠国关税税率 5.5%。请计算应纳关税税额。

10. 某贸易公司于 2015.5.13(周三) 申报进口一批货物，海关于当日开出税款缴款书，其中关税税款 RMB 24 000，增值税税款 RMB 35 100，消费税税款 RMB 8 900，该公司实际缴纳税款日期 6 月 9 日 (周二)。该公司应纳的滞纳金是多少？

三、实务思考

中方某外贸公司派遣贸易小组赴美购买设备，双方在纽约就设备规格、单价、数量等主要条款达成口头协议。小组离美时向对方表示，回京后缮制合同，双方签字后生效。回京后，用户撤回进口委托，合同无法签署，信用证也未开出。美方敦促中方履约，否则将在美起诉中方公司。试分析中方公司如何处理此案。

实训项目3
缮制形式发票

操作练习

根据下列资料制作形式发票，要求格式清楚、条款明确、内容完整。

1. 国外客户资料：

NEO GENERAL TRADING CO.

P.O. BOX 99552，RIYADH 22766，KSA

TEL：00966-1-4659220

FAX：00966-1-4659213

2. 我方出口公司资料：

GUANGDONG FOREIGN TRADE IMP. & EXP. CORP.

15-18/F.，GUANGDONG FOREIGN ECONOMIC AND TRADE BUILDING

351 TIANHE ROAD GUANGZHOU，CHINA

3. 我方通知行资料：

BANK OF CHINA GUANGZHOU BRANCH

HEAD OFFICE 148 ZHONGSHAN SOUTH ROAD GUANGZHOU

TELEX：34226/34327 BOCJS CN

4. 合同签订时间及地点：Feb. 28，2015 GUANGZHOU，CHINA

5. 我方对押汇银行的要求：可在中国任何银行押汇。

6. 编号要求：合同号从 NEO2001026 起编；发票号从 2001STD001 起编。

7. 装运港：中国广州。

8. 对付款方式的要求：买方应通过一家卖方可以接受的银行于装运月份前30天开立并送达卖方不可撤销即期信用证，有效至装运日后15天内在中国议付。

9. 交易磋商中客户的最后来函。

NEO GENERAL TRADING CO.

P. O. BOX 99552，RIYADH 22766，KSA TEL：00966-1-4659220 FAX：00966-1-4659213

E-MAIL：neo@neogeneral.com

Feb. 27，2015

Dear Mr. Chang：

We have received your E-Mail of Feb. 26，2015.

After the consideration，we have pleasure in confirming the following offer and accepting below：

1. Commodity：canned mushrooms pieces & stems
2. Specifications：24 tins per carton，425 grams net weight each tin，227 grams drain weight each tin
3. Package：exported brown carton，with ROSE brand.
4. Quantity：1 700 cartons，one 20'FT CONTAINER
5. Quality：2001 new Crop product
6. Price：USD 7.80/CARTON CFR DAMMAM PORT ON FULL LINER TERMS
7. Payment：L/C AT SIGHT
8. Shipment：Not later than Apr. 30，2015
9. Shipping Marks：ROSE BRAND

                178/2001

                RIYADH

Please send us your SALES CONTRACT and PROFORMA INVOICE，and we hope both of us may have a wonderful beginning.

Best Regards，

NEO GENERAL TRADING CO.，

Tom Smith

PROFORMA INVOICE

TO:

TERM OF PAYMENT:

PORT OF LOADING:

PORT OF DESTINATION:

TIME OF DELIVERY:

INSURANCE:

VALIDITY:

Marks and Numbers	Number and Kind of Package Description of Goods	Quantity	Unit Price	Amount
	Total Amount:			

SAY TOTAL:

BENEFICIARY:

ADVISING BANK:

NEGOTIATING BANK:

实训项目4

缮制销售确认书

操作练习

请根据下列资料填写 Sales Confirmation，要求格式清楚、条款明确、内容完整。

1. 买方：

NICHIEN CORPORATION

2-2 NAKANOSHIMA 3-CHOME，KITA-KU OSAKA，632-8620，JAPAN

2. 卖方：

SHANDONG TEXTILES IMPORT & EXPORT CORP.

4 YING CHUN STREET，QINGDAO，CHINA

3. 合同签订时间：2015 年 1 月 20 日。

4. 合同签订地点：中国青岛。

5. 合同份数：一式三份。

6. 唛头：无。

7. 信用证有效期：信用证在装运日期后 21 天内在中国议付有效。

8. 卖方提交单据：整套正本清洁提单、商业发票一式三份、装箱单一式三份。

9. 注意：转运、付款条件等选项，须以"☒"标注。

10. 函电。

SHANDONG TEXTILES IMPORT & EXPORT CORP.
4 YING CHUN STREET，QINGDAO，CHINA

20-Jan-2015

Dear sirs：

Thanks for your Acceptance of Jan 18th. And hereby we are pleased to send you our sales confirmation No.03DRA207 for your signing，please.

| Portable Mixer Pm-23 | $ 23 FOB Dalian/Set | 100Sets | $ 2 300.00 |
| Vacuum cleaner Vc-18 | $ 47 FOB Dalian/Set | 100Sets | $ 4 700.00 |

Terms：As usual

Packing：to be effected by the sellers.

Transshipment：not allowed

Partial shipments：not allowed

We hope that the goods will be shipped by June 30th. And we ensure L/C will reach you not later than April 30.

Yours Faithfully

SALES CONFIRMATION

卖方:
Seller:

买方:
Buyer:

合同号码:
NO.:

日期:
DATE:

地点:
SIGNED IN :

经买卖双方同意成交下列商品，订立条款如下：

This contract is made by and agreed between the BUYER and SELLER，in accordance with the terms and conditions stipulated below.

唛头 Marks and Numbers	名称及规格 Description of goods	数量 Quantity	单价 Unit Price	金额 Amount
	总值 TOTAL:			

Transshipment（转运）:

☐ Allowed（允许） ☐ Not allowed（不允许）

Partial shipments（分批装运）:

☐ Allowed（允许） ☐ Not allowed（不允许）

Shipment date（装运期）:

Insurance（保险）:

由____按发票金额110%投保____险，另加保____险至____为止。

To be covered by the____FOR 110% of the invoice value covering____additional____from____ to____.

Terms of payment（付款条件）:

☐买方不迟于____年____月____日前将100%的货款用即期汇票/电汇送抵卖方。

The buyers shall pay 100% of the sales proceeds through sight(demand) draft/by T/T remittance to the sellers not later than____.

☐买方须于____年____月____日前通过____银行开出以卖方为受益人的不可撤销____天期信用证，并注明在上述装运日期后____天内在中国议付有效，信用证须注明合同编号。

The buyers shall issue an irrevocable L/C at____sight through____in favor of the sellers prior to____indicating L/C shall be valid in China through negotiation within____day after the shipment effected，the L/C must mention the Contract Number.

☐付款交单：买方应对卖方开具的以买方为付款人的见票后____天付款跟单汇票付款，付款时交单。

Documents against payment(D/P): The buyers shall duly make the payment against documentary draft made out to the buyers at____sight by the sellers.

☐承兑交单：买方应对卖方开具的以买方为付款人的见票后____天承兑跟单汇票承兑，承兑时交单。

Documents against acceptance (D/A)：The buyers shall duly accept the documentary draft made out to the buyers at____days by the sellers.

Documents required（单据）：

卖方应将下列单据提交银行议付／托收。

The sellers shall present the following documents required for negotiation/collection to the banks.

□整套正本清洁提单。

　　Full set of clean on Board Ocean Bills of Lading.

□商业发票一式____份。

　　Signed commercial invoice in____copies.

□装箱单或重量单一式____份。

　　Packing list/weight memo in____copies.

□由____签发的质量与数量证明书一式____份。

　　Certificate of quantity and quality in____copies issued by____.

□保险单一式____份。

　　Insurance policy in____copies.

□由____签发的产地证一式____份。

　　Certificate of Origin in____copies issued by____.

Shipping advice（装运通知）：

一旦装运完毕，卖方应立即电告买方合同号、商品号、已装载数量、发票总金额、毛重、运输工具名称及启运日期等。

The sellers shall immediately，upon the completion of the loading of the goods，advise the buyers of the Contract No.，names of commodity，loaded quantity，invoice values，gross weight，names of vessel and shipment date by TLX/FAX.

Inspection and Claims（检验与索赔）：

1. 卖方在发货前由_____检验机构对货物的品质、规格和数量进行检验，并出具检验证明书。

　　The buyers shall have the qualities，specifications，quantities of the goods carefully inspected by the____Inspection Authority，which shall issue Inspection Certificate before shipment.

2. 货物到达目的口岸后，买方可委托当地的商品检验机构对货物进行复检。如果发现货物有损坏、残缺或规格、数量与合同规定不符，买方须于货到目的口岸的____天内凭____检验机构出具的检验证明书向卖方索赔。

　　The buyers have right to have the goods inspected by the local commodity inspection authority after the arrival of the goods at the port of destination if the goods are found damaged/short/their specifications and quantities not in compliance with that specified in the contract，the buyers shall lodge claims against the sellers based on the Inspection Certificate issued by the Commodity____Inspection Authority within____days after the goods arrival at the destination.

3. 如买方提出索赔，凡属品质异议须于货到目的口岸之日起____天内提出；凡属数量异议须于货到目的口岸之日起____天内提出。对货物所提任何异议应由保险公司、运输公司或邮递机构负责的，卖方不负任何责任。

　　The claims，if any regarding to the quality of the goods，shall be lodged within____days after arrival of the goods at the destination，if any regarding to the quantities of the goods，shall be lodged within____days after arrival of the goods at the destination. The sellers shall not take any responsibility if any claims concerning the shipping goods is up to the responsibility of Insurance Company/Transportation Company/Post Office.

Force Majeure（人力不可抗拒）：

如因人力不可抗拒的原因造成本合同全部或部分不能履约，卖方概不负责但卖方应将上述发生的情况及时通知买方。

The sellers shall not hold any responsibility for partial or total non-performance of this contract due to Force Majeure. But the sellers advise the buyers on time of such occurrence.

（续表）

Disputes settlement（争议之解决方式）:

凡因执行本合约或有关本合约所发生的一切争执，双方应协商解决。如果协商不能得到解决，应提交仲裁。仲裁地点在被告方所在国内，或者在双方同意的第三国。仲裁裁决是终局的，对双方都有约束力，仲裁费用由败诉方承担。

All disputes in connection with this contract of the execution thereof shall be amicably settled through negotiation. In case no amicable settlement can be reached between the two parties，the case under dispute shall be submitted to arbitration，which shall be held in the country where the defendant resides，or in third country agreed by both parties. The decision of the arbitration shall be accepted as final and binding upon both parties. The Arbitration Fees shall be borne by the losing party.

Law application（法律适用）:

本合同之签订地或发生争议时货物所在地，在中华人民共和国境内或被诉人为中国法人的，适用中华人民共和国法律，除此规定外，适用《联合国国际货物销售公约》。

It will be governed by the law of the People's Republic of China under the circumstances that the contract is signed or the goods while the disputes arising are in the People's Republic of China or the defendant is Chinese legal person，otherwise it is governed by Untied Nations Convention on Contract for the International Sale of Goods.

本合同使用的价格术语系根据国际商会《INCOTERMS 2010》。

The terms in the contract based on INCOTERMS 2010 of the International Chamber of Commerce.

Versions（文字）:

本合同中、英两种文字具有同等法律效力，在文字解释上，若有异议，以中文解释为准。

This contract is made out in both Chinese and English of which version is equally effective. Conflicts between these two languages arising there from，if any，shall be subject to Chinese version.

本合同共____份，自双方代表签字（盖章）之日起生效。

This contract is in____copies，effective since being singed/sealed by both parties.

　　　　　　　　　　　　　The Buyer　　　　　　　　The Seller

实训项目5

签订进口合同

一、操作练习

根据下列资料制作进口合同，要求格式清楚、条款明确、内容完整。

1. 国外客户资料：

ARELLA AND CO. SPA

PLAZZA COLLEGIO CAIROLIN. 3 27100 PAVIA，ITALY

2. 我方进口公司资料：

SHENZHEN OCDA FOOD CO.，LTD.

7/F，OCDA BLDG，KEYUAN RD.，SHENZHEN，CHINA

TEL：86-755-2626268　FAX：86-755-2626269

3. 合同号：OA010602

4. 签订日期：JUNE 2，2015

5. 签订地点：SHENZHEN

6. 交易磋商中 ARELLA AND CO. SPA 的最后来函。

PLAZZA COLLEGIO CAIROLIN. 327100 PAVIA，ITALY

MAY. 25，2015

Dear Mr. Chang,

We have received your E-Mail of MAY. 24，2015.

After the consideration，we have pleasure in confirming the following offer and accepting it:

1. Commodity：CANNED MUSHROOMS

2. Packing：CARTON

3. Specification：24 TINS×425 GRAMS

4. Quantity：1 700 CARTONS/FCL

5. Price：USD 7.80/CTN CFR C 2% DAMMAM PORT.

6. 5% more or less in quantity and value allowed.

7. Payment: The buyers shall issue an irrevocable L/C at 90 days sight through BANK in favour of the sellers prior to JUNE 6，2015 indicating L/C shall be valid in PAVIA，ITALY through negotiation within 10 days after the shipment effected，the L/C must mention the Contract Number.

8. Shipment Time：WITHIN 20 DAYS AFTER RECEIPT OF IRREVOCABLE SIGHT L/C.Transhipment not allowed，Partial shipment not allowed. Shipment from PAVIA，ITALY to SHENZHEN，CHINA.

9. Insurance：to be covered by the seller for 110 % of the invoice value covering Institute Cargo Clauses(A) 1/1/82 additional Institute War and Strikes Clauses-Cargo 1/1/82 from PAVIA，ITALY to SHENZHEN .

Please send us a contract and thank you for your cooperation.

Yours sincerely,

ARELLA AND CO. SPA

Tom Smith

购 货 合 同
PURCHASE CONTRACT

合同编号： Contract No.:	签订日期： Date:	签订地点： Signed at:

1. 买方：
   The Buyers:
   地址：
   Address:

电话： Tel:	传真： Fax:

2. 卖方：
   The Sellers:
   地址：
   Address:

电话： Tel:	传真： Fax:

经买卖双方确认根据下列条款订立本合同：

The undersigned Sellers and Buyers have confirmed this contract in accordance with the terms and conditions stipulated below:

3. 商品名称及规格 Name of Commodity & Specification	4. 数量 Quantity	5. 单价 Unit Price	6. 总金额 Amount

7. 总值（大写）：
   Total Value (in words):

8. 允许溢短_____%。
   ____% more or less in quantity and value allowed.

9. 成交价格术语：
   Terms of Price:
   □ FOB   □ CFR   □ CIF   □ DDU

10. 包装：
    Packing:

11. 运输唛头：
    Shipping Mark:

12. 运输起讫：由_____（装运港）到_____（目的港）。
    Shipment from_____(Port of Shipment) to _____(Port of Destination).

13. 转运：□允许　□不允许；　　　　　分批：□允许　□不允许
    Transshipment: □ allowed　□ not allowed　Partial shipment: □ allowed　□ not allowed

14. 运输时间：
    Shipment Time：WITHIN 20DAYS AFTER RECEIPT OF IRREVOCABLE SIGHT L/C.

15. 保险：由_____方按发票金额的_____% 投保_____，加保_____从_____到_____。
    Insurance：to be covered by the_____for_____% of the invoice value covering_____ additional
    from _____.

16. 付款条件:

Terms of Payment:

□买方应不迟于＿＿＿＿＿年＿＿＿＿＿月＿＿＿＿＿日前将100%货款用即期汇票／电汇支付给卖方。

The buyers shall pay 100% of the sales proceeds through sight (demand) draft/by T/T remittance to the sellers not later than＿＿＿＿＿/＿＿＿＿＿.

□买方应于＿＿＿＿＿年＿＿＿＿＿月＿＿＿＿＿日前通过＿＿＿＿＿＿＿＿＿＿＿银行开立以卖方为受益人的＿＿＿＿＿天不可撤销信用证，有效期至装运后＿＿＿＿＿天在中国议付，并注明合同号。

The buyers shall issue an irrevocable L/C at ＿＿＿＿＿sight through＿＿＿＿＿in favour of the sellers prior to ＿＿＿＿＿indicating L/C shall be valid in＿＿＿＿＿though negotiation within＿＿＿＿＿days after the shipment effected，the L/C must mention the Contract Number.

□付款交单：买方应凭卖方开立给买方的＿＿＿＿＿期跟单汇票付款，付款时交单。

Documents against payment (D/P): the buyers shall dully make the payment against documentary draft made out to the buyers at＿＿＿＿＿ / ＿＿＿＿＿sight by the sellers.

□承兑交单：买方应凭卖方开立给买方的＿＿＿＿＿期跟单汇票付款，承兑时交单。

Documents against acceptance (D/A): the buyers shall dully accept the documentary draft made out to the buyers at＿＿＿＿＿ /＿＿＿＿＿days by the sellers.

17. 装运通知：一旦装运完毕，卖方应立即电告买方合同号、品名、已装载数量、发票总金额、毛重、运输工具名称及启运日期等。

Shipping advice: the sellers shall immediately，upon the completion of the loading of the goods advise the buyers of the Contract No.，names of commodity，loaded quantity，invoice value，gross weight，names of vessel and shipment date by TLX/FAX.

18. 检验与索赔:

Inspection and Claims:

□卖方在发货前由＿＿＿＿＿检验机构对货物的品质、规格和数量进行检验，并出具检验证明。

The buyer shall have the qualities，specifications，quantities of the goods carefully inspected by the ＿＿＿＿＿ /＿＿＿＿＿ Inspection Authority，which shall issues Inspection Certificate before shipment.

□货物到达目的口岸后，买方可委托当地的商品检验机构对货物进行复验。如果发现货物有损坏、残缺或规格、数量与合同规定不符，买方须于货物到达目的口岸的＿＿＿＿＿天内凭＿＿＿＿＿检验机构出具的检验证明书向卖方索赔。

The buyers have right to have the goods inspected by the local commodity inspection authority after the arrival of the goods at the port of destination. If the goods are found damaged/short/their specifications and quantities not in compliance with that specified in the contract，the buyers shall lodge claims against the sellers based on the Inspection Certification issued by the Commodity Inspection Authority within＿＿＿＿＿/＿＿＿＿＿ days after the goods arrival at the destination.

□ 如买方提出索赔，凡属品质异议须于货物到达目的口岸之日起＿＿＿＿＿天内提出；凡属数量异议须于货物到达目的口岸之日起＿＿＿＿＿天内提出。对所装货物所提任何异议应由保险公司、运输公司或邮递机构负责的，卖方不负任何责任。

The claims，if any regarding to the quality of the goods，shall be lodged within＿＿＿＿＿days after arrival of the goods at the destination，if any regarding to the quantities of the goods，shall be lodged within＿＿＿＿＿days after arrival of the goods at the destination. The sellers shall not take any responsibility if any claims concerning the shipping goods up to the responsibility of Insurance Company/Transportation Company/Post office.

19. 不可抗力：如因人力不可抗拒的原因造成本合同全部或部分不能履约，卖方概不负责，但卖方应将上述发生的情况及时通知买方。

Force Majeure: the sellers shall not hold any responsibility for partial or total non-performance of this contract due to Force Majeure. But the sellers shall advise the buyers on time of such occurrence.

（续表）

20. 争议的解决方式：任何因本合同而发生或与本合同有关的争议，应提交中国国际经济贸易仲裁委员会，按该会的规则进行仲裁。仲裁裁决是终局的，对双方均有约束力。

Disputes settlement: All disputes arising out of the contract or in connection with the contract, shall be submitted to the China International Economic and Trade Arbitration Commission for arbitration in accordance with its Rules of Arbitration. The arbitral award is final and binding upon both parties.

21. 法律适用：本合同的签订地、或发生争议时货物所在地在中华人民共和国境内或被诉人为中国法人的，适用于中华人民共和国法律，除此规定外，适用《联合国国际货物销售合同公约》。本合同使用的 FOB、CFR、CIF、DDU 术语系根据国际商会《INCOTERMS 2010》。

Law applications：it will be governed by the law of the People's Republic of China under the circumstances that the contract is signed or the goods while the disputes arising are in the People's Republic of China or the defendant is Chinese legal person，otherwise it is governed by United Nations Convention on Contract for the International Sale of Goods. The terms in the contract based on INCOTERMS 2010 of the International Chamber of Commerce.

22. 文字：本合同中、英文两种文字具有同等法律效力，在文字解释上，若有异议，以中文解释为准。

Versions: This contract is made out in both Chinese and English of which version is equally effective. Conflicts between these two languages arising therefrom，if any，shall be subject to Chinese version.

23. 附加条款：本合同上述条款与本附加条款有抵触时，以本附加条款为准。

Additional Clauses: conflicts between contract clause hereabove and this additional clause，if any，it is subject to this additional clause.

24. 本合同共_____份，自双方代表签字／盖章之日起生效。

This contract is in_____copies，effective since being signed/sealed by both parties.

买方代表人：	卖方代表人：
Representative of the buyers:	Representative of the sellers:
签字：	签字：
Authorized signature:	Authorized signature:
（买方公司盖章）	（卖方公司盖章）

二、实务思考

中国 A 公司与美国 B 公司签订进口 1 000 吨小麦合同。事后 A 公司与中国其他两家公司分别签订转售 500 吨小麦合同。合同履行期内，B 公司因故明确众承无法履行合同。A 公司多次交涉未果，遂向 B 公司提出如下赔偿要求：① B 公司无法履行合同造成的利润损失；②支付给国内两家公司的违约金；③催促 B 公司履行合同等文电、办公费用；④其他国 B 公司违反合同造成的损失。请问：A 公司的要求是否合理？为什么？

实训项目6

签订买卖合同(产品采购合同)

操作练习

根据下列条件签订采购合同，要求格式清楚、条款明确、内容完整。

1. 广州天丽国际贸易公司与 STORY SHARP CO.，LTD. 是长期工作关系，2015 年 9 月 15 日，STORY SHARP CO.，LTD. 在确认了天丽公司寄出的货品初样后直接向天丽公司下了订货单。2015 年 9 月 20 日天丽公司立即根据客户订单及生产制造单与广东源达工贸有限公司签订了采购合同。

2. 需方：广州天丽国际贸易公司 (广州中山南路 324 号 3 楼)。

3. 供方：广东源达工贸有限公司 (广州市中山路 112 号)。

4. 合同号：2005/LT098

5. 货号品名：IDW—504 女牛仔夹克。

6. 单价：￥62.00。

7. 结算方式：出货后 45 个工作日付款。

8. 合同号：JHW 2005/02。

（一）

采 购 合 同

合同编号：

需方：

日期：

供方：

下列签字双方同意按以下条款达成交易

颜色		尺寸	等级		唛头
寸密		花样	重量		
纱支		缝边	件数		
交货日期		结算方式			
备注	(1) 详细要求参见 SILU 订货单，工艺制造单。 (2) SILU 订货单、工艺制造单为本合同附件，与本合同具有同等的法律效力。 (3) 本公司委托 SILU 公司验货，并凭合格检验报告出运和付款。				

海关编码	品名及规格	数量	含税单价	含税金额
			总金额	

一、运输方式和交货地点：按客户指定上海仓库。

二、本合同规定之花样颜色搭配出口商标、包装、印刷等项，如因国外临时特殊需要可以书面修正。

三、供方经济责任：

(1) 应按合同规定，按时、按质、按量生产及发货，否则需方因此所受的经济损失，由供方负责。

(2) 如发生未按合同规定数量交货的情况，除按规定赔偿需方的经济损失外，对未交的货物是否需要补交、何时补交，均按需方要求办理。

(3) 不符合合同规定的产品，在需方代保管期内支付需方实际支付的仓储费。

(4) 供方所供产品必须为供方自产产品，如供方所开具的增值税发票所涉及的商品是属非自产产品，因而造成需方不能出口退税或已退税款被追回、处罚等，一切经济损失由供方承担。

(5) 其他。

四、需方经济责任：

(1) 变更产品品种、规格给供方造成损失的，应偿付供方实际损失，但以直接损失为限。

(2) 未按合同规定时间和要求提供有关资料，包装物等，交货日期应该推迟。

(3) 货到需方指定目的地，由于装运延期而造成的损失，由供方负责。

(4) 其他。

五、工厂在交货时必须提供厂检合格证。

六、未经需方同意，供方不得使用、生产、销售合同规定数量之外的属于需方的商标、花形和款式，否则需承担一切经济责任。

七、供需双方由于人力不可抗拒和企业本身造成的原因而不能履行合同时，由双方协商或由上级机构认定，可免予承担经济责任。

八、供需双方因履行本合同发生纠纷时，应尽力协商解决，协商不成，任何一方均可向需方所在地法院起诉。

九、出运数量不得超出合同数量的±5%。

（二）

STORY SHARP CO.，LTD.
生产制造单

工厂			单位					
款号	IDW-504		品名	女牛仔夹克				
订单号	SL5058		数量	1 400				
图示		尺寸部位	30	32	34	36	38	40	42
		后领高	8.5	8.5	8.5	8.5	8.5	8.5	8.5
		后领宽	16.2	16.6	17	17.6	18.2	18.8	19.4
面料：97%COTTON，3% LYCRA 同原样加弹力。		后背宽	34.5	35.5	36.5	37.7	38.9	40.3	41.7
		前胸宽	33	34	35	36.2	37.4	38.8	40.2
洗水：同原样。		胸围	44.5	46.5	48.5	51	53.5	56.5	59.5
缝线：粗细，颜色，风格同原样。		腰围	37.5	39.5	41.5	44	46.5	49.5	52.5
洗标号码：3506096 56995 w05		下摆	42.5	44.5	46.5	49	51.5	54.5	57.5
套结位置：袖叉×2，前侧袋口×4。		小肩	11.9	20.2	21	21.8	22.6	23.4	24.2
		袖长	61.2	61.6	62	62.6	63.2	63.8	64.4
钮门：有尾圆头凤眼。		袖笼	19.4	20.2	21.	21.8	22.6	23.4	24.2
吊牌：吊牌，弹力吊牌用7.5cm长胶钉打在左袖克夫上中缝中。注意洗水标要用胶纸包，防止印字掉色。警告贴纸贴在左前口袋。		袖肥	17.4	18.2	19	19.8	20.6	21.4	22.2
		袖口	10.5	10.5	11	11.5	11.5	12	12
		前长	54	55	56	57	58	59	60
		中后长	54	55	56	57	58	59	60

	缝制指示：平车车前侧袋，袋口车1.2cm双线。袋贴布边车边线。平车车前侧缝，拷边后面车1.2cm双线在前中片上。平车车前盲克，拷边后面车1.2cm双线。平车做装前幅贴袋，袋口还口车1.8cm线一道。袋中车花型线，袋袋面车1.2cm双线。平车车后中，后侧缝，拷边后面车1.2cm双线在后肩克及肩缝，拷边后面车1.2cm双线在袖大片商，袖侧缝袖口位开叉，叉边车1.2cm双线在衫身上，五线拷边车袖底，侧缝，内缝倒向后。平车车前门襟贴，面车3.3双线，平车做装下摆，装位处车1.2cm双线，其他三边车0.15cm边，平车做装领，领外口车1.2cm双线。装领领位车0.15cm边线。后领中吊装原身挂耳，主标吊车于后中领下，原身布挂耳中间。尺寸标吊车与主标左旁领下，原身布挂耳外边，洗水表车在左侧骨脚上12cm(穿起计)。

辅料表	主唛：（刷两面） STYTLE: DW-353 QTY: SIZE: COLOR: ORDER: PALE BLUE	侧唛：（刷两面） MEAS: G.W.：22 KGS N.W.：21 KGS						
主标	红底织黑字对折	1枚/件						
尺寸标	红底织黑字编号 TRU 2013	1枚/件						
吊牌	打印：IDW	1枚/件						
胶袋正面印尺码	反面印警告语	1件/袋						
拷贝纸	白色防潮纸	1张/件	30	32	34	36	38	40	42
防水袋	空白无内容	1个/箱	126	255	322	238	154	112	196
纸箱	出口三瓦楞	1件/箱	1 400						

包装指示：一件一胶袋，修袖对折，内落拷贝纸。独色独码装，数量自定。胶袋反面印警告语，正面右上角印尺寸，胶袋上放两个气眼，每箱内有一个大防水袋，用出口三瓦楞纸箱，箱内上下放划板，透明封箱带工字形封口。

（三）

STORY SHARP CO., LTD.
订货单

ORDER NO：SL5058　　　　STYLE NO：IDW-504　　　　2015 年 9 月 5 日

公司			品名	CARAMEL CLIPPED CORDUROY JKT	商标	IDE	重要说明
出运日期	2015 年 12 月 5 日		尺寸 / 数量	TAN 同初样	30；32；34；36；38；40；42		1. 工厂大货生产之前，必须得到 SILU 公司对产品书面确认及生产通知，方可大货生产。
交货地点	约堡				126；252；322；238；154；112；196		2. 供应商如违约或由于产品质量问题而使需方不能按时、按质、按量收到货物的，供应商应向需方支付违约金，以该批货物货款每天 2% 来计算。
包装要求	独色独码一胶带；独色独码一纸箱 (数量自定)；客户同意订单号的尾箱允许同色混码；胶带上要有尺寸和气孔；三瓦楞出口纸箱，四面封口，"井"字形打包带。				1 400		3. 请熟读"两单""两要求"。
面料要求	同初样		外箱唛头	主唛：(刷两面) 侧唛：(刷两面) STYTLE：IDW-353 MEAS： QTY： ORDER：27319 SIZE： G.W.： COLOR： N.W.：			4. 工厂未得 SILU 公司许可不得外发订单。 5. 工厂在生产过程中如发现或发生问题必须及时通知我司有关人员，以便双方及时沟通和解决。 6. 注意尺寸表上的允许公差范围。
要求	1. 洗标号码：673211456998W06 2. 尺寸要通过的 DATA SHEET 3. 收到正本订单一个月后寄出正确的面料、水洗、辅料、尺寸产前样 4. SHOWING DATE：收到订单一个月 5. 生产国、RN 号码						
	出货后		特别注意				
	请 10 天内 DHL 本司 1. 提单正本 2. 发票 3. 装箱单 4. 质检书		请工厂在包装的同时，必须确保外包装质量。纸箱的大小和质量由 SILU 公司确认方可出运，装箱清单与实际出货装箱情况必须一致，并提前将包装明细及体积数量通知我司，如发生未经我司允许的随意混箱、溢短装等类似情况，由此带来的费用将由工厂承担。					

实训项目7

签订产品购销合同

操作练习

根据下列条件签订购销合同，要求格式清楚、条款明确、内容完整。

1. 合同号：JHW2005102。

2. 山东鑫宏包装印刷有限公司无自主进口权，在得知青岛长安化工实业有限公司从德国 BASF 进口了一批三羟甲基丙烷后，立即致电询问，经过磋商，于 2015 年 10 月 17 日达成购销协议。

3. 卖方：青岛长安化工实业有限公司（青岛中山南路 224 号诺亚大厦 7 楼）。

4. 买方：山东鑫宏包装印刷有限公司（青岛市文化路 24 号）。

5. 货号品名：三羟甲基丙烷。

6. 单价：900 元/袋。

7. 包装：25kg/袋。

8. 数量：1 吨。

9. 质量标准：按照原厂生产标准。

10. 交货方式：供方送货。

11. 交货地点：需方工厂。

12. 付款方式：需方以电汇方式支付所有货款，供方见电汇底单传真确认后发货。

13. 供方代表：李涛；需方代表：黄东。

产品购销合同

合同编号：

签订日期：

供方：

地址：

需方：

地址：

一、产品名称、产地、规格型号、包装、数量、价款

产品名称	产地	规格型号	包装	数量	单价	总金额

总金额合计（大写）：人民币

二、质量标准：

三、交（提）货方式：

四、交货时间和地点：

五、付款方式及时间：

六、合同履行地：

七、本合同适用《合同法》有关买卖合同的有关规定。

八、本合同一式二份，双方各执一份，自双方签字盖章后生效。

九、本合同手写或有任何修改均无效。

供方：   需方：

代表：   代表：

实训项目8

填写开证申请书

一、操作练习

根据下列资料填写开证申请书，要求格式清楚、条款明确、内容完整。

THE BUYER：GUANGDONG FOREIGN TRADE IMP. & EXP. CORP.

15-18/F.，GUANGDONG FOREIGN ECONOMIC AND TRADE BUILDING，351 TIANHE ROAD GUANGZHOU，CHINA

THE SELLER：ROYAL TRADERS LTD.

333 BARRON BLVD.，INGLESIDE，ILLINOIS（UNITED STATES）

NAME OF COMMODITY：MEN'S DENIM UTILITY SHORT

SPECIFICATIONS：

COLOR：MEDDEST SANDBLAST

FABRIC CONTENT：100% COTTON

QUANTITY：2 000 CARTON

PRICE TERM：FOB NEW YORK USD 285/CARTON

TOTAL AMOUNT：USD 570 000.00

COUNTRY OF ORIGIN AND MANUFACTURERS：

UNITED STATES OF AMERICA，

VICTORY FACTORY

PARTIAL SHIPMENT AND TRANSSHIPMENT ARE PROHIBITTED

SHIPPING MARK：ST

NO.1…UP

TIME OF SHIPMENT：BEFORE JULY 15，2015

PLACE AND DATE OF EXPIRY：CHINA，JULY 30，2015

PORT OF SHIPMENT：NEW YORK

PORT OF DESTINATION：XINGANG PORT，TIANJING OF CHINA

INSURANCE：TO BE COVERED BY BUYER.

PAYMENT：BY IRREVOCABLE FREELY NEGOTIABLE L/C AGAINST SIGHT DRAFTS FOR 100 PCT OF INVOICE VALUE AND THE DOCUMENTS DETAILED HEREUNDER.

DOCUMETNS:

1. INVOICES IN TRIPLICATE

2. PACKING LIST IN TRIPLICATE

3. FULL SET OF CLEAN ON BOARD BILLS OF LADING MADE OUT TO ORDER AND BLANK ENDORSED NOTIFYING THE APPLICANT WITH FULL NAME AND ADDRESS MARKED FREIGHT COLLECT.

4. CERTIFICATE OF ORIGIN IN DUPLICATE.

5. BENEFICIARY'S CERTIFIED COPY OF FAX TO THE APPLICANT WITHIN 1 DAY AFTER SHIPMENT ADVISING GOODS NAME OF VESSEL，INVOICE VALUE, AND DATE OF SHIPMENT，QUANTITY AND WEIGHT.

OTHER TERMS AND CONDITIONS:

1. L/C TO BE ISSUED BY TELETRANSMISSION.

2. THE BUYER SHALL BEAR ALL BANKING CHARGES INCURRED INSIDE THE ISSUING BANK.

3. ALL DOCUMENTS MUST BE MAILED IN ONE LOT TO THE ISSUING BANK BY COURIER SERVICE.

4. PRESENTATION PERIOD：WITHIN 10 DAYS AFTER THE DATE OF SHIPMENT.

IRREVOCABLE DOCUMENTARY CREDIT APPLICATION

TO:	Date:
□ Issue by airmail □ With brief advice by teletransmission □ Issue by express delivery □ Issue by teletransmission (which shall be the operative instrument)	Credit No. Date and place of expiry
Applicant	Beneficiary (Full name and address)
Advising Bank	Amount

Partial shipments □ allowed　□ not allowed	Transshipment □ allowed　□ not allowed	Credit available with By □ sight payment □ acceptance □ negotiation □ deferred payment at against the documents detailed herein □ and beneficiary's draft(s) fo_____% of invoice value at _____sight drawn on
Loading on board/dispatch/taking in charge at/from not later than For transportation to： □ FOB　□ CFR　□ CIF　□ or other terms		

Documents required：(marked with X)

1. (　) Signed commercial invoice in_____copies indicating L/C No. and Contract No..

2. (　) Full set of clean on board Bills of Lading made out to order and blank endorsed，marked "freight [　] to collect / [　]prepaid [　]showing freight amount" notifying _____.

(　) Airway bills/cargo receipt/copy of railway bills issued by_____showing "freight [　] to collect/[　] prepaid [　] indicating freight amount" and consigned to_____ .

3. (　) Insurance Policy/Certificate in_____copies for_____% of the invoice value showing claims payable in_____currency of the draft，blank endorsed，covering All Risks，War Risks and_____.

4. (　) Packing List/Weight Memo in_____copies indicating quantity，gross and weights of each package.

5. (　) Certificate of Quantity/Weight in_____copies issued by _____.

6. (　) Certificate of Quality in_____copies issued by [　] manufacturer/[　] public recognized surveyor_____.

7. (　) Certificate of Origin in_____copies .

8. (　) Beneficiary's certified copy of fax / telex dispatched to the applicant within_____days after shipment advising L/C No.，name of vessel，date of shipment，name，quantity，weight and value of goods.

Other documents，if any

Description of goods：

Additional instructions：

1. (　) All banking charges outside the opening bank are for beneficiary's account.

2. (　) Documents must be presented within_____days after date of issuance of the transport documents but within the validity of this credit.

3. (　) Third party as shipper is not acceptable，Short Form/Blank back B/L is not acceptable.

4. (　) Both quantity and credit amount_____% more or less are allowed.

5. (　) All documents must be sent to issuing bank by courier/speed post in one lot.

6. (　) Other terms，if any

二、实务思考

1. 我海口某外贸公司从马来西亚某公司进口一批商品，双方签订的合同中规定：数量 2 000 吨，单价 150 美元吨。分批装运不允许，没有数量增减幅度。我外贸公司在填开证申请书时，填写信用证总金额为 300 000 美元，数量 2 100 吨。开证行按申请书内容开出信用证，马来西亚公司未要求改证，直接发货 2 000 吨。请问：如果按发货数量制单，马来西亚受益人能否安全收汇？为什么？

2. 我某进出口公司从美国进口大豆一批，合同规定：最后装船朗为 2015 年 9 月 30 日，信用证有效期为 2015 年 10 月 15 日，交单期为提单日期后 15 天内，但必须在信用证有效期之内。我公司于 2015 年 8 月 31 日按合同规定向本地银行申请开立信用证，美国出口公司于 2015 年 8 月 30 日装船完毕，提单日期为 2015 年 8 月 30 日。2015 年 8 月 31 日美方收到我方银行开出的信用证，美国公司将做好的全套单证送银行兑用。问：美国出口商能否顺利结汇？为什么？

实训项目9

缮制出口货物托运订舱单

操作练习

2015 年 3 月 22 日，中国银行广东省分行通知广东对外贸易有限公司，收到利雅得银行转来的信用证，经审核，广东对外贸易有限公司认为其符合要求，随即开始根据信用证的有关规定备货出运。4 月 12 日，广东对外贸易有限公司委托货运代理人（上海凯通国际货运代理有限公司）向船公司订舱。

广东公司银行账号：8546253956321

联系人：张立

电话 / 传真：020-86521548

根据信用证和合同的规定填写"货物出运委托书"。

（一）

销售合同
SALES CONTRACT

卖方 SELLER:	GUANGDONG FOREIGN TRADE IMP. & EXP. CORP. 15-18/F.，351 TIANHE ROAD，GUANGZHOU，CHINA TEL：0086-20-4715004 FAX：0086-20-4711363	编号： NO.: 日期： DATE:	NEO2001026 Feb. 28，2015
买方 BUYER:	YINSHEN TRADING CO. LTD. P.O. BOX 99552，RIYADH 22766，KSA TEL：00966-1-4659220 FAX：00966-1-4659213	地点： SIGNED IN:	GUANGZHOU，CHINA

买卖双方同意以下条款达成交易：

This contract is made by and agreed between the BUYER and SELLER，in accordance with the terms and conditions stipulated below.

1. 品名及规格 Commodity & Specification	2. 数量 Quantity	3. 单价及价格条款 Unit Price & Trade Terms	4. 金额 Amount
			CFR DAMMAM PORT
ABOUT 1 700 CARTONS CANNED MUSRHOOMS PIECES & STEMS 24 TINS X 425 GRAMS NET WEIGHT (D.W. 227 GRAMS) AT USD7.80 PER CARTON. ROSE BRAND. G.W.：19 074.44KGS	1 700 CARTONS	USD 7.80	USD 13 260.00
Total:	1 700 CARTONS		USD 13 260.00

允许 With	溢短装，由卖方决定 More or less of shipment allowed at the sellers' option
5. 总值 Total Value	USD THIRTEEN THOUSAND TWO HUNDRED AND SIXTY ONLY.
6. 包装 Packing	EXPORTED BROWN CARTON
7. 唛头 Shipping Marks	ROSE BRAND 178/2001 RIYADH
8. 装运期及运输方式 Time of Shipment & means of Transportation	Not Later Than Apr.30，2015 BY VESSEL
9. 装运港及目的地 Port of Loading & Destination	From：GUANGZHOU，CHINA To：DAMMAM，SAUDI ARABIA
10. 保险 Insurance	TO BE COVERED BY THE BUYER.
11. 付款方式 Terms of Payment	The Buyers shall open through a bank acceptable to the Seller an Irrevocable Letter of Credit payable at sight of reach the seller 30 days before the month of shipment，valid for negotiation in China until the 15th day after the date of shipment.
12. 备注 Remarks	

The Buyer	The Seller
YINSHEN TRADING CO. LTD.	GUANGDONG FOREIGN TRADE IMP. & EXP. CORP.
(signature)	(signature)

（二）

2015 MAR22 09：18：11			LOGICAL TERMINAL E102

ISSUE OF A DOCUMENTARY CREDIT

MT S700

PAGE　00001
FUNC MSG700
UMR　06881051

MSGACK　DWS765I AUTH OK，KEY B198081689580FC5，BKCHCNBJ RJHISARI RECORO

BASIC HEADER	F 01 BKCHCNBJA940 0588 550628
APPLICATION HEADER	0 700　1057 010320 RJHISARIAXXX 7277 977367 020213 1557 N
	*ALRAJHI BANKING AND INVESTMENT
	*CORPORATION
	*RIYADH
	*(HEAD OFFICE)
USER HEADER	SERVICE CODE　　103：（银行盖信用证通知专用章）
	BANK. PRIORITY　113：
	MSG USER REF.　　108：
	INFO. FROM CI　　115：

SEQUENCE OF TOTAL	*27	1 / 1
FORM OF DOC. CREDIT	*40 A	IRREVOCABLE
DOC. CREDIT NUMBER	*20	0011LC123756
DATE OF ISSUE	31 C	150320
DATE/PLACE EXP.	*31 D	DATE 150515 PLACE CHINA
APPLICANT	*50	YINSHEN TRADING CO. LTD.
		P.O. BOX 99552，RIYADH 22766，KSA
		TEL：00966-1-4659220 FAX：00966-1-4659213
BENEFICIARY	*59	GUANGDONG FOREIGN TRADE IMP. & EXP. CORP.
		15-18/F.，351 TIANHE ROAD，GUANGZHOU，CHINA
		TEL：0086-20-4715004 FAX：0086-20-4711363
AMOUNT	*32 B	CURRENCY USD AMOUNT 13 260
AVAILABLE WITH/BY	*41 D	ANY BANK IN CHINA，
		BY NEGOTIATION
DRAFTS AT ...	42 C	SIGHT
DRAWEE	42 A	RJHISARI
		*ALRAJHI BANKING AND INVESTMENT
		*CORPORATION
		*RIYADH
		*(HEAD OFFICE)
PARTIAL SHIPMTS	43 P	NOT ALLOWED
TRANSSHIPMENT	43 T	NOT ALLOWED
LOADING ON BRD	44 A	CHINA MAIN FORT，CHINA
	44 B	DAMMAM PORT，SAUDI ARABIA
LATEST SHIPMENT	44 C	150430

（续表）

GOODS DESCRIPT.	45 A	ABOUT 1 700 CARTONS CANNED MUSRHOOM PIECES & STEM S 24 TINS X 425 GRAMS NET WEIGHT (D.W. 227 GRAMS) AT USD7.80 PER CARTON. ROSE BRAND.
DOCS REQUIRED	46 A	DOCUMENTS REQUIRED:
		+SIGNED COMMERCIAL INVOICE IN TRIPLICATE ORIGINAL AND MUST SHOW BREAK DOWN OF THE AMOUNT AS FOLLOWS: FOB VALUE, FREIGHT CHARGES AND TOTAL AMOUNT C AND F.
		+FULL SET CLEAN ON BOARD BILL OF LADING MADE OUT TO THE ORDER OF AL RAJHI BANKING AND INVESTMENT CORP, MARKED FREIGHT PREPAID AND NOTIFY APPLICANT，INDICATING THE FULL NAME, ADDRESS AND TEL NO. OF THE CARRYING VESSEL'S AGENT AT THE PORT OF DISCHARGE.
		+PACKING LIST IN ONE ORIGINAL PLUS 5 COPIES，ALL OF WHICH MUST BE MANUALLY SIGNED.
		+INSPECTION (HEALTH) CERTIFICATE FROM C.I.Q. (ENTRY-EXIT INSPECTION AND QUARANTINE OF THE PEOPLES REP. OF CHINA) STATING GOODS ARE FIT FOR HUMAN BEING.
		+CERTIFICATE OF ORIGIN DULY CERTIFIED BY C.C.P.I.T.STATING THE NAME OF THE MANUFACTURERS OF PRODUCERS AND THAT GOODS EXPORTED ARE WHOLLY OF CHINESE ORIGIN.
		+THE PRODUCTION DATE OF THE GOODS NOT TO BE EARLIER THAN HALF MONTH AT TIME OF SHIPMENT. BENEFICIARY MUST CERTIFY THE SAME.
		+SHIPMENT TO BE EFFECTED BY CONTAINER AND BY REGULAR LINE. SHIPMENT COMPANY'S CERTIFICATE TO THIS EFFECT SHOULD ACCOMPANY THE DOCUMENTS.
DD. CONDITIONS	47 A	ADDITIONAL CONDITION:
		A DISCREPANCY FEE OF USD50.00 WILL BE IMPOSED ON EACH SET OF DOCUMENTS PRESENTED FOR NEGOTIATION UNDER THIS L/C WITH DISCREPANCY. THE FEE WILL BE DEDUCTED FROM THE BILL AMOUNT.
CHARGES	71 B	ALL CHARGES AND COMMISSIONS OUTSIDE KSA ON BENEFICIARIES' ACCOUNT INCLUDING REIMBURSING, BANK COMMISSION，DISCREPANCY FEE (IF ANY) AND COURIER CHARGES.
CONFIRMAT INSTR	*49	WITHOUT
REIMBURS. BANK RIYADH (HEAD OFFICE)	53 D	AL RAJHI BANKING AND INVESTMENT CORP

（续表）

INS PAYING BANK	78	DOCUMENTS TO BE DESPATCHED IN ONE LOT BY COURIER.ALL CORRESPONDENCE TO BE SENT TO ALRAJHI BANKING AND INVESTMENT CORPORATION RIYADH (HEAD OFFICE)
SEND REC INFO	72	REIMBURSEMENT IS SUBJECT TO ICC URR 525
		ORDER IS <MAC：> <PAC：> <ENC：> <CHK：> <TNG：>
TRAILER		<PDE：>
		MAC：E55927A4　CHK：7B505952829A　HOB：

（三）

出口货物订舱委托书						
日期：　　年　月　日						
1. 发货人	4. 信用证号码					
	5. 开证银行					
	6. 合同号码		7. 成交金额			
	8. 装运口岸		9. 目的港			
2. 收货人	10. 转船运输		11. 分批装运			
	12. 信用证有效期		13. 装船期限			
	14. 运费		15. 成交条件			
	16. 公司联系人		17. 电话 / 传真			
3. 通知人	18. 公司开户行		19. 银行账号			
	20. 特别要求					
21. 标记唛码	22. 货号规格	23. 包装件数	24. 毛重	25. 净重	26. 数量	27. 单价	28. 总价
29. 总件数	30. 总毛重	31. 总净重	32. 总尺码		33. 总金额	
34. 备注						

实训项目10

缮制国际货物托运书

操作练习

2015 年 3 月 12 日，江苏长宏物流有限公司受南京纺织公司委托，填制国际货物托运书，以航空方式出口女式棉运动上衣。根据商业发票内容，制作国际货物托运书，要求格式清楚、内容完整。

（一）

ISSUER NANJING TEXTILE CO.，LTD. HUARONG MANSION RM2901 NO.85 GUANJIAQIAO， NANJING 210005，CHINA		商业发票 COMMERCIAL INVOICE	
TO FASHION FORCE CO.，LTD. P. O. BOX 8935 NEW TERMINAL，ALTA，VISTA OTTAWA， CANADA		NO. NT01FF004	DATE Mar. 9，2015
TRANSPORT DETAILS SHIPMENT FROM SHANGHAI，CHINA TO MONTREAL， CANADA BY AIR FREIGHT PREPAID		S/C NO. F01LCB05127	L/C NO. 63211020049
		TERMS OF PAYMENT L/C AT SIGHT	

Marks and Numbers	Number and kind of package Description of goods	Quantity	Unit Price USD	Amount
FASHION FORCE F01LCB05127 CTN NO. MONTREAL MADE IN CHINA				CIF MONTREAL
	LADIES COTTON BLAZER (100% COTTON，40S×20/140×60)	2 550 PCS	USD 12.80	USD 32 640.00
	Total:	2 550 PCS		USD 32 640.00

SAY TOTAL：USD THIRTY-TWO THOUSAND SIX HUNDRED AND FORTY ONLY
SALES CONDITIONS：CIF MONTREAL/CANADA
      SALES CONTRACT NO. F01LCB05127
      LADIES COTTON BLAZER (100% COTTON，40S×20/140×60)

STYLE NO.	PO NO.	QTY/PCS	USD/PC
46-301A	10337	2 550	12.80

PAKAGE	N. W.	G. W.
85 CARTONS	17 KGS	19 KGS

TOTAL PACKAGE：85 CARTONS
TOTAL MEAS：21 583 CBM

NANJING TEXTILE CO.，LTD.

李好

（二）

国际货物托运书
SHIPPER'S LETTER OF INSTRUCTION

TO:　　　　　　　　　　　　　　　　　　　　　进仓编号：

托运人	
发货人 SHIPPER	
收货人 CONSIGNEE	
通知人 NOTIFY PARTY	

起运港		目的港		运费	
标记唛头 MARKS	件数 NUMBER	中英文品名 DESCRIPTION OF GOODS		毛重（公斤） G. W (KGS)	尺码（立方米） SIZE (M³)

1. 货单到达时间：3.17 报关	2. 航班：OZ/3.18	运价：29/KG+50
电　话：021-84217836 传　真：021-84217835 联系人：张海 地　址：上海市三环路 60 号世贸大厦 2401 室 托运人签字：	★如改配航空公司请提前通知我司 （公章） 制单日期：　　　年　　　月　　　日	

实训项目11

缮制出口货物明细单

操作练习

2015 年 3 月 22 日，中国银行山东省分行通知宏鑫国际贸易有限公司，收到利雅得银行转来的信用证，经审核，宏鑫公司认为其符合要求，随即开始根据信用证的有关规定备货出运。4 月 12 日，宏鑫公司向船公司订舱。商品毛重 19 074.44KGS；体积 36.85CBM。

根据合同和信用证制作出口货物明细单，要求格式清楚、内容完整。

（一）

销售合同
SALES CONTRACT

卖方 SELLER： HONGXIN TRADING CO.，LTD. 　　编号 NO.： NEO2001026

HUARONG MANSION RM2901 NO.85 　　日期 DATE： Feb. 28，2015

GUANJIAQIAO，NANJING 210005，CHINA

TEL：0086-25-4715004

FAX：0086-25-4711363

买方 BUYER： NEO GENERAL TRADING CO. 　　地点 SIGNED IN：NANJING，CHINA

P.O. BOX 99552，RIYADH 22766，KSA

TEL：00966-1-4659220

FAX：00966-1-4659213

买卖双方同意以下条款达成交易：

This contract is made by and agreed between the BUYER and SELLER，in accordance with the terms and conditions stipulated below.

1. 品名及规格 Commodity & Specification	2. 数量 Quantity	3. 单价及价格条款 Unit Price & Trade Terms	4. 金额 Amount
			CFR DAMMAM PORT
ABOUT 1 700 CARTONS CANNED MUSRHOOMS PIECES & STEMS 24 TINS×425 GRAMS NET WEIGHT (D.W. 227 GRAMS). ROSE BRAND.	1 700 CARTONS	USD 7.80	USD 13 260.00
Total：	1 700 CARTONS		USD 13 260.00

允许 　　　　溢短装，由卖方决定

With 　　　　More or less of shipment allowed at the sellers' option

5. 总值 Total Value 　　USD THIRTEEN THOUSAND TWO HUNDRED AND SIXTY ONLY.

6. 包装 Packing 　　EXPORTED BROWN CARTON

7. 唛头 　　　　ROSE BRAND

Shipping Marks 　　178/2001

RIYADH

8. 装运期及运输方式 　　　　Not Later Than Apr.30，2015

Time of Shipment & means of Transportation 　　BY VESSEL

9. 装运港及目的地 　　From：SHANGHAI，CHINA

Port of Loading & Destination 　　To：DAMMAM PORT，SAUDI ARABIA

10. 保险 Insurance 　　TO BE COVERED BY THE BUYER.

11. 付款方式 　　The Buyers shall open through a bank acceptable to the Seller an

Terms of Payment 　　Irrevocable Letter of Credit payable at sight of reach the seller 30 days before the month of shipment，valid for negotiation in China until the 15th day after the date of shipment.

12. 备注 Remarks

　　The Buyer 　　　　　　　　　　The Seller

NEO GENERAL TRADING CO. 　　　　HONGXIN TRADING CO.，LTD.

　　(signature) 　　　　　　　　　　(signature)

（二）

```
2015 MAR22 09：18：11 LOGICAL TERMINAL        E102
MT S700            ISSUE OF A DOCUMENTARY CREDIT      PAGE      00001
                                                     FUNC     MSG700
                                                     UMR      06881051
```

MSGACK DWS765I AUTH OK，KEY B198081689580FC5，BKCHCNBJ RJHISARI RECORO		
BASIC HEADER		F 01 BKCHCNBJA940 0588 550628
APPLICATION HEADER		0 700 1057 010320 RJHISARIAXXX 7277 977367 020213 1557 N
		*ALRAJHI BANKING AND INVESTMENT
		*CORPORATION
		*RIYADH
		*(HEAD OFFICE)
USER HEADER		SERVICE CODE 103： （银行盖信用证通知专用章）
		BANK. PRIORITY 113：
		MSG USER REF. 108：
		INFO. FROM CI 115：
SEQUENCE OF TOTAL	*27	1 / 1
FORM OF DOC. CREDIT	*40 A	IRREVOCABLE
DOC. CREDIT NUMBER	*20	0011LC123756
DATE OF ISSUE	31 C	150322
DATE/PLACE EXP.	*31 D	DATE 150515 PLACE CHINA
APPLICANT	*50	NEO GENERAL TRADING CO.
		P. O. BOX 99552，RIYADH 22766，KSA
		TEL：00966-1-4659220 FAX：00966-1-4659213
BENEFICIARY	*59	HONGXIN TRADING CO.，LTD.
		HUARONG MANSION RM2901 NO.85 GUANJIAQIAO，NANJING
		210005，CHINA
		TEL：0086-25-4715004
		FAX：0086-25-4711363
AMOUNT	*32 B	CURRENCY USD AMOUNT 13260，
AVAILABLE WITH/BY	*41 D	ANY BANK IN CHINA，BY NEGOTIATION
DRAFTS AT ...	42 C	SIGHT
DRAWEE	42 A	RJHISARI
		*AL RAJHI BANKING AND INVESTMENT CORPORATION
		*RIYADH
		*(HEAD OFFICE)
PARTIAL SHIPMTS	43 P	NOT ALLOWED
TRANSSHIPMENT	43 T	NOT ALLOWED
LOADING ON BRD	44 A	CHINA MAIN FORT，CHINA
	44 B	DAMMAM PORT，SAUDI ARABIA
LATEST SHIPMENT	44 C	150430
GOODS DESCRIPT	45 A	ABOUT 1 700 CARTONS CANNED MUSRHOOM PIECES & STEMS
		24 TINS×425 GRAMS NET WEIGHT (D.W. 227 GRAMS) AT USD
		7.80 PER CARTON.
		ROSE BRAND.

（续表）

DOCS REQUIRED	46 A	DOCUMENTS REQUIRED:
		+ SIGNED COMMERCIAL INVOICE IN TRIPLICATE ORIGINAL AND MUST SHOW BREAK DOWN OF THE AMOUNT AS FOLLOWS: FOB VALUE，FREIGHT CHARGES AND TOTAL AMOUNT C AND F.
		+ FULL SET CLEAN ON BOARD BILLS OF LADING MADE OUT TO THE ORDER OF AL RAJHI BANKING AND INVESTMENT CORP，MARKED FREIGHT PREPAID AND NOTIFY APPLICANT，INDICATING THE FULL NAME，ADDRESS AND TEL NO. OF THE CARRYING VESSEL'S AGENT AT THE PORT OF DISCHARGE.
		+ PACKING LIST IN ONE ORIGINAL PLUS 5 COPIES，ALL OF WHICH MUST BE MANUALLY SIGNED.
		+ INSPECTION (HEALTH) CERTIFICATE FROM C.I.Q. (ENTRY-EXIT INSPECTION AND QUARANTINE OF THE PEOPLES REP. OF CHINA) STATING GOODS ARE FIT FOR HUMAN BEING.
		+ CERTIFICATE OF ORIGIN DULY CERTIFIED BY C.C.P.I.T. STATING THE NAME OF THE MANUFACTURERS OF PRODUCERS AND THAT GOODS EXPORTED ARE WHOLLY OF CHINESE ORIGIN.
		+ THE PRODUCTION DATE OF THE GOODS NOT TO BE EARLIER THAN HALF MONTH AT TIME OF SHIPMENT. BENEFICIARY MUST CERTIFY THE SAME.
		+SHIPMENT TO BE EFFECTED BY CONTAINER AND BY REGULAR LINE. SHIPMENT COMPANY'S CERTIFICATE TO THIS EFFECT SHOULD ACCOMPANY THE DOCUMENTS.
DD. CONDITIONS	47 A	ADDITIONAL CONDITION: A DISCREPANCY FEE OF USD50.00 WILL BE IMPOSED ON EACH SET OF DOCUMENTS PRESENTED FOR NEGOTIATION UNDER THIS L/C WITH DISCREPANCY. THE FEE WILL BE DEDUCTED FROM THE BILL AMOUNT.
CHARGES	71 B	ALL CHARGES AND COMMISSIONS OUTSIDE KSA ON BENEFICIARIES' ACCOUNT INCLUDING REIMBURSING, BANK COMMISSION，DISCREPANCY FEE (IF ANY) AND COURIER CHARGES.
CONFIRMAT INSTR	*49	WITHOUT
REIMBURS. BANK	53 D	AL RAJHI BANKING AND INVESTMENT CORP RIYADH (HEAD OFFICE)
INS PAYING BANK	78	DOCUMENTS TO BE DESPATCHED IN ONE LOT BY COURIER. ALL CORRESPONDENCE TO BE SENT TO ALRAJHI BANKING AND INVESTMENT CORPORATION RIYADH (HEAD OFFICE)
SEND REC INFO	72	REIMBURSEMENT IS SUBJECT TO ICC URR 525
TRAILER		ORDER IS <MAC：> <PAC：> <ENC：> <CHK：> <TNG：> <PDE：>

（三）

出口货物明细单				银行编号		外运编号	
年 月 日				核销单号		许可证号	
经营单位 （装船人）				合同号			
				信用证号			
				收汇方式			
提单或 承运收据	抬头人			开证日期		金额	
				贸易性质		贸易国别	
	通知人			出口口岸		目的港	
				可否转运		可否分批	
	运费			装运期限		有效期限	
标记唛头	货名规格及货号		件数及 包装式样	毛重	净重	价格 （成交条件）	
				KG		单价	总价
	TOTAL:						
SAY TOTAL:								
本公司注意事项				总体积		
				保险单	险别		
					保额		
					赔款 地点		
外运外轮注意事项				船名			
				海关编号			
				放行日期			
				制单员			

实训项目12
缮制出境货物报检单

一、操作练习

2015年3月12日，江西国际进出口贸易公司填写出境货物报检单，随附合同、信用证、发票、箱单等申请报检，要求签发出境货物换证凭单、品质证书与质量证书。出口商品为H6-59940BS GOLF CAP，产地为江西，存放于工厂仓库。商品海关编码为84151021，用三个40尺集装箱装运上COSTCO542632，经香港转船运至日本横滨港口。

根据合同、信用证，制作出境货物报检单，要求格式清楚、内容完整。

（一）

售货确认书
SALES CONFIRMATION

卖方 Sellers：JIANGXI INTERNATONAL CO.，LTD

ROOM 2501，JIAFA MANSTION，BEIQIAO 合同号 Contract No.：03TG28711

WEST ROAD，NANCHANG 日期 Date：JULY，22，2015

买方 Buyers：EAST AGENT COMPANY 地点 Signed at：NANCHANG，

3-72，OHTAMACHI，NAKA-KU，YOKOHAMA， CHINA

JAPAN

This Sales Contract is made by and between the Sellers and Buyers，whereby the sellers agree to sell and the buyers agree to buy the under-mentioned goods according to the terms and conditions stipulated below：

品名及规格 NAME OF COMMODITY & SPECIFICATION	单价 UNIT PRICE	数量 QUANTITY	金额及术语 AMOUNT & PRICE TERMS
H6-59940BS GOLF CAP	CIF AKITA USD 8.10	1 800 DOZS	CIF AKITA USD 14 580.00
10% more or less both in amount and quantity allowed	TOTAL：	1 800 DOZS	USD 14 580.00

Packing：CARTON

Delivery：From NANCHANG，CHINA to AKITA，JAPAN

Shipping Marks：V.H

LAS PLAMS

C/NO.

Time of Shipment：Within_30_days after receipt of L/C allowing transshipment and partial shipment.

Terms of Payment：By 100% Irrevocable Letter of Credit on favor of the Sellers to be available. By sight draft to be opened and to reach China before___JULY 30，2015___and to remain valid for negotiation in China until the 15th days after the foresaid Time of Shipment.

L/C must mention this contract number. L/C advised by BANK OF CHINA NANJING BRANCH.TLX: 44U4K NJBC，CN. ALL banking charges outside China (the mainland of China) are for account of the Drawee.

Insurance：To be effected by Sellers for 110% of full invoice value covering_F.P.A_up to_AKITA_.To be effected by the Buyers.

Arbitration：All disputes arising from the execution of or in connection with this contract shall be settled amicable by negotiation. In case of settlement can be reached through negotiation the case shall then be submitted to China International Economic & Trade Arbitration Commission. In Nanjing for arbitration in act with its sure of procedures. The arbitral award is final and binding upon both parties for setting the Dispute. The fee，for arbitration shall be borne by the losing party unless otherwise awarded.

THE SELLER：   THE BUYER：

（二）

ISSUE OF DOCUMENTARY CREDIT	
ISSUING BANK	METITABANKLED., JAPAN
DOC. CREDIT NUMBER	LTR0505457
DATE OF ISSUE	150727
EXPIRY	DATE 150908 PLACE NANJING，CHINA
APPLICANT	EAST AGENT COMPANY
	3-72，OHTAMACHI，NAKA-KU，YOKOHAMA，JAPAN231
BENEFICIARY	JIANGXI INTERNATONAL CO.，LTD
	ROOM 2501，JIAFA MANSTION，BEIJING WEST ROAD，NANCHANG
AMOUNT	CURRENCY USD AMOUNT 14 580.00
POS. /NEG. TOL. (%)	5/5
AVAILABLE WITH/BY	ANY BANK IN ADVISING COUNTRY
	BY NEGOTIATION
DRAFT AT…	DRAFTS AT SIGHT FOR FULL INVOICE VALUE
PARTIAL SHIPMENTS	ALLOWED
TRANSSHIPMENT	ALLOWED
LOADING IN CHARGE	NANJING
FOR TRANSPORT TO	AKITA
SHIPMENT PERIOD	AT THE LATEST AUG 30，2015
DESCRIPT. OF GOODS	1 800DOZS OF H6-59940BS GOLF CAPS，USD 8.10 PER DOZ AS PER SALES CONTRACT 03TG28711 DD 22，7，03 CIF AKITA

DOCUMENTS REQUIRED

*COMMERCIAL INVOICE 1 SIGNED ORIGINAL AND 5 COPIES

*PACKING LIST IN 2 COPIES

*FULL SET OF CLEAN ON BOARD，MARKED "FREIGHT PREPAID" AND NOTIFY APPLICANT (AS INDICATE ABOVE)

*GSP CERTIFICATE OF ORIGIN FORM A，CERTIFYING GOODS OF ORIGIN IN CHINA，ISSUED BY COMPETENT AUTHORITIES

*INSURANCE POLICY/CERTIFICATE COVERING F.P.A. OF PICC. INCLUDING WAREHOUSE TO WAREHOUSE CLAUSE UP TO FINAL DESTINATION AT AKITA，FOR AT LEAST 110 PCT OF CIF-VALUE.

*SHIPPING ADVICES MUST BE SENT TO APPLICANT WITH 2 DAYS AFTER SHIPMENT ADVISING NUMBERE OF PACKAGES，GROSS & NET WEIGHT，VESSEL NAME，BILL OF LADING NO. AND DATE，CONTRACT NO.，VALUE.

PRESENTATION PERIOD	21 DAYS AFTER ISSUANCE DATE OF SHIPPING DOCUMENT
CONFIRMATION	WITHOUT
INSTRUCTIONS	THE NEGOTIATION BANK MUST FORWARD THE DRAFTS AND ALL DOCUMENTS BY REGISTERED AIRMAIL.DIRECT TO US IN TWO CONSECUTIVE LOTS，UPON RECEIPT OF THE DRAFTS AND DOCUMENTS IN ORDER，WE WILL REMIT THE PROCEEDS AS INSTRUCTED BY THE NEGOTIATING BANK.

（三）

中华人民共和国出入境检验检疫 出境货物报检单					

报检单位（加盖公章）　　　　　　　　　　　　　　　　编　　号

报检单位登记号：　　　　联系人：　　　电话：　　　　报检日期：　年　月　日

发货人	（中文）				
	（外文）				
收货人	（中文）				
	（外文）				

货物名称（中/外文）	H.S.编码	产地	数/重量	货物总值	包装种类 及数量

运输工具名称号码		贸易方式		货物存放地点	
合同号		信用证号		用途	
发货日期		输往国家 （地区）		许可证/审批号	
启运地		到达口岸		生产单位注册号	

集装箱规格、数量及号码		

合同、信用证订立的检验检疫 条款或特殊要求	标记及号码	随附单据（划"√"或补填）
		□合同　　　　　　　□信用证 □发票　　　　　　　□换证凭单 □装箱单　　　　　　□厂检单 □包装性能结果单　　□许可/审批文件

需要证单名称（划"√"或补填）	*检验检疫费
□品质证书　　　__正__副　　□卫生证书　　　　__正__副 □重量证书　　　__正__副　　□动物卫生证书　　__正__副 □数量证书　　　__正__副　　□熏蒸/消毒证书　　__正__副 □兽医卫生证书__正__副　　□出境货物换证凭单__正__副 □健康证书　　　__正__副　　□植物检疫证书　　__正__副	总金额 （人民币元）
	计费人
	收费人

报检人郑重声明： 　　1.本人被授权报检。 　　2.上列填写内容正确属实，货物无伪造或冒用他人的厂 名、标志、认证标志，并承担货物质量责任。 　　　　　　　　　　　　　　签名：_____	领取证单
	日期
	签名

注：有"*"号栏由出入境检验检疫机关填写。

二、报检单审单练习

请根据以下资料修改一份出境货物报检单。

GUANGDONG TEXTILES IMPORT & EXPORT KNITWEARS COMPANY LIMITED

15/F，GUANGDONG TEXTILES MANSION，168 XIAOBEI ROAD，GUANGZHOU CHINA

COMMERCIAL INVOICE

Messrs.: CURRENT FUNDS LIMITED   INVOICE NO.: 9703S9023

     ROOM 1110 CHINACHEM GOLDEN PLAZA   INVOICE DATE: NOV. 2，2014

     NO. 77 MODY ROAD，TSM SHA TSUI EAST   L/C NO.: WFH515950F

     KOWLOON，HONGKONG   S/C N O.: DY-039

Transport details: FROM GUANGZHOU TO SANTOS W/T   Terms of payment: BY L/C

     HONGKONG BY VESSEL

Mark & number	Description of goods	Quantity	Unit price	Amount
N/M	MEN'S 100 PCT COTTON WOVEN UNDER PANTS	7 200 DOZ	USD 4.2/DOZ	USD 30 240.00
			CIF SANTOS	USD 30 240.00

TOTAL QUANTITY：7 200 DOZ

PACKING：240CTNS

TOTAL WEIGHT：N.G：720 KGS；G.W 800 KGS

SHIPPED PER：XINDA/FANDU V.336

SHIPPED ON BOAD：NOV.10，2014

         GUANGDONG TEXTILES IMPORT & EXPORT

         KNITWEARS COMPANY LIMITED

有关资料：

商品编码：6207.1100

货物存放地点：大朗仓库

报检人：何涛

报检时提交的随附单据：合同、信用证、发票、装箱单

需要的单据：品质证书1正1副

用途：其他

产地：广州

报检日期：2014.11.3

中华人民共和国出入境检验检疫
出境货物报检单

报检单位（加盖公章）　　　　　　　　　　　　　　　　　编　　号

报检单位登记号：　　　　联系人：何涛　电话：　　　报检日期：2014 年 11 月 3 日

发货人	（中文）	广东纺织品进出口针织有限公司
	（外文）	GUANGDONG TEXTILES IMPORT & EXPORT KNITWEARS COMPANY LIMITED
收货人	（中文）	
	（外文）	CURRENT FUNDS LIMITED

货物名称（中 / 外文）	H.S. 编码	产地	数 / 重量	货物总值	包装种类及数量
男式内裤 MEN'S 100 PCT COTTON WOVEN		广东省 广州市	7 200 件	30 240 美元	240 纸箱

运输工具名称号码	XINDA/FANDU V.336	贸易方式	来料加工	货物存放地点	大朗仓库
合同号	DY-093	信用证号	WFH515950F	用途	其他
发货日期	2014-11-3	输往国家（地区）	巴西	许可证 / 审批号	
启运地	广州	到达口岸	圣保罗	生产单位注册号	

集装箱规格、数量及号码		
合同、信用证订立的检验检疫条款或特殊要求	标记及号码	随附单据（划"√"或补填）
	N/M	☑合同　　　　☑信用证 ☑发票　　　　□换证凭单 ☑装箱单　　　□厂检单 □包装性能结果单 □许可 / 审批文件

需要证单名称（划"√"或补填）	* 检验检疫费	
☑品质证书　　1 正 1 副　□卫生证书　　　正　副 □重量证书　　正　副　□动物卫生证书　　正　副 □数量证书　　正　副　□熏蒸 / 消毒证书　　正　副 □兽医卫生证书　正　副　□出境货物换证凭单　正　副 □健康证书　　正　副　□植物检疫证书　　正　副	总金额（人民币元）	
	计费人	
	收费人	

报检人郑重声明： 1. 本人被授权报检。 2. 上列填写内容正确属实，货物无伪造或冒用他人的厂名、标志、认证标志，并承担货物质量责任。 签名：何涛	领取证单	
	日期	
	签名	何涛

注：有"*"号栏由出入境检验检疫机关填写。

三、实务思考

1. 2014 年 11 月 20 日国内银行 A 收到出口商交来一套出口单据，金额 USD 385 000.00，开证行为某国 B 银行，经审单，单单相符，单证相符，信用证明确规定受 UCP 600 约束，A 银行议付后向开证行寄单索偿。12 月 2 日，A 银行收到 B 银行发来的拒付电文，理由如下：①检验证书没有显示收货人名称构成不符点，并造成该货不能通关；②开证行不允许在检验证书上不显示收货人的名称。请问：B 银行的做法是否妥当？为什么？

2. 2014 年 11 月 20 日国内银行 A 受理了出口商 B 一笔出口业务，金额 USD 380 000.00，银行 A 审单后认为单证相符，于 11 月 21 日监督给开证行，11 月 27 日银行 A 收到开证行拒付通知，提出不符点：certificate of analysis showing quantity not complied with L/C，信用证描述药品数量为 105BAU，而检验分析单上的数量为 600 BAU。请问：开证行拒付是否正确？为什么？

实训项目13

缮制全套报检单据

操作练习

宏鑫国际贸易公司委托徐州通达食品厂报检。根据下列资料，制作报检所需全套单据（出境货物报检单、商业发票、装箱单），要求格式清楚、内容完整。

1. 宏鑫国际贸易公司资料

地址：南京市中山路 85 号华荣大厦 2901 室

邮编：210005

法人代表：张宝

业务联系人：黄爱玲

联系电话：025-4715004

企业性质：私营有限责任公司

2. 商品资料

中文名称：碎片蘑菇罐头

英文名称：CANNED MUSRHOOMS PIECES & STEMS

商品描述：24 TINS×425 GRAMS NET WEIGHT (D.W. 227 GRAMS)

包装纸箱：长 45mm，宽 20mm，高 14.9mm

海关编码：2003.1011

有关重量及体积计算：此项商品按净重的 1.1 倍来估算毛重；所有计算结果保留两位小数。

（一）

销售合同
SALES CONTRACT

卖方 SELLER: HONGXIN TRADING CO., LTD.
　　　　　HUARONG MANSION RM2901 NO.85
　　　　　ZHONGSHAN ROAD, NANJING 210005, CHINA
　　　　　TEL: 0086-25-4715004 FAX: 0086-25-4711363

编号 NO.: NEO2001026
日期 DATE: Feb. 28, 2015
地点 SIGNED IN: NANJING, CHINA

买方 BUYER: NEO GENERAL TRADING CO.
　　　　　P.O. BOX 99552, RIYADH 22766, KSA
　　　　　TEL: 00966-1-4659220 FAX: 00966-1-4659213

买卖双方同意以下条款达成交易：

This contract is made by and agreed between the BUYER and SELLER, in accordance with the terms and conditions stipulated below.

1. 品名及规格 Commodity & Specification	2. 数量 Quantity	3. 单价及价格条款 Unit Price & Trade Terms	4. 金额 Amount
			CFR DAMMAM PORT
ABOUT 1 700 CARTONS CANNED MUSRHOOMS PIECES & STEMS 24 TINS × 425 GRAMS NET WEIGHT (D.W. 227 GRAMS) ROSE BRAND.	1 700 CARTONS	USD 7.80	USD 13 260.00
Total:	1 700 CARTONS		USD 13 260.00

允许 With	溢短装，由卖方决定 More or less of shipment allowed at the sellers' option
5. 总值 Total Value	USD THIRTEEN THOUSAND TWO HUNDRED AND SIXTY ONLY.
6. 包装 Packing	EXPORTED BROWN CARTON
7. 唛头 Shipping Marks	ROSE BRAND 178/2001 RIYADH
8. 装运期及运输方式 Time of Shipment & means of Transportation	Not Later Than Apr. 30, 2015 BY VESSEL
9. 装运港及目的地 Port of Loading & Destination	From: SHANGHAI, CHINA To: DAMMAM PORT, SAUDI ARABIA
10. 保险 Insurance	TO BE COVERED BY THE BUYER.
11. 付款方式 Terms of Payment	The Buyers shall open through a bank acceptable to the Seller an Irrevocable Letter of Credit payable at sight of reach the seller 30 days before the month of shipment, valid for negotiation in China until the 15th day after the date of shipment.
12. 备注 Remarks	

　　　　The Buyer
　NEO GENERAL TRADING CO.
　　　(signature)

　　　　The Seller
　HONGXIN TRADING CO., LTD.
　　　(signature)

（二）

```
2015 MAR22 09：18：11                          LOGICAL TERMINAL E102
MT S700        ISSUE OF A DOCUMENTARY CREDIT       PAGE    00001
                                                   FUNC    MSG700
                                                   UMR     06881051
```

MSGACK DWS765I AUTH OK，KEY B198081689580FC5，BKCHCNBJ RJHISARI RECORO		
BASIC HEADER		F 01 BKCHCNBJA940 0588 550628
APPLICATION HEADER		0 700 1057 010320 RJHISARIAXXX 7277 977367 020213 1557 N
		*ALRAJHI BANKING AND INVESTMENT
		*CORPORATION
		*RIYADH
		*(HEAD OFFICE)
USER HEADER		SERVICE CODE 103：（银行盖信用证通知专用章）
		BANK. PRIORITY 113：
		MSG USER REF. 108：
		INFO. FROM CI 115：
SEQUENCE OF TOTAL	*27	1 / 1
FORM OF DOC. CREDIT	*40 A	IRREVOCABLE
DOC. CREDIT NUMBER	*20	0011LC123756
DATE OF ISSUE	31 C	150320
DATE/PLACE EXP.	*31 D	DATE 150920 PLACE CHINA
APPLICANT	*50	NEO GENERAL TRADING CO.
		P.O. BOX 99552，RIYADH 22766，KSA
		TEL：00966-1-4659220
		FAX：00966-1-4659213
BENEFICIARY	*59	HONGXIN TRADING CO.，LTD.
		HUARONG MANSION RM2901 NO.85 ZHONGSHAN ROAD，
		NANJING 210005，CHINA
		TEL：0086-25-4715004 FAX：0086-25-4711363
AMOUNT	*32 B	CURRENCY USD AMOUNT 13 260.00
AVAILABLE WITH/BY	*41 D	ANY BANK IN CHINA，
		BY NEGOTIATION
DRAFTS AT ...	42 C	SIGHT
DRAWEE	42 A	RJHISARI
		*ALRAJHI BANKING AND INVESTMENT
		*CORPORATION
		*RIYADH
		*(HEAD OFFICE)
PARTIAL SHIPMTS	43 P	NOT ALLOWED
TRANSSHIPMENT	43 T	NOT ALLOWED
LOADING ON BRD	44 A	CHINA MAIN PORT，CHINA
	44 B	DAMMAM PORT，SAUDI ARABIA
LATEST SHIPMENT	44 C	150430
GOODS DESCRIPT.	45 A	ABOUT 1 700 CARTONS CANNED MUSRHOOM PIECES &
		STEMS 24 TINS X 425 GRAMS NET WEIGHT (D.W. 227 GRAMS)

（续表）

		AT USD7.80 PER CARTON. ROSE BRAND.
DOCS REQUIRED	46 A	DOCUMENTS REQUIRED: + SIGNED COMMERCIAL INVOICE IN TRIPLICATE ORIGINAL AND MUST SHOW BREAK DOWN OF THE AMOUNT AS FOLLOWS: FOB VALUE，FREIGHT CHARGES AND TOTAL AMOUNT C AND F. + FULL SET CLEAN ON BOARD BILL OF LADING MADE OUT TO THE ORDER OF ALRAJHI BANKING AND INVESTMENT CORP，MARKED FREIGHT PREPAID AND NOTIFY APPLICANT，INDICATING THE FULL NAME，ADDRESS AND TEL NO. OF THE CARRYING VESSEL'S AGENT AT THE PORT OF DISCHARGE. + PACKING LIST IN ONE ORIGINAL PLUS 5 COPIES，ALL OF WHICH MUST BE MANUALLY SIGNED. + INSPECTION (HEALTH) CERTIFICATE FROM C.I.Q. (ENTRY-EXIT INSPECTION AND QUARANTINE OF THE PEOPLE'S REP. OF CHINA) STATING GOODS ARE FIT FOR HUMAN BEING. + CERTIFICATE OF ORIGIN DULY CERTIFIED BY C.C.P.I.T. STATING THE NAME OF THE MANUFACTURERS OF PRODUCERS AND THAT GOODS EXPORTED ARE WHOLLY OF CHINESE ORIGIN. + THE PRODUCTION DATE OF THE GOODS NOT TO BE EARLIER THAN HALF MONTH AT TIME OF SHIPMENT. BENEFICIARY MUST CERTIFY THE SAME. +SHIPMENT TO BE EFFECTED BY CONTAINER AND BY REGULAR LINE. SHIPMENT COMPANY'S CERTIFICATE TO THIS EFFECT SHOULD ACCOMPANY THE DOCUMENTS.
DD. CONDITIONS	47A	ADDITIONAL CONDITION: A DISCREPANCY FEE OF USD50.00 WILL BE IMPOSED ON EACH SET OF DOCUMENTS PRESENTED FOR NEGOTIATION UNDER THIS L/C WITH DISCREPANCY. THE FEE WILL BE DEDUCTED FROM THE BILL AMOUNT.
CHARGES	71 B	ALL CHARGES AND COMMISSIONS OUTSIDE KSA ON BENEFICIARIES' ACCOUNT INCLUDING EIMBURSING，BANK COMMISSION，DISCREPANCY FEE (IF ANY) AND COURIER CHARGES.
CONFIRMAT INSTR	*49	WITHOUT
REIMBURS. BANK	53 D	AL RAJHI BANKING AND INVESTMENT CORP RIYADH (HEAD OFFICE)
INS PAYING BANK	78	DOCUMENTS TO BE DESPATCHED IN ONE LOT BY COURIER. ALL CORRESPONDENCE TO BE SENT TO ALRAJHI BANKING AND INVESTMENT CORPORATION RIYADH (HEAD OFFICE)
SEND REC INFO	72	REIMBURSEMENT IS SUBJECT TO ICC URR 600

TRAILER ORDER IS <MAC：> <PAC：> <ENC：> <CHK：> <TNG：> <PDE：>

MAC：E55927A4

CHK：7B505952829A HOB

（三）

中华人民共和国出入境检验检疫 出境货物报检单						
报检单位(加盖公章)：					*编 号	
报检单位登记号：		联系人：		电话：	报检日期：年 月 日	
发货人	(中文)					
	(外文)					
收货人	(中文)					
	(外文)					
货物名称(中/外文)	H.S.编码	产地	数/重量	货物总值		包装种类及数量
运输工具名称号码		贸易方式		货物存放地点		
合同号		信用证号		用途		
发货日期		输往国家 (地区)		许可证/审批号		
启运地		到达口岸		生产单位注册号		
集装箱规格、数量及号码						
合同、信用证订立的检验 检疫条款或特殊要求	标记及号码		随附单据(划"√"或补填)			
			□合同 □发票 □装箱单 □包装性能结果单		□信用证 □换证凭单 □厂检单 □许可/审批文件	
需要证单名称(划"√"或补填)			*检验检疫费			
□品质证书 ＿正＿副 □重量证书 ＿正＿副 □数量证书 ＿正＿副 □兽医卫生证书 ＿正＿副 □健康证书 ＿正＿副 □卫生证书 ＿正＿副 □动物卫生证书 ＿正＿副 □熏蒸/消毒证书 ＿正＿副 □出境货物换证凭单 ＿正＿副 □植物检疫证书 ＿正＿副			总金额 (人民币元)			
			计费人			
			收费人			
报检人郑重声明： 1. 本人被授权报检。 2. 上列填写内容正确属实，货物无伪造或冒用他人 的厂名、标志、认证标志，并承担货物质量责任。 签名：＿＿＿＿＿＿＿			领取证单			
			日期			
			签名			

注：有"*"号栏由出入境检验检疫机关填写。

（四）

商业发票
COMMERCIAL INVOICE

To

日期 Date

发票号 Invoice No.

合约号 Contract No.

信用证号 L/C No. _____

开船日期 Sailing about _____

装由 Shipped per _____

出 From _____

至 To _____

唛头 SHIPPING MARK	货 名 数 量 QUANTITIES AND DESCRIPTIONS	单价 UNIT PRICE	金额 AMOUNET

（五）

标志 SHIPPING MARK	货物描述 DESCRIPTIONS OF GOODS	数量 QUANTITY	件数 PACKAGE	毛重 G.W	净重 N.G	尺码 M
TOTAL:						

装箱单

PACKING LIST

发票号码 Invoice No.: 　　　　　　　　　　　日期 Date: _____

实训项目14

缮制出口货物报关单

操作练习

根据新的海关报关规定，货物出口报关必须在货物进入装货码头仓库后才能进行。由于南京纺织公司的船期是 2015 年 3 月 20 日，所以 2015 年 3 月 9 日南京纺织公司按上海凯通国际货运代理有限公司的要求，将报关委托书、出口货物报关单及上述单据寄到上海委托代理报关。

根据下列资料填写出口货物报关单。

公司名称：南京纺织服装有限公司

地址：南京市中山路 85 号华荣大厦 2901 室

邮编：210005

联系电话：025-4715004

经办人：李宝华

公司十位编码：73314338-5

公司海关代码：3201004261

税务登记号码：320102134773852

报关单预录入编号：DS9110002

出运日期：2015-03-20

运费 1 500 美元，保费 360 美元，杂费 60 美元。

此份报关单是给报关行或代理公司委托报关之用，报关单上的海关编码、报关单填制日期可不写。

（一）

中华人民共和国出入境检验检疫
出境货物换证凭单

类别：口岸申报换证   编号：320100202007610

发货人	南京纺织服装有限公司	标记及号码 FASHION FORCE F01LCB05127 CTN NO. MONTREAL MADE IN CHINA
收货人	***	
品名	女式全棉上衣	
H.S. 编码	62043200.90	
报检数／重量	2 550 件	
包装种类及数量	纸箱—201	
申报总值	32 640 美元	

产地	江苏省无锡市	生产单位（注册号）	无锡季节制衣有限公司
生产日期	2015 年 3 月	生产批号	3201FZ21802003
包装性能检验结果单号	340400301000200	合同／信用证号	F01LCB05127/63211020049
		运输工具名称及号码	COSCO548796
输往国家或地区	加拿大	集装箱规格及数量	20'×1
发货日期	2015.03	检验依据	SN/T0557-1996 及合同

检验检疫结果	本批货物共 201 箱 2 550 件，经按 SN/T0557-1996 标准的要求，随机抽取代表性样品 8 箱 101 件，根据上述检验依据进行检验，结果如下： 款号：46-301A 色号：黑色、白色 规格：10-12-14-16-18 上述货物经检验，符合检验依据要求。 ******** （出入境检验检疫局检验检疫专用章） 签字：黄海 日期：2015 年 3 月 13 日

本单有效期	截止于 2015 年 3 月 12 日
备注	产地标识查验符合规定

分批出境核销栏	日期	出境数／重量	结存数／重量	核销人	日期	出境数／重量	结存数／重量	核销人

说明：1. 货物出境时，经口岸检验检疫机关查验货证相符，且符合检验检疫要求的予以签发通关单或换发检验检疫证书；2. 本单不作为国内贸易的品质或其他证明；3. 涂改无效。

（二）

出口收汇核销单
出口退税专用

（苏）编号：327636262

出口单位：南京纺织有限公司

单位代码：3201004261

货物名称	数量	币种总价
女式全棉上衣	2 550 件	USD 32 640.00

报关单编号：

外汇局签注栏：

（海关盖章）

年　　月　　日（盖章）

未经核销此联不得撕开

出口收汇核销单

（苏）编号：327636262

出口单位：南京纺织有限公司

单位代码：3201004261

类别	币种金额	日期	盖章

银行签注栏

海关签注栏：

外汇局签注栏：

（出口单位盖章）

年　　月　　日（盖章）

出口收汇核销单
存根

（苏）编号：327636262

出口单位：南京纺织有限公司

单位代码：3201004261

出口币种总价：USD 32 640.00

收汇方式：L/C AT SIGHT

预计收款日期：2015.4.12

报关日期：2015.3.16

备注：

此单报关有效期截止到

（出口单位盖章）

（三）

销售合同
SALES CONTRACT

卖方 SELLER：NANJING TEXTILE CO.，LTD.   编号 NO.：F01LCB05127
HUARONG MANSION RM2901   日期 DATE：Jan. 26，2015
NO.85 ZHONGSHAN ROAD，   地点 SIGNED IN：NANJING，CHINA
NANJING 210005，CHINA
买方 BUYER：FASHION FORCE CO.，LTD
P. O. BOX 8935 NEW TERMINAL，
ALTA，VISTA TTAWA，CANADA

买卖双方同意以下条款达成交易：

This contract is made by and agreed between the BUYER and SELLER，in accordance with the terms and conditions stipulated below.

1. 商品号 Art No.	2. 品名及规格 Commodity & Specification	3. 数量 Quantity	4. 单价及价格条款 Unit Price & Trade Terms	5. 金额 Amount
				CIF MONTREAL
46-301A	LADIES COTTON BLAZER (100% COTTON，40S×20/140×60)	2 550 PCS	USD 12.80	USD 32 640.00
		Total:	USD 12.80	USD 32 640.00

允许   3% 溢短装，由卖方决定
With   More or less of shipment allowed at the sellers' option

6. 总值 Total Value   USD THIRTY-TWO THOUSAND SIX HUNDRED AND FORTY ONLY.

7. 包装 Packing   CARTON

8. 唛头 Shipping Marks   FASHION FORCE
                               F01LCB05127
                               CTN NO.
                               MONTREAL
                               MADE IN CHINA

9. 装运期及运输方式   NOT LATER THAN MAR. 25，2015
   Time of Shipment & means of Transportation   BY VESSEL

10. 装运港及目的地   FROM：SHANGHAI，CHINA
    Port of Loading & Destination   TO: MONTREAL，CANADA

11. 保险   FOR 110% CIF INVOICE VALUE COVERING ALL RISKS，INSTITUTE
    Insurance   CARGO CLAUSES，INSTITUTE STRIKES，INSTITUTE WAR CLAUSES
                       AND CIVIL COMMOTIONS CLAUSES.

12. 付款方式   BY IRREVOCABLE LETTER OF CREDIT TO BE OPENED BY FULL
    Terms of Payment   AMOUNT OF S/C，PAYMENT AT SIGHT DOCUMENT TO BE PRESENTED
                       WITHIN 21 DAYS AFTER DATE OF B/L AT BENEFICIARY'S ACCOUNT.

13. 备注   PARTIAL SHIPMENTS：NOT ALLOWED.
    Remarks   TRANSSHIPMENT：ALLOWED.

            The Buyer   The Seller
FASHION FORCE CO.，LTD   NANJING TEXTILE CO.，LTD.

（四）

DEAILED PACKING LIST

TO:		INVOICE NO.		NT01FF004
FASHION FORCE CO.，LTD		INVOICE DATE		Mar. 9，2015
P. O. BOX 8935 NEW TERMINAL，ALTA，VISTA		S/C NO.		F01LCB05127
OTTAWA，CANADA		S/C DATE		Dec. 26，2014

FROM: SHANGHAI，CHINA		TO: MONTREAL，CANADA
Letter of Credit No.: 63211020049		Date of Shipment: Mar. 20，2015

CTN NO	CTNS	DESIGNS/ COLORS	STYLE NO	SIZE ASSORTMENT PER CARTON						PCS/ CNT	TOTAL PCS/ CNTS	G.W./ CTN	N.W./ CTN	MEAS./ CTN	CBM/ CTN
				10	12	14	16	18	20						
1/18	18	BLACK	46-301A	14						14	252	15	10	97×72×12	0.084
19/56	38	BLACK			14					14	532				
57/106	50	BLACK				13				13	650			98×76×12	0.089
107/149	43	BLACK					12			12	516				
150/175	25	BLACK						12		12	300			99×80×11	0.087
176/194	19	BLACK							12	12	228				
196	1	WHITE		11						11	11				0.084
197	1	WHITE			9	3				12	12				
198	1	WHITE				13				13	13				0.089
199	1	WHITE				3	9			12	12				
200	3	WHITE						4		4	12				0.087
201	1	WHITE						2	10	12	12				
1/201ex															
TOTAL	201										2 550	3 015	2 010		17.51

SHIPPING MARKS:

FASHION FORCE

F01LCB05127

CTN NO.

MONTREAL

MADE IN CHINA

SALES CONDITIONS: CIF MONTREAL/CANADA

SALES CONTRACT NO. F01LCB05127

LADIES COTTON BLAZER (100% COTTON，40S×20/140×60)

STYLE NO.	PO NO.	QTY/PCS	USD/PC
46-301A	10337	2 550	12.80

（五）

中华人民共和国海关出口货物报关单

预录入编号： 海关编号：

出口口岸	备案号	出口日期		申报日期
经营单位	运输方式	运输工具名称		提运单号
发货单位	贸易方式	征免性质		结汇方式
许可证号	运抵国（地区）	指运港		境内货源地
批准文号	成交方式	运费	保费	杂费
合同协议号	件数	包装种类	毛重（千克）	净重（千克）
集装箱号	随附单据	生产厂家		

标记唛码及备注

项号	商品编号	商品名称	规格型号	数量及单位	最终目的国（地区）	单价	总价	币制	征免

税费征收情况

录入员　录入单位	兹声明以上申报无讹并承担法律责任	海关审单批注及放行日期（签章）
		审单　　　　　　审价
报关员		
	申报单位（签章）	征税　　　　　　统计
单位地址		查验　　　　　　放行
邮编　　　电话　　　填制日期		

实训项目15

缮制出口货物报关单(空运单)

操作练习

根据空运单内容及相关信息，填写出口货物报关单。

商品编码：2003.1011

预录入号：2350219

经营单位编号：3201003830

成交方式：CNF

批准文号：2999456

合同协议号：JD021021

单价：USD 3.92/CARTON

净重（公斤）：16 895.26 KGS

2015 年 4 月 7 日出口，2015 年 4 月 5 日由发货单位向南京海关申报。

999		999 —										
Shipper's Name and Address	Shipper's Account Number	Not Negotiable **Air Waybill** Issued by 中国国际航空公司 **AIR CHINA** BEIJING CHINA										

Copies 1，2 and 3 of this Air Waybill are originals and have the same validity.

Consignee's Name and Address	Consignee's Account Number	It is agreed that the goods described herein are accepted for carriage in apparent good order. And condition (except as noted) and SUBJECT TO THE CONDITIONS OF CONTRACT ON. THE REVERSE HEREOF. ALL GOODS MAY BE CARRIED BY AND OTHER MEANS INCLUDING ROAD OR ANY OTHER CARRIER UNLESS SPECIFIC CONTRARY INSTRUCTIONS ARE GIVEN HEREON BY THE SHIPPER. THE SHIPPER'S ATTENTION IS DRAWN TO THE NOTICE CONCERNING CARRIER'S LIMITATION OF LIABILITY. Shipper may increase such limitation of liability by declaring a higher value for carriage and paying a supplemental charge if required.

Issuing Carrier's Agent Name and City		Accounting Information
Agent's IATA Code	Account No.	

Airport of Departure (Addr. of First Carrier) and Requested Routing

To	By First Carrier Routing and Destination	to	by	to	by	Currency	CHGS Code	WT/VAL		Other		Declared Value for Carriage	Declared Value for Customs
								PPD	COLL	PPD	COLL		

Airport of Destination	Flight/Date For carrier Use Only Flight/Date		Amount of Insurance	INSURANCE - If Carrier offers insurance，and such insurance is requested in accordance with the conditions thereof，indicate amount to be insured in figures in box marked "Amount of Insurance".

Handing Information

(For USA only) These commodities licensed by U.S. for ultimate destination ……………………………………………………………………

Diversion contrary to U.S. law is prohibited

No. of Pieces RCP	Gross Weight	Kg lb	Rate lass	Commodity Item No.	Chargeable Weight		Rate Charge	Total	Nature and Quantity of Goods (incl. Dimensions or Volume)

Prepaid Collect Weight Charge	Other Charges
Valuation Charge	
Tax	
Total other Charges Due Agent	Shipper certifies that the particulars on the face hereof are correct and that insofar as any part of the consignment contains dangerous goods，such part is properly described by name and is in proper condition for carriage by air according to the applicable Dangerous Goods Regulations.
Total other Charges Due Carrier	
	…………………………………………………………………… Signature of Shipper or his Agent

Total Prepaid	Total Collect		
Currency Conversion Rates	CC Charges in Dest. Currency		
For Carrier's Use only at Destination	Charges at Destination	………………………………………………………………… Executed on (date) at(place) Signature of Issuing Carrier or its Agent	
		Total Collect Charges	999 —

ORIGINAL 3 (FOR SHIPPER)

实训项目16

缮制全套出口货物报关单

操作练习

这是一笔出口到加拿大的食品业务，由于要从上海出运，因此鑫宏国际贸易公司委托上海凯通国际货运代理有限公司代理报关。到目前为止，鑫宏国际贸易公司已经拿到了出口收汇核销单和商检换证凭单。请根据下列资料和单据，配齐出口报关所需的全套单证寄往上海。

1. **鑫宏国际贸易公司资料**

地址：南京市中山路 85 号华荣大厦 2901 室

邮编：210005

联系电话：025-4715004

公司十位编码：73314337-5

公司海关代码：3201003830

税务登记号码：320102200118388

2. **加拿大公司资料**

FASHION FORCE CO.，LTD

P. O. BOX 8935 NEW TERMINAL，ALTA，VISTA OTTAWA，CANADA

3. **报关单资料**

报关单预录入编号：DS9110008

出运日期：2015-04-25

制单日期：2015-04-18

此份报关单是给报关行或代理公司委托报关之用，报关单上的海关编码、报关单填制日期可不写。

（一）

<table>
<tr><td colspan="4" align="center">中华人民共和国出入境检验检疫
出境货物换证凭单</td></tr>
<tr><td colspan="2">类别：口岸申报换证</td><td colspan="2">编号：3200000202000368</td></tr>
<tr><td>发货人</td><td>鑫宏国际贸易有限公司</td><td colspan="2" rowspan="2">标记及号码

ROSE BRAND</td></tr>
<tr><td>收货人</td><td>***</td></tr>
<tr><td>品名</td><td>碎片蘑菇罐头 24×425G</td><td colspan="2">178/2001</td></tr>
<tr><td>H. S. 编码</td><td>2003.1011</td><td colspan="2">RIYADH</td></tr>
<tr><td>报检数 / 重量</td><td colspan="3">1 700 箱 /17 340 克</td></tr>
<tr><td>包装种类及数量</td><td colspan="3">纸箱 1 700</td></tr>
<tr><td>申报总值</td><td colspan="3">13 260 美元</td></tr>
<tr><td>产地</td><td>江苏省徐州市</td><td>生产单位（注册号）</td><td>6500/554433</td></tr>
<tr><td>生产日期</td><td>2015/04</td><td>生产批号</td><td>***</td></tr>
<tr><td>包装性能检
验结果单号</td><td>320100381005836</td><td>合同 / 信用证号</td><td>NEO2001026 / 0011LC123756</td></tr>
<tr><td></td><td></td><td>运输工具名称及号码</td><td>船舶</td></tr>
<tr><td>输往国家或地区</td><td>加拿大</td><td>集装箱规格及数量</td><td>*** ***</td></tr>
<tr><td>发货日期</td><td>***</td><td>检验依据</td><td>合同、SN0400-1995</td></tr>
<tr><td>检
验
检
疫
结
果</td><td colspan="3">本批商品经按 QB1006—90 抽取代表性样品检验结果如下：
一、物理检验
1. 外观无膨胀，无损坏，密封良好。
2. 罐外无锈，罐内壁无腐蚀，罐内无杂质。
3. 内容物，形状，块粒，色泽，香味正常。
4. 净重 425 克，固形物大于等于 70%。
5. NACL：1.75%。
二、化学检验（重金属含量：每公斤制品中含量）
锡不超过 200 毫克、铜不超过 5 毫克、铅不超过 1 毫克、砷不超过 0.5 毫克。
三、细菌检验：商业无菌
结论：本批商品符合上述检验依据，适合人类食用。
********（出入境检验检疫局检验检疫专用章）
签字：张宝天   日期：2015 年 4 月 17 日</td></tr>
<tr><td>本单有效期</td><td colspan="3">截止于 2015 年 8 月 17 日</td></tr>
<tr><td>备注</td><td colspan="3">查验合格</td></tr>
</table>

<table>
<tr><td rowspan="2">分
批
出
境
核
销
栏</td><td rowspan="2">日期</td><td>出境数 /
重量</td><td>结存数 /
重量</td><td rowspan="2">核销人</td><td rowspan="2">日期</td><td>出境数 /
重量</td><td>结存数 /
重量</td><td rowspan="2">核销人</td></tr>
<tr><td></td><td></td><td></td><td></td></tr>
<tr><td></td><td></td><td></td><td></td><td></td><td></td><td></td><td></td></tr>
<tr><td></td><td></td><td></td><td></td><td></td><td></td><td></td><td></td></tr>
<tr><td></td><td></td><td></td><td></td><td></td><td></td><td></td><td></td></tr>
<tr><td></td><td></td><td></td><td></td><td></td><td></td><td></td><td></td></tr>
</table>

说明：1. 货物出境时，经口岸检验检疫机关查验货证相符，且符合检验检疫要求的予以签发通关单或换发检验检疫证书；2. 本单不作为国内贸易的品质或其他证明；3. 涂改无效。

（二）

出口收汇核销单

（苏）编号：32765696960

3 2 7 6 5 6 9 6 0

未经核销此联不得撕开

出口收汇核销单
出口退税专用

（苏）编号：32765696960

出口单位：鑫宏国际贸易有限公司

单位代码：3201003830

货物名称	数量	币种总价
碎片蘑菇罐头	1 700 箱	USD 13 260.00

报关单编号：

外汇局签注栏：

（海关盖章）

年　　月　　日（盖章）

出口单位：鑫宏国际贸易有限公司

单位代码：3201003830

类别	币种金额	日期	盖章

银行签注栏

（出口单位盖章）

海关签注栏：

外汇局签注栏：

年　　月　　日（盖章）

出口收汇核销单
存根

（苏）编号：32765696960

出口单位：鑫宏国际贸易有限公司

单位代码：3201003830

出口币种总价：USD 32 640.00

收汇方式：L/C AT SIGHT

预计收款日期：2015.5.21

报关日期：2015.4.23

备注：

此单报关有效期截止到

（出口单位盖章）

（三）

中华人民共和国海关出口货物报关单

预录入编号：   海关编号：

出口口岸	备案号	出口日期	申报日期	
经营单位	运输方式	运输工具名称	提运单号	
发货单位	贸易方式	征免性质	结汇方式	
许可证号	运抵国（地区）	起运港	境内货源地	
批准文号	成交方式	运费	保费	杂费
合同协议号	件数	包装种类	毛重（千克）	净重（千克）
集装箱号	随附单据	生产厂家		

标记唛码及备注

项号	商品编号	商品名称、规格型号	数量及单位	最终目的国（地区）	单价	总价	币制	征免

税费征收情况

录入员　录入单位	兹声明以上申报无讹并承担法律责任	海关审单批注及放行日期（签章）
		审单　　　　　　　审价
报关员		
	申报单位（签章）	
单位地址		征税　　　　　统计
邮编　　　　电话	填制日期	查验　　　　　放行

（四）

商业发票
COMMERCIAL INVOICE

To

日期
Date

发票号
Invoice No.

合约号
Contract No.

信用证号
L/C No.

装由
Shipped per_____

开船日期
Sailing about_____

出
From_____

至
To _____

唛头 SHIPPING MARK	货 名 数 量 QUANTITIES AND DESCRIPTIONS	单价 UNIT PRICE	金额 AMOUNET

（五）

装箱单
PACKING LIST

Invoice No: _____   Date：_____

标志及箱号	品名及规格	数量	件数	毛重	净重	尺码
TOTAL:						

实训项目17

缮制出口货物投保单

一、操作练习

2015 年 3 月 9 日，上海大通国际货运代理有限公司通知上海纺织服装有限公司其所订舱位已经确认，该批货物将于 3 月 20 日装上由上海港开往加拿大蒙特利尔港的"HUA CHANG"轮第 09981 船次。在得到了船公司关于确认订舱的配舱回单后，上海纺织有限公司即于 3 月 16 日按照信用证的有关规定填写"投保单"，并随附商业发票向中国人民保险公司上海分公司办理保险手续。

根据信用证要求填写出口投保单。

（一）

ISSUER SHANGHAI TEXTILE GARMENT CO., LTD. HUARONG MANSION RM2901 NO.85 ZHONGSHAN ROAD, SHANGHAI 210005, CHINA		商业发票 COMMERCIAL INVOICE		
TO FASHION FORCE CO., LTD. P. O. BOX 8935 NEW TERMINAL, ALTA, VISTA OTTAWA, CANADA		NO. NT01FF004		DATE Mar. 9, 2015
TRANSPORT DETAILS SHIPMENT FROM SHANGHAI，CHINA TO MONTREAL, CANADA BY VESSEL		S/C NO. F01LCB05127		L/C NO. 63211020049
		TERMS OF PAYMENT L/C AT SIGHT		
Marks and Numbers	Number and kind of package Description of goods	Quantity	Unit Price	Amount
				USD
FASHION FORCE F01LCB05127 CTN NO. MONTREAL MADE IN CHINA				CIF MONTREAL
	LADIES COTTON BLAZER (100% COTTON，40S×20/140×60)	2 550 PCS	USD 12.80	USD 32 640.00
	Total：	2 550 PCS		USD 32 640.00

SAY TOTAL：USD THIRTY TWO THOUSAND SIX HUNDRED AND FORTY ONLY

SALES CONDITIONS：CIF MONTREAL/CANADA
SALES CONTRACT NO. F01LCB05127
LADIES COTTON BLAZER (100% COTTON，40S×20/140×60)

STYLE NO.	PO NO.	QTY/PCS	USD/PC
46-301A	10337	2 550	12.80

（出口商签字和盖单据章）

（二）

2015 JAN31 15：23：4		LOGICAL TERMINALE102

MT S700　　ISSUE OF A DOCUMENTARY CREDIT　　PAGE　00001
　　　　　　　　　　　　　　　　　　　　　　　　　　　FUNC　MSG700
　　　　　　　　　　　　　　　　　　　　　　　　　　　UMR　06607642

MSGACK DWS765I AUTH OK，KEY B110106173BAOC53B，BKCHCNBJ BNPA**** RECORO

BASIC HEADER		F 01 BKCHCNBJA940 0542 725524
APPLICATION HEADER		0 700 1122 010129 BNPACAMMAXXX 4968 839712 010130 0028 N
		*BNP PARIBAS (CANADA)
		*MONTREAL
USER HEADER		SERVICE CODE 103：
		BANK. PRIORITY 113：
		MSG USER REF. 108：（银行盖信用证通知专用章）
		INFO. FROM CI 115：
SEQUENCE OF TOTAL	*27	1／1
FORM OF DOC. CREDIT	*40 A	IRREVOCABLE
DOC. CREDIT NUMBER*	20	63211020049
DATE OF ISSUE	31 C	150129
EXPIRY	*31 D	DATE 150410 PLACE IN BENEFICIARY'S COUNTRY
APPLICANT	*50	FASHION FORCE CO.，LTD P. O. BOX 8935 NEW TERMINAL，ALTA，VISTA OTTAWA，CANADA
BENEFICIARY	*59	SHANGHAI TEXTILE GARMENT CO.，LTD. HUARONG MANSION RM2901 NO.85 ZHONGSHAN ROAD，SHANGHAI 210005，CHINA
AMOUNT	*32 B	CURRENCY USD AMOUNT 32640，
AVAILABLE WITH/BY	*41 D	ANY BANK BY NEGOTIATION
DRAFTS AT ...	42 C	SIGHT
DRAWEE	42 A	BNPACAMMXXX *BNP PARIBAS (CANADA) *MONTREAL
PARTIAL SHIPMTS	43 P	NOT ALLOWED
TRANSSHIPMENT	43 T	ALLOWED
LOADING ON CHARGE	44 A	CHINA
FOR TRANSPORT TO...	44 B	MONTREAL
LATEST DATE OF SHIP.	44 C	150325
DESCRIPT OF GOODS	45 A	

SALES CONDITIONS: CIF MONTREAL/CANADA

SALES CONTRACT NO. F01LCB05127

LADIES COTTON BLAZER (100% COTTON，40S×20/140×60)

STYLE NO.	PO NO.	QTY/PCS	USD/PC
46-301A	10337	2 550	12.80

（续表）

| DOCUMENTS REQUIRED | 46 A | +COMMERCIAL INVOICES IN 3 COPIES SIGNED BY BENEFICIARY'S REPRESENTATIVE.

+CANADA CUSTOMS INVOICES IN 4 COPIES.

+FULL SET OF ORIGINAL MARINE BILLS OF LADING CLEAN ON BOARD PLUS 2 NON NEGOTIABLE COPIES MADE OUT OR ENDORSED TO ORDER OF BNP PARIBAS (CANADA) MARKED FREIGHT PREPAID AND NOTIFY APPLICANT'S FULL NAME AND ADDRESS.

+DETAILED PACKING LISTS IN 3 COPIES.

+COPY OF CERTIFICATE OF ORIGIN FORM A.

+COPY OF EXPORT LICENCE.

+BENEFICIARY'S LETTER STATING THAT ORIGINAL CERTIFICATE OF ORIGIN FORM A, ORIGINAL EXPORT LICENCE, COPY OF COMMERCIAL INVOICE, DETAILED PACKING LISTS AND A COPY OF BILL OF LADING WERE SENT DIRECT TO APPLICANT BY COURIER WITHIN 5 DAYS AFTER SHIPMENT.THE RELEATIVE COURIER RECEIPT IS ALSO REQUIRED FOR PRESENTATION.

+COPY OF APPLICANT'S FAX APPROVING PRODUCTION SAMPLES BEFORE SHIPMENT.

+LETTER FROM SHIPPER ON THEIR LETTERHEAD INDICATING THEIR NAME OF COMPANY AND ADDRESS, BILL OF LADING NUMBER, CONTAINER NUMBER AND THAT SHIPMENT, INCLUDING ITS CONTAINER, DOES NOT CONTAIN ANY NON-MANUFACTURED WOODEN MATERIAL, DUNNAGE, BRACING MATERIAL, PALLETS, CRATING OR OTHER NON-MANUFACTURED WOODEN PACKING MATERIAL.

+INSPECTION CERTIFICATE ORIGINAL SINGED AND ISSUED BY FASHION FORCE CO., LTD STATING THE SAMPLES OF FOUR STYLE GARMENTS HAS BEEN APPROVED, WHICH SEND THROUGH DHL BEFORE 15 DAYS OF SHIPMENT.

+INSURANCE POLICY OR CERTIFICATE IN 1 ORIGINAL AND 1 COPY ISSUED OR ENDORSED TO THE ORDER OF BNP PARIBAS (CANADA) FOR THE CIF INVOICE PLUS 10 PERCENT COVERING ALL RISKS, INSTITUTE STRIKES, INSTITUTE WAR CLAUSES AND CIVIL COMMOTIONS CLAUSES. |
| ADDITIONAL COND. | 47 A | +IF DOCUMENTS PRESENTED ARE FOUND BY US NOT TO BE IN FULL COMPLIANCE WITH CREDIT TERMS. WE WILL ASSESS A CHARGE OF USD 55.00 PER SET OF DOCUMENTS.

+ALL CHARGES IF ANY RELATED TO SETTLEMENTS ARE FOR ACCOUNT OF BENEFICIARY. |

（续表）

		+3 PCT MORE OR LESS IN AMOUNT AND QUANTITY IS ALLOWED.
		+ALL CERTIFICATES/LETTERS/STATEMENTS MUST BE SIGNED AND DATED
		+FOR INFORMATION ONLY, PLEASE NOTE AS OF JANUARY 4, 2015 THAT ALL SHIPMENTS FROM CHINA THAT ARE PACKED WITH UNTREATED WOOD WILL BE BANNED FROM CANADA DUE TO THE THREAT POSED BY THE ASIAN LONGNORNED BEETLE.
		+THE CANADIAN GOVERNMENT NOW INSIST THAT EVERY SHIPMENT ENTERING CANADA MUST HAVE THE ABOVE DOCUMENTATION WITH THE SHIPMENT.
		+BILL OF LADING AND COMMERCIAL INVOICE MUST CERTIFY THE FOLLOWING: THIS SHIPMENT, INCLUDING ITS CONTAINER DOES NOT CONTAIN ANY NON-MANUFACTURED WOODEN MATERIAL, DUNNAGE, BRACING MATERIAL PALLETS, CRATING OR OTHER NON MANUFACTURED WOODEN PACKING MATERIAL.
		+BENEFICIARY'S BANK ACCOUNT NO. 07773108201140121
CHARGES	71 B	OUTSIDE COUNTRY BANK CHARGES TO BE BORNE BY THE BENEFICIARY OPENING BANK CHARGES TO BE BORNE BY THE APPLICANT
CONFIRMATION	*49	WITHOUT
INSTRUCTIONS	78	
		+WE SHALL COVER THE NEGOTIATING BANK AS PER THEIR INSTRUCTIONS
		+FORWARD DOCUMENTS IN ONE LOT BY SPECIAL COURIER PREPAID TO BNP PARIBAS (CANADA) 1981 MCGILL COLLECE AVE.MONTREAL QC H3A 2W8 CANADA.
SEND. TO REC. INFO.	72	THIS CREDIT IS SUBJECT TO UCP FOR DOCUMENTARY CREDIT 2007 REVISION ICC PUBLICATION 600 AND IS THE OPERATIVE INSTRUMENT
TRAILER		ORDER IS <MAC：> <PAC：> <ENC：> <CHK：> <TNG：> <PDE：> MAC：F344CA36 CHK：AA6204FFDFC2

（三）

出口货物运输保险投保单			
发票号码		投保条款和险别	
被保险人	客户抬头	（　）PICC CLAUSE （　）ICC CLAUSE （　）ALL RISKS （　）W. P. A./W. A.	
	过户	（　）F. P. A. （　）WAR RISKS （　）S. R. C. C. （　）STRIKE	
保险金额	USD（　）	（　）ICC CLAUSE A	
	HKD（　）	（　）ICC CLAUSE B	
	（　）（　）	（　）ICC CLAUSE C	
启运港		（　）AIR TPT ALL RISKS	
目的港		（　）AIR TPT RISKS	
转内陆		（　）O/L TPT ALL RISKS	
开航日期		（　）O/L TPT RISKS	
		（　）TRANSHIPMENT RISKS	
		（　）W TO W	
船名航次		（　）T. P. N. D.	
赔款地点		（　）F. R. E. C.	
赔付币别		（　）R. F. W. D.	
正本份数		（　）RISKS OF BREAKAGE	
		（　）I. O. P.	
其他特别条款			
以下由保险公司填写			
保单号码		费率	
签单日期		保费	
投保日期：		投保人签章：	

（四）

中保财产保险有限公司
The People's Insurance (Property) Company of China，Ltd

发票号码
Invoice No.

保险单号次
Policy No.

海 洋 货 物 运 输 保 险 单
MARINE CARGO TRANSPORTATION INSURANCE POLICY

被保险人：中保财产保险有限公司(以下简称本公司)根据被保险人的要求，及其所缴付约定的保险费，按照本保险单承担险别和背面所载条款与下列特别条款承保下列货物运输保险，特签发本保险单。

Insured：This policy of Insurance witnesses that the People's Insurance (Property) Company of China，Ltd. (hereinafter called "The Company")，at the request of the Insured and in consideration of the agreed premium paid by the Insured，undertakes to insure the under mentioned goods in transportation subject to conditions of the Policy as per the Clauses printed overleaf and other special clauses attached hereon.

保险货物项目 Descriptions of Goods	包装 单位 数量 Packing Unit Quantity	保险金额 Amount Insured

承保险别：
Conditions:

货物标记：
Marks of Goods:

总保险金额：
Total Amount Insured:

保费：
Premium As arranged:

载运输工具：
Per conveyance S.S:

开航日期：
Slg. on or abt:

起运港：
Form:

目的港：
To:

所保货物，如发生本保险单项下可能引起索赔的损失或损坏，应立即通知本公司下述代理人查勘。如有索赔，应向本公司提交保险单正本(本保险单共有_____份正本)及有关文件。如一份正本已用于索赔，其余正本则自动失效。

In the event of loss or damage which may result in acclaim under this Policy，immediate notice must be given to the Company's Agent as mentioned hereunder. Claims，if any，one of the Original Policy which has been issued in_____ original (s) together with the relevant documents shall be surrendered to the Company. If one of the Original Policy has been accomplished，the others to be void.

赔款偿付地点：
Claim payable at:

日期：
Date:

地址：
Address:

二、实务思考

1. 中国纺织品进出口公司与希腊商人在 2015 年 1 月 5 日按 CIF 条件签订出口 10 万码棉布合同，支付方式为不可撤销即期信用证。希腊商人于 2015 年 6 月通过银行开来信用证，经审核与合同相符，其中保险金额为发票金额加 10%。我方正在备货，希腊商人传递给我方一份信用证修改书，内容为将投保金额改为按发票金额加 15%。我方按原证规定投保、发货，并于货物装运后在信用证有效期内，向议付行提交全套装运单据。议付行议付后将全套单据寄开证行，开证行以保险单与信用证修改书不符为由拒付。请问：开证行拒付是否正确？

2. 直达运输是否须投保转船险的争议案：

C 轻工业品进出口公司对日本 Y 株式会社出口一笔玻璃器皿。2015 年 3 月 11 日国外开来信用证，信用证有关保险条款规定保险单一式两份，投保海洋运输货物平安险，包括破碎险和转船险。在特别条款中又规定：装船后须向开证申请人发装运通知电报。一份该电报的经检验的抄本应随同议付单据一起交单。

C 轻工业品进出口公司根据信用证要求，在装运后备齐单据向国外寄单办理收汇手续。3 月 26 日开证行提出异议：你第 ××× 号单据已收到，经审核发现如下不符点：①保险单的险别中漏保转船险 (transshipment risk)。②信用证要求提供 "inspected copy of cable"（经检验的电报抄本）。该抄本须经过原发的电报局盖章证实电文的内容，才能符合我信用证要求。上述不符点我行无法接受，单据仍在我行代保管，速告你处理意见。

C 轻工业品进出口公司接到开证行的上述拒付意见后，经研究认为开证行意见毫无道理。所谓漏保转船险事，该货系直达运输，根本不转船。至于电报抄本，我所提供的单据完全符合信用证要求。C 轻工业品进出口公司即于 3 月 28 日向开证行做如下答复：关于第 ××× 号信用证项下的单据，我们认为：①该批货物是由起运港直达目的港，中途不转船，所以就不投保转船险，并非漏保。②对于信用证要求 "inspected copy of cable"，我提供的单据名称也是 "inspected copy of cable"，所以单证已经相符。至于是否须经过原发电机构盖章证实，信用证上并没有这样要求。根据《UCP 600》规定：银行审核单据是依据单据表面上是否与信用证条款相符合，以确定是否接受单据。所以我单据表面上与你信用证相符合，你应该接受单据。

4 月 1 日开证行又提出仍然不同意接受单据，其电文如下：你 3 月 28 日电悉。经研究，我们认为：①银行不管实际运输是否转船或直达，只管单据表面上是否相符。信用证要求投保转船险；而保险单缺转船险，就是单证不符。②经检验的电报抄本，不仅在单据名称上表示，而且在实际上也要经过原发电部门盖章表示经检验。你未经发电部门检验，怎能构成 "经检验的电报抄本"？所以它并未满足信用证的要求。上述不符点是明显存在的，速告单据处理意见。

C 轻工业品进出口公司又再三与买方交涉，最后按 80% 付款，赔偿对方 20% 而结案。

实训项目18

缮制海洋货物运输保险单

一、操作练习

SHANGHAI FORGIGN TRADE IMP. AND EXP. CORP. 向英国CBD贸易公司出口LADIES LYCRA LONG PANT 共2 400件，每件20美元CIF伦敦，纸箱包装，每箱12件。

合同规定按发票金额加一成投保英国伦敦保险协会ICC(A)和战争险，运输标志(唛头)为：CBD/LONDON/NOS1—200。

该货物于2015年10月20日在南京装"大丰"号轮运往伦敦。

发票号码：INV52148。

根据上述条件用英文填制一份保险单。

中保财产保险有限公司

The People's Insurance (Property) Company of China，Ltd

发票号码
Invoice No.

保险单号次
Policy No.

海 洋 货 物 运 输 保 险 单
MARINE CARGO TRANSPORTATION INSURANCE POLICY

被保险人：中保财产保险有限公司 (以下简称本公司) 根据被保险人的要求，及其所缴付约定的保险费，按照本保险单承担险别和背面所载条款与下列特别条款承保下列货物运输保险，特签发本保险单。

Insured: This policy of Insurance witnesses that the People's Insurance (Property) Company of China，Ltd. (hereinafter called "The Company")，at the request of the Insured and in consideration of the agreed premium paid by the Insured，undertakes to insure the under mentioned goods in transportation subject to conditions of the Policy as per the Clauses printed overleaf and other special clauses attached hereon.

保险货物项目 Descriptions of Goods	包装 Packing	单位 Unit	数量 Quantity	保险金额 Amount Insured

承保险别：
Conditions:

货物标记：
Marks of Goods:

总保险金额：
Total Amount Insured:

保费：
Premium As arranged:

载运输工具：
Per conveyance S.S:

开航日期：
Slg. on or abt:

起运港：
Form:

目的港：
To:

所保货物，如发生本保险单项下可能引起索赔的损失或损坏，应立即通知本公司下述代理人查勘。如有索赔，应向本公司提交保险单正本 (本保险单共有_____份正本) 及有关文件。如一份正本已用于索赔，其余正本则自动失效。

In the event of loss or damage which may result in acclaim under this Policy，immediate notice must be given to the Company's Agent as mentioned hereunder. Claims，if any，one of the Original Policy which has been issued in_____original (s) together with the relevant documents shall be surrendered to the Company. If one of the Original Policy has been accomplished，the others to be void.

赔款偿付地点：
Claim payable at:

日期：
Date:

地址：
Address:

二、审单练习

1. 信用证条款：

DOCUMENTS REQUIRED：INSURANCE POLICY COVERING MARINE TRANSPORTATION ALL RISKS AS PER INSTITUTE CARGO CLAUSES(A) WITH CLAIMS PAY- ABLE AT NEW YORK.

保险单据显示：<u>CERTIFICATE OF INSUANCE</u>
                       A

COVERING MAR INE TRANSPORTATION <u>ALL RISKS</u> AS PER
                                     B

<u>INSTITUTE CARGO CLAUSES(A)</u> WITH CLAIMS PAY- ABLE <u>AT NEW YORK.</u>
          C   D

2. 信用证条款：

SHIPMENT FROM SHANGHAI TO NEW YOR BY SEA

TRANSHIPMENT：ALLOWED IN HONGKONG ONLY

DOCUMENTS REQUIRED：INSURANCE POLICY COVERING MARINE TRANSPORTATION ALL RISKS AS PER INSTITUTE CARGO CLAUSES(A).

信用证未对保险单据做出任何其他规定。

保险单据显示：<u>INSUANCE POLICY</u>
                    A

COVERING SHIPMENT FROM <u>SHANGHAI</u> TO <u>HONGKONG</u>
                             B   C

RISKS COVERED：MARINE TRANSPORTATION <u>ALL RISKS AS PER ICC(A)</u>
                                               D

三、实务思考

1. 福建某货代公司接受货主委托，安排一批茶叶海运出口，货代公司在提取了船公司提供的集装箱并装箱后，将整箱货交船公司。同时，货主自行办理了货物运输保险。收货人在目的港拆箱提货时发现集装箱内异味较浓，经查明，该集装箱前一航次所载货物为硫酸，致使茶叶受污染。请问：①收货人应该向谁索赔？为什么？②最终由谁对茶叶受污染事故承担赔偿责任？

2. 某外贸公司进口散装化肥一批，曾向保险公司投保海运一切险。货抵目的港后，全部卸至运输公司仓库。在卸货过程中，外贸公司与装卸公司签订了一份灌装协议，并开始灌装。某日，由装卸公司根据协议将已灌装成包的半数货物堆放在港区内铁路边堆场，等待铁路转运至其他地方交付不同买主。另一半留在仓库等待灌装的散货，因受台风袭击，遭受严重湿损。于是，外贸公司就遭受湿损部分向保险公司索赔，被拒绝。请问：保险公司的做法是否正确？

实训项目19
缮制多式海运提单

一、操作练习

SHANGHAI FORGIGN TRADE IMP. AND EXP. CORP. 向英国 EAST AGENT COMPANY，126 Rome street，ANTERWEIP，Belgium 出口 LADIES LYCRA LONG PANT 共 2 400 件，每件 20 美元 CIF 伦敦，纸箱包装，每箱 12 件。箱件尺寸为 50cm×20cm×30cm，毛重为 10 千克 / 箱，运输标志（唛头）为：CBD/LONDON/NOS1-200。

该货物于 2015 年 10 月 20 日在上海装 E002 航次 "DAFENG" 号轮运往伦敦。

请根据上述条件填制一份 "清洁、已装船、空白抬头" 的提单，要求通知 EAST AGENT COMPANY，并注明 "运费预付"。

Shipper	B/L NO.: KFT2582588
	COMBINED TRANSPORT BILL OF LADING
Consignee	Received in apparent good order and condition except as otherwise noted the total number of container or other packages or units enumerated below for transportation from the place of receipt to the place of delivery subject to the terms hereof. One of the signed Bills of Lading must be surrendered duly endorsed in exchange for the Goods or delivery order. On presentation of this document (duly) Endorsed to the Carrier by or on behalf of the Holder，the rights and liabilities arising in accordance with the terms hereof shall (without prejudice to any rule of common law or statute rendering them binding on the Merchant) become binding in all respects between the Carrier and the Holder as though the contract evidenced hereby had been made between them.
Notify Party	
	SEE TERMS ON ORIGINAL B/L

PRE-CARRIAGE BY	Place of Receipt	FOR DELIVERY OF GOODS PLEASE APPLY TO:
OCEAN Vessel and Voyage NO.	Port of Loading	
Port of Discharge	Place of Delivery	FINAL DESTINATION FOR THE MERCHANT'S REFERENCE ONLY

Container Nos/Seal Nos. Marks and Numbers	No. of Container / Packages / Description of Goods	Gross Weight (Kilos)	Measurement (cu-metres)

FREIGHT & CHARGES	REVENUE TONS.	RATE PER	PREPAID	COLLECT
	PREPAID AT	PAYABLE AT	PLACE AND DATE OF ISSUE	
	TOTAL PREPAID	NO. of Original Bs/L	STAMPS & SIGNATURE	
			AS MASTER	

LADEN ON BOARD THE VESSEL

DATE

BY··

(TERMS CONTINUED ON BACK HEROF)

二、审单练习

广东荣华贸易有限公司与芬兰 ABC 公司成交一笔出口交易。ABC 公司按期开来信用证，荣华公司按期出运，并填制好海运提单，请根据下面信用证提供的内容审核海运提单编号① - ⑧的内容，对单证不符的内容在单据上进行修改。

ISSUING BANK：METITA BANK LTD.

FIN-00020 METITA FINLAND

FORM OF DOC. CREDIT：IRREVOCABLE

CREDIT NUMBER：LRT9802457

DATE OF ISSUE：150505

EXPIRY：DATE 150716

APPLICANT：ABC CORP. AKEKSAN TERINK AUTO

P. O. BOX 9，FINLAND

BENEFICIARY：GUANGDONG RONGHUA TRADE CO.，LTD.

168 DEZH ENG ROAD SOUTH，GUANGZHOU，CHINA

AMOUNT：CURRENCY USD AMOUNT 36 480.00 (SAY US DOLLARS THIRTY SIX THUSAND FOU HUNDRED AND EIGHTY ONLY.)

POS./NEG. TOL.(%)：5/5

AVAILABLE WITH/BY：ANY BANK IN ADVISING COUNTRY

BY NEGOTIATION

PARTIAL SHIPMENTS：NOT ALLOWED

TRANSHIPENT：ALLOWED

LOADING IN CHARGE：GUANGZHOU

FOR TRANSPORT TO：HELSINKI

SHIPMENT PERIOD：AT THE LATEST JULY 10，2015

DESCRIPTION OF GOODS：9 600 PCS OF WOMEN'S SWEATERS

UNIT PRICE：USD 3.80/PC

PHACKING：12PCS/CTN TOTAL 800CTNS OTHER DETAILS AS PER S/C NO.98SGQ468001 CFR HELSINKI

DOCUMENTS REQUIRED：FULL SET OF CLEAN ON BOARD MARINE BILLS OF LADING, MADE OUT TO ORDEROF METITA BANK LTD., FINLAND，MARKED "FREIGHT PREPAID" AND NOTIFY APPLICANT(AS INDICATE ABOVE)

ADDITIONAL COND.：1. T. T. REIBURSEMENT IS PROHIBITED.

2. ALL DOCUMENTS MUST BE MARKDED THE S/C NO.

3. SHIPPING MARKS：ABC

HELSINKI

NO. 1-800.

Shipper GUANGDONG RONGHUA TRADE CO., LTD. 168 DEZH ENG ROAD SOUTH, GUANGZHOU, CHINA ①	B/L NO.: KFT2582588

COMBINED TRANSPORT BILL OF LADING

Received in apparent good order and condition except as otherwise noted the total number of container or other packages or units enumerated below for transportation from the place of receipt to the place of delivery subject to the terms hereof. One of the signed Bills of Lading must be surrendered duly endorsed in exchange for the Goods or delivery order. On presentation of this document (duly) Endorsed to the Carrier by or on behalf of the Holder, the rights and liabilities arising in accordance with the terms hereof shall (without prejudice to any rule of common law or statute rendering them binding on the Merchant) become binding in all respects between the Carrier and the Holder as though the contract evidenced hereby had been made between them.

SEE TERMS ON ORIGINAL B/L

Consignee	
ABC CORP. AKEKSAN TERINK AUTO P. O. BOX 9, FINLAND ②	

Notify Party	
METITA BANK LTD. FIN-00020 METITA FINLAND ③	

PRE-CARRIAGE BY DONGFAHONG	Place of Receipt	FOR DELIVERY OF GOODS PLEASE APPLY TO:
OCEAN Vessel and Voyage NO. SUSUN 103	Port of Loading GUANGZHOU	
Port of Discharge HELSINKI VIA HONGKONG	Place of Delivery	FINAL DESTINATION FOR THE MERCHANT'S REFERENCE ONLY

Container Nos/Seal Nos. Marks and Numbers	No. of Container / Packages / Description of Goods	Gross Weight (Kilos)	Measurement (cu-metres)
N/M ④	9 600 PCS WOMEN'S SWEATERS ⑤ TOTAL: EIGHT HUNDRED CARTONS ONLY ⑥ S/C NO.: LRT9802457 ⑦	13 600.00 KGS FREIGHT COLLECT ⑧	25CBM

FREIGHT & CHARGES	REVENUE TONS.	RATE PER	PREPAID	COLLECT
	PREPAID AT	PAYABLE AT	PLACE AND DATE OF ISSUE GUANGZHOU MAY 20, 2015	
	TOTAL PREPAID	NO. of Original Bs/L THREE(3)	STAMPS & SIGNATURE ABC SHIPPING CO. 刘五 AS MASTER	

LADEN ON BOARD THE VESSEL
DATE   BY·····························
(TERMS CONTINUED ON BACK HEROF)

三、实务思考

　　某公司接到国外开来的信用证，规定"于或约于 5 月 15 日装船"。该公司于 5 月 8 日装船，并向银行提交了一份 5 月 8 日签发的提单，但却遭到银行拒付。请问这是为什么？

实训项目20

缮制外运海运提单

一、操作练习

根据下列资料，填写海运提单。

1. 信用证资料

FROM：UFJ BANK，TOKYO

TO：BANK OF CHINA，SHANDONG BR.

DD：DEC. 28，2014

L/C NO. UF789

DATE AND PLACE OF EXPIRY：FEB. 28，2015

APPLICANT：XYZ COMPANY，6-2 OHTEMACHI，1-CHOME，CHIYADA-KU，
　　　　　　TOKYO

BENEFICIARY：ABC COMPANY，NO.128 ZHONGSHAN XILU，SHANDONG

CREDIT AMOUNT：USD 22 912.50

SHIPMENT FROM：QINGDAO，CHINA

FOR TRANSPORTATION TO：TOKYO，JAPAN

LATEST DATE OF SHIPMENT：JAN. 18，2015

　　　　　　　　　　　　PARTIAL SHIPMENTS AND TRANSHIPMENT
　　　　　　　　　　　　ALLOWED

COVERING：CONTRACT NO. 04GD002

　　　　　　3 000 PCS HOSPITAL UNIFORM REF-6002T-XL AT USD 1.85/PC

　　　　　　750 PCS HOSPITAL UNIFORM REF-1602-UNICA AT USD 2.15/PC

　　　　　　1 500 PCS HOSPITAL UNIFORM REF-3009T-XL AT USD 3.85/PC

PRICE TERMS：CIP TOKYO

DOCUMENTS REQUIRED：

+ FOR GOODS UNDER CONTRACT NO.04GD002：

FULL SET (3/3) OF CLEAN SHIPPED ON BOARD OCEAN BILL OF LADING
MADE OUT TO ORDER OF ISSUNG BANK，NOTIFYING APPLICANT AND MARKED
FREIGHT PREPAID SHOWING FINAL DESTINATION AS KYOTO.

　　……

2. 海运方式运输下：

发票显示：

CONTRACT NO. 04GD002

DESCRIPTION OF GOODS: 5 250 PCS HOSPITAL UNIFORM

SHIPPING MARKS: XYZ

TOKYO

04GD002

1-88 CTNS

船长签发的装货单显示：

PLACE OF RECEIPT FROM QINGDAO THEN BY DIRECT SHIPMENT FROM QINGDAO，CHINA TO TOKYO，JAPAN，FINAL DESTINATION TO BE KYOTO

SHIPPER：V-STAR COMPANY，QINGDAO

5 250 PCS HOSPITAL UNIFORM

OCEAN VESSEL VOYAGE：VICTORY V.666

ON BOARD DATE：JAN. 18，2015

G.W.：1 232 KGS，MEAS.：4.20CBM

PACKED IN 88 CARTONS.

SHIP END IN ONE (1×20') CONTAINER (CONTAINER ON. APLU1234567, SEAL NO.006789，CY/CY)

海运提单由承运人的代理人 PERFECT LOGISTICS COMPANY 签发。

签发地点：青岛

签发日期：2015 年 1 月 17 日

签发人：李好

Shipper		B/L No.		
Consignee or order		<div align="center">SINOTRANS</div><div align="center">中 国 外 运 广 东 公 司</div>**SINOTRANS GUANGDONG COMPANY**<div align="center">**OCEAN BILL OF LADING**</div>		
Notify address				
Pre-carriage by	Port of loading	SHIPPED on board in apparent good order and condition (unless otherwise indicated) the goods or packages specified herein and to be discharged at the mentioned port of discharge or as near thereto as the vessel may safely get and be always afloat. The weight，measure，marks and numbers，quality，contents and value，being particulars furnished by the Shipper，are not checked by the Carrier on loading.		
Vessel	Port of transshipment			
Port of discharge	Final destination	The Shipper，Consignee and the Holder of this Bill of Lading hereby expressly accept and agree to all printed，written or stamped provisions，exceptions and conditions of this Bill of Lading，including those on the back hereof. IN WITNESS whereof the number of original Bills of Lading stated below have been signed，one of which being accomplished the other(s) to be void.		
Container seal No. or marks and Nos.	Number and kind of package	Description of goods	Gross weight (kgs.)	Measurement (m^3)
Freight and charges		REGARDING TRANSHIPMENT INFORMATION PLEASE CONTACT		
Ex. rate	Prepaid at	Freight payable at	Place and date of issue	
	Total prepaid	Number of original Bs/L	Signed for or on behalf of the Master As Agent	

二、根据信用证进行审单练习

Issuing Bank：METITA BANK LTD.FIN – 00020 METITA，FINLAND

Term of Doc. Credit：IRREVOCABLE

Credit Number：LRT9802457

Date of Issue：150505

Expiry：Date 150716 Place CHINA

Applicant：ABC CORP. AKEKSANTERINK AUTO

P. O. BOX 9，FINLAND

Beneficiary：GUANGDONG RONGHUA TRADE CO.，LTD.

168 DEZHENG ROAD SOUTH，GUANGZHOU，CHINA

Amount：Currency USD Amount 36 480.00 (SAY US DOLLARS THIRTY SIX THOUSAND FOUR HUNDRED AND EIGHTY ONLY)

Pos. /Nag. Toll. (%)：5/5

Available with/by：ANY BANK IN ADVISING COUNTRY BY NEGOTIATION

Partial Shipments：Not Allowed

Transshipment：Allowed

Loading in Charge：GUANGZHOU

For Transport to：HELSINKI

Shipment Period：AT THE LATEST JULY 10，2015

Descript. of Goods：9 600 PCS OF WOMEN'S SWEATERS

UNIT PRICE：USD 3.80/PC

PACKING：12PCS/CTN TOTAL 800CTNS

OTHER DETAILS AS PER S/C NO. 98SGQ468001 CFR HELSINKI

Documents Required：

FULL SET OF CLEAN ON BOARD MARINE BILLS OF LADING，MADE OUT TO ORDER OF METITA BANK LTD.，FINLAND，MARKED "FREIGHT PREPAID" AND NOTIFY APPLICANT (AS INDICATE ABOVE)

Additional Cond.：

(1) T. T. REIMBURSEMENT IS PROHIBITED

(2) ALL DOCUMENTS MUST BE MARKED THE S/C NO.

(3) SHIPPING MARKS：ABC

HELSINKI

NO. 1-800

Shipper GUANGDONG RONGHUA TRADE CO., LTD. 168 DEZHENG ROAD SOUTH, GUANGZHOU, CHINA ①			B/L No.KFT2582588
Consignee ABC CORP. AKEKSANTKRINK AUTO P. O. BOX9, FINLAND ②			**BILL OF LADING** 中国远洋运输公司 中 国 远 洋 运 输 公 司 CHINA OCEAN SHIPPING ORIGINAL
Notify Party METTA BANK LTD., FIN-00020 METTA, FINLAND ③			
Pre carriage by DONGFANGHONG ⑨	Place of Receipt ⑩		
Ocean Vessel Vow. No. SUISUN 103 ⑪	Port of Loading GUANGZHOU ⑫		
Port of discharge HELSINKI VIA	Final destination	Freight payable at	Number original Bs/L
Marks and Numbers N/M ④	Number and kind of packages; Description 9 600 PCS WOMEN'S SWEATERS ⑤ TOTAL: EIGHT HUNDRED CARTONS ONLY. ⑥ S/C NO.LRT9802457 ⑦		Gross weight 13 600.00 KGS FREIGHT COLLECT ⑧	Measurement 25 CBM
Applicable only when document used as a Through Bill of Loading			
Freight & Charges	Revenue Tons.	Rate Per	Prepaid	Collect ⑬
		Prepaid at	Payable at	P1ace and Date of Issue GUANGZHOU MAY20, 2011
		Total Prepaid	No.of Original Bs/L THREE(3)	Stamp & Signature ABC SHIPPING CO. 刘五 AS MASTER

三、案例分析

浙江粮油食品进出口公司与美国 H 公司订立一份出口 360 吨冷冻品合同，规定 2014 年 4—9 月平均交货 60 吨，即期信用证付款，信用证规定货物装运前有出口口岸商检局出具船边测温证书作为议付不可缺少的单据之一。4—7 月交货正常，顺利结汇。8 月因船期延误至 9 月 6 日才实际装运出口。海运提单倒签为 8 月 31 日，但送银行议付的商检证中填写的船边测温日期为 9 月 6 日。9 月 7 日，出口方在同一艘船又装运了 60 吨，开证行收到单据后来电表示对这两批货拒付。试分析我方有什么失误及开证行拒付的依据是什么？

实训项目21

缮制中远海运提单

一、操作练习

SHANGHAI GLOVES CO.，LTD.

Shanghai International Trade Center 2201 Yan An Road (W)，SHANGHAI 200336

TEL：+86 21 6278 9099

FAX：+86 21 6278 9569

向加拿大公司

YINSHEN TRADING CO.，LTD.

#304-310 JaJa Street，Toronto，Canada

TEL：(1)7709910

FAX：(1)7701100

出口 1521A Latex Full Coated Cotton Woven，Knit Wrist Liner 共 1 000 箱，每件 2.2 美元 CIF 伦敦，纸箱包装，每箱 12 件。毛重为 16.65 千克 / 箱，体积为 10.8 立方米。运输标志 (唛头) 为：N/M

该货物于 2014 年 11 月 25 日在上海装 V.26GW 航次 "CMA CGM" 号轮运往蒙特利尔。

根据上述资料填制一份 "清洁、已装船、空白抬头" 的提单，要求通知 YINSHEN TRADING CO. LTD.。

1. Shipper Insert Name，Address and Phone		B/L No.
2. Consignee Insert Name，Address and Phone		中远集装箱运输有限公司 COSCO CONTAINER LINES TLX：33057 COSCO CN FAX：+86(021) 6545 8984 ORIGINAL
3. Notify Party Insert Name，Address and Phone (It is agreed that no responsibility shall attach to the Carrier or his agents for failure to notify)		Port-to-Port or Combined Transport **BILL OF LADING** RECEIVED in external apparent good order and condition except as other-Wise noted. The total number of packages or unites stuffed in the container，the description of the goods and the weights shown in this Bill of Lading are furnished by the Merchants，and which the carrier has no reasonable means of checking and is not a part of this Bill of Lading contract. The
4. Combined Transport *	5. Combined Transport*	carrier has Issued the number of Bills of Lading stated below，all of this tenor and date，One of the original Bills of Lading
Pre - carriage by	Place of Receipt	must be surrendered and endorsed or signed against the delivery
6. Ocean Vessel Voy. No.	7. Port of Loading	of the shipment and whereupon any other original Bills of Lading
8. Port of Discharge	9. Combined Transport *	shall be void. The Merchants agree to be bound by the terms and conditions of this Bill of Lading as if each had personally signed this Bill of Lading.
	Place of Delivery	SEE clause 4 on the back of this Bill of Lading (Terms continued on the back hereof，please read carefully). *Applicable Only When Document Used as a Combined Transport Bill of Lading.
Marks & Nos. Container / Seal No.	No. of Containers or Packages	Description of Goods (If Dangerous Goods，See Clause 20)	Gross Weight (Kgs)	Measurement
		Description of Contents for Shipper's Use Only (Not part of This B/L Contract)		

10. Total Number of containers and/or packages (in words)					
Subject to Clause 7 Limitation					
11. Freight & Charges	Revenue Tons	Rate	Per	Prepaid	Collect
Declared Value Charge					
Ex. Rate	Prepaid at	Payable at		Place and date of issue	
Total Prepaid	No. of Original B(s)/L	Signed for the Carrier，COSCO CONTAINER LINES			
LADEN ON BOARD THE VESSEL					
DATE		BY			

二、实务思考

1. 中国浙江矿产进出口公司以 FOB 宁波与香港远东公司成交一批钢材，港商即转手以 CFR 釜山价售给韩国 A 公司。港商开来信用证以 FOB 中国口岸，要求货运釜山，并在提单上表明"FREIGHT PREPAID"（运费预付）。试分析港商为什么这么做？我方应如何处理？

2. 港至港海运提单与联合运输提单名称引起争议的问题：

某进出口公司向泰国巴伐利亚有限公司出口一批电器电料，国外开来信用证有关条款规定"100 cases of electric good sand materials，shipment from Chinese port to Bangkok，partial shipments and transshipment are prohibited. Full set clean on board marine bill of lading marked freight prepaid to order of shipper endorsed to K.T Bank notifying buyers."（"电器电料 100 箱，从中国港口至曼谷。禁止分批装运和转运。全套清洁已装船海运提单，注明'运费预付'，发货人抬头，背书给 K．T．银行，通知买方。"）某进出口公司接到上述信用证，经审查认为没有什么问题，即装集装箱运输，随后备妥各种单据向议付行交单议付。单据寄到国外却被开证行拒付，其理由为：①信用证要求的是清洁已装上船的海运提单，你们提交的却是"联合运输提单"。②我信用证规定不许转运，但根据你们提单上的记载，显然是经过转运到曼谷港。以上两项构成不符交单，现开证行无法付款。

某进出口公司接到开证行上述拒付货款的意见后审核留底单据，认为是故意挑剔，做如下答复：先引用联合运输单据统一规则（国际商会第 600 号出版物）说明联合运输提单也可以适用于港至港海运提单。关于转运的问题，如货物系由集装箱运输，根据 UCP 600 第 19 条 b 款规定，即使信用证禁止转运，只要提单证实有关货物已由集装箱运输，银行予以接受。开证行对此提出，"即使货物由集装箱运输可以接受转运提单，但也解决不了问题，信用证规定提交已装上船的海运提单。我行收到的却是联合运输提单，单据名称相差甚远。我行审单依据是单据表面上是否与信用证条款相符。我行只受 UCP 600 约束。你方强调依据国际商会第 600 号出版物联合运输单据统一规则，但我行不受其约束"。请问：我方公司应该如何处理？

3. 某土产进出口公司向 John Wilson & bros co.，出口一笔蜂蜜，对方开来信用证装运条款规定"…Full set of clean 'on board' marine bill of lading covering a port shipment made out to our order and marked 'freight prepaid' notify buyers M/S John Wilson & Bros. co.，…Beneficiary certified copy of telex dispatched to the accountee within two days after the date of shipment on the bill of lading advising name of commodity，quantity，weight，value，vessel name，B/L No. sailing date… evidencing the following merchandise：25/tons of bee honey…shipment not later than March 31，2015.transhipment is prohibited …"（"……全套清洁港至港已装船海运提单，做成我行指示抬头，注明'运费预付'，通知买方 John Wilson & Bros，Co.……受益人证实的电传副本，受益人必须在提单的装运日后

两天内发电传给开证申请人，通知品名、数量、重量、价值、船名、提单号和开航日期……证明装运下列货物：25吨蜂蜜……于2015年3月31日之前装运，不许转船。")某土产进出口公司根据信用证要求于2015年3月16日安排装运完毕，并备妥各种所要求的单据向议付行交单议付。议付行审查后认为单证相符，向开证行寄出单据。未料到开证行于3月28日却提出单证不符，拒受单据。其电文如下："①我信用证规定全套清洁港至港已装船海运提单，你提交的运输单据的名称为联合运输提单。②我信用证规定不许转运，你提交的运输单据说明在香港转运。③我信用证规定提单日后两天内发出装运通知。你提单日为3月15日，即最晚应于3月17日发出，根据电传副本证实你方于3月18日才发出装运通知，所以晚一天。以上3点与我信用证不符，故我行无法接受你单据"。请问：我方公司应该如何处理？

实训项目22
缮制空运提单

一、操作练习

2015 年 4 月 7 日，宏鑫贸易公司 (HONGXIN TRADING CO.，LTD.) 的货物从南京起运，航班为 FX0910，请根据信用证制作空运提单，要求格式清楚、内容完整。

补充资料：

商品毛重：19 074.44 KGS

体积：36.85CBM

Rate Class 运价分类代号：M

Rate/Charge 费率：20.61

Other Charge 其他费用：AWC(运单费)50.00

（一）

2015MAR22 09：18：11		LOGICAL TERMINAL	E102

MT S700 **ISSUE OF A DOCUMENTARY CREDIT** PAGE 00001
FUNC MSG700
UMR 06881051

MSGACK DWS765I AUTH OK，KEY B198081689580FC5，BKCHCNBJ RJHISARI RECORO

BASIC HEADER		F 01 BKCHCNBJA940 0588 550628
APPLICATION HEADER		0 700 1057 010320 RJHISARIAXXX 7277 977367 020213 1557 N
		*ALRAJHI BANKING AND INVESTMENT
		*CORPORATION
		*RIYADH
		*(HEAD OFFICE)
USER HEADER		SERVICE CODE 103： （银行盖信用证通知专用章）
		BANK. PRIORITY 113：
		MSG USER REF. 108：
		INFO. FROM CI 115：
SEQUENCE OF TOTAL	*27	1／1
FORM OF DOC. CREDIT	*40	IRREVOCABLE
DOC. CREDIT NUMBER	*20	0011LC123756
DATE OF ISSUE	31 C	150122
DATE/PLACE EXP.	*31 D	DATE 150515 PLACE CHINA
APPLICANT	*50	NEO GENERAL TRADING CO.
		P.O. BOX 99552，RIYADH 22766，KSA
		TEL：00966-1-4659220
		FAX：00966-1-4659213
BENEFICIARY	*59	HONGXIN TRADING CO.，LTD.
		HUARONG MANSION RM2901 NO.85 ZHONGSHAN ROAD，
		NANJING 210005，CHINA
		TEL：0086-25-4715004
		FAX：0086-25-4711363
AMOUNT	*32 B	CURRENCY USD AMOUNT 13260，
AVAILABLE WITH/BY	*41 D	ANY BANK IN CHINA，
		BY NEGOTIATION
DRAFTS AT ...	42 C	SIGHT
DRAWEE	42 A	RJHISARI
		*ALRAJHI BANKING AND INVESTMENT
		*CORPORATION
		*RIYADH
		*(HEAD OFFICE)
PARTIAL SHIPMTS	43 P	NOT ALLOWED
TRANSSHIPMENT	43 T	NOT ALLOWED
LOADING ON BRD	44 A	NANJING，CHINA
	44 B	DAMMAM PORT，SAUDI ARABIA
LATEST SHIPMENT	44 C	150430

（续表）

GOODS DESCRIPT.	45 A	ABOUT 1700 CARTONS CANNED MUSRHOOM PIECES & STEMS 24 TINS X 425 GRAMS NET WEIGHT (D.W. 227 GRAMS) AT USD7.80 PER CARTON.
ROSE BRAND.		
DOCS REQUIRED	46 A	+ SIGNED COMMERCIAL INVOICE IN TRIPLICATE ORIGINAL AND MUST SHOW BREAK DOWN OF THE AMOUNT AS FOLLOWS: FOB VALUE, FREIGHT CHARGES AND TOTAL AMOUNT C AND F.
		+ FULL SET AIR WAYBILL EVIDENCING NEO GENERAL TRADING CO., MARKED FREIGHT PREPAID.
		+ PACKING LIST IN ONE ORIGINAL PLUS 5 COPIES, ALL OF WHICH MUST BE MANUALLY SIGNED.
		+ INSPECTION (HEALTH) CERTIFICATE FROM C.I.Q. (ENTRY-EXIT INSPECTION AND QUARANTINE OF THE PEOOPLES REP. OF CHINA) STATING GOODS ARE FIT FOR HUMAN BEING.
		+ CERTIFICATE OF ORIGIN DULY CERTIFIED BY C.C.P.I.T. STATING THE NAME OF THE MANUFACTURERS OF PRODUCERS AND THAT GOODS EXPORTED ARE WHOLLY OF CHINESE ORIGIN.
		+ THE PRODUCTION DATE OF THE GOODS NOT TO BE EARLIER THAN HALF MONTH AT TIME OF SHIPMENT. BENEFICIARY MUST CERTIFY THE SAME.
		+SHIPMENT TO BE EFFECTED BY CONTAINER AND BY REGULARE LINE. SHIPMENT COMPANY'S CERTIFICATE TO THIS EFFECT SHOULD ACCOMPANY THE DOCUMENTS.
DD. CONDITIONS	47 A	ADDITIONAL CONDITION: A DISCREPANCY FEE OF USD50.00 WILL BE IMPOSED ON EACH SET OF DOCUMENTS PRESENTED FOR NEGOTIATION UNDER THIS L/C WITH DISCREPANCY. THE FEE WILL BE DEDUCTED FROM THE BILL AMOUNT.
CHARGES	71 B	ALL CHARGES AND COMMISSIONS OUTSIDE KSA ON BENEFICIARIES' ACCOUNT INCLUDING REIMBURSING, BANK COMMISSION, DISCREPANCY FEE (IF ANY) AND COURIER CHARGES.
CONFIRMAT INSTR	*49	WITHOUT REIMBURS. BANK53 D// AL RAJHI BANKING AND INVESTMENT CORP RIYADH (HEAD OFFICE)
		INS PAYING BANK 78 DOCUMENTS TO BE DESPATCHED IN ONE LOT BY COURIER.
		ALL CORRESPONDENCE TO BE SENT TO ALRAJHI BANKING AND INVESTMENT COPRORATION RIYADH (HEAD OFFICE)
SEND REC INFO	72	REIMBURSEMENT IS SUBJECT TO ICC URR 600
TRAILER		ORDER IS <MAC: > <PAC: > <ENC: > <CHK: > <TNG: > <PDE: > MAC: E55927A4 CHK: 7B505952829A HOB:

（二）

999													999 —	

Shipper's Name and Address	Shipper's Account Number	Not Negotiable Air Waybill Issued by 中国国际航空公司 AIR CHINA BEIJING CHINA

Copies 1，2 and 3 of this Air Waybill are originals and have the same validity.

Consignee's Name and Address	Consignee's Account Number	It is agreed that the goods described herein are accepted for carriage in apparent good order And condition (except as noted) and SUBJECT TO THE CONDITIONS OF CONTRACT ON THE REVERSE HEREOF. ALL GOODS MAY BE CARRIED BY AND OTHER MEANS INCLUDING ROAD OR ANY OTHER CARRIER UNLESS SPECIFIC CONTRARY INSTRUCTIONS ARE GIVEN HEREON BY THE SHIPPER. THE SHIPPER'S ATTENTION IS DRAWN TO THE NOTICE CONCERNING CARRIER'S LIMITATION OF LIABILITY. Shipper may increase such limitation of liability by declaring a higher value for carriage and paying a supplemental charge if required.

Issuing Carrier's Agent Name and City		Accounting Information
Agent's IATA Code	Account No.	

Airport of Departure (Add. of First Carrier) and Requested Routing

To	By First Carrier Routing and Destination	to	by	to	by	Currency	CHGS Code	WT/VAL		Other		Declared Value for Carriage	Declared Value for Customs
								PPD	COLL	PPD	COLL		

Airport of Destination	Flight/Date For carrier Use Only Flight/Date	Amount of Insurance	INSURANCE - If Carrier offers insurance，and such insurance is requested in accordance with the conditions thereof，indicate amount to be insured in figures in box marked "Amount of Insurance".

Handing Information

(For USA only) These commodities licensed by U.S. for ultimate destination ·······························Diversion contrary to U.S. law is prohibited

No of Pieces RCP	Gross Weight	KG lb	Rate Class Commodity Item No.	Chargeable Weight	Rate Charge	Total	Nature and Quantity of Goods (incl. Dimensions or Volume)

Prepaid Weight Charge Collect	Other Charges
Valuation Charge	
Tax	

Total other Charges Due Agent	Shipper certifies that the particulars on the face hereof are correct and that insofar as any part of the consignment contains dangerous goods，such part is properly described by name and is in proper condition for carriage by air according to the applicable Dangerous Goods Regulations.
Total other Charges Due Carrier	

....
Signature of Shipper or his Agent

Total Prepaid	Total Collect	
Currency Conversion Rates	CC Charges in Dest. Currency	

....
Executed on (date)　　　　at(place)　　　　Signature of Issuing Carrier or its Agent

For Carrier's Use only at Destination	Charges at Destination	Total Collect Charges 999 —

二、实务思考

1. 国内 A 贸易公司出口货物，并通过 B 货代公司向某国外班轮 C 订舱出运货物，货装船后，C 公司向 A 公司签发一式三份记名提单。货到目的港，记名提单上的收货人未取得正本提单情况下，从 C 公司手中提走全部货物。A 公司以承运人无单放货为由，在国内起诉 C 公司。(提单注明适用美国法律。在美国，承运人向记名提单的记名收货人交付货物时，不负有要求记名收货人出示或提交记名提单的义务) 请问：①本案适用哪个国家法律？为什么？②承运人是否承担无单放货责任？为什么？

2. 某一货主将一批货交由无船承运人运输，并签发 H-B/L，无船承运人将货交船公司，并由船公司签发 H-B/L，目的港的无船承运人在收货人未调换 B/L 的情况下将货交给收货人。请问：①这种放货行为将产生什么后果？②无船承运人将承担什么样的责任？

实训项目23

缮制商业发票

一、操作练习

根据合同、信用证及下列资料，制作商业发票，要求格式清楚、内容完整。

2014年8月12日，山西宏发贸易公司填制编号为2003SDT009的商业发票。

（一）

售货确认书
SALES CONFIRMATION

卖方：　　　　　　　　　　　　　　　　　合同号码：
Sellers：SHANXI HONGFA CO.，LTD　　　　Contract No.：03TG28711
买方：　　　　　　　　　　　　　　　　　日期：
Buyers：YAHALUCHI CO.，LTD.　　　　　　 Date：JULY. 22，2014
　　　　3-72，OHTAMACHI，NAKA-KU，　　地点：
　　　　YOKOHAMA，JAPAN231　　　　　　 Signed at：TAIYUAN，CHINA

　　This Sales Contract is made by and between the Sellers and Buyers，whereby the Sellers agree to sell and the Buyers agree to buy the under-mentioned goods according to the terms and conditions stipulated below：

品名及规格 NAME OF COMMODITY & SPECIFICATION	单价 UNIT PRICE	数量 QUANTITY	金额及术语 AMOUNT & PRICE TERMS
H6-59940BS GOLF CAPS	USD 8.10	1 800 DOZS	CIF AKITA USD 14 580.00
		TOTAL	USD 14 580.00

10% more or less both in amount and quantity allowed

Packing：CARTON

Delivery：From TAIYUAN，CHINA to AKITA，JAPAN

Shipping Marks：V.H
　　　　　　　　LAS PLAMS
　　　　　　　　C/NO.

Time of Shipment：Within 30 days after receipt of L/C. allowing transshipment and partial shipment.

Terms of Payment：By 100% Irrevocable Letter of Credit on favor of the Sellers to be available. By sight draft to be opened and to reach China before   JULY 30，2014   and to remain valid for negotiation in China until the 15th days after the foresaid Time of Shipment.

　　　　　　　　L/C must mention this contract number L/C advised by BANK OF CHINA NANJING BRANCH.

TLX：44U4K NJBC，CN. ALL banking Charges outside China (the mainland of China) are for account of the Drawee.

Insurance：To be effected by Sellers for 110% of full invoice value covering   F.P.A up to AKITA To be effected by the Buyers.

Arbitration：All disputes arising from the execution of or in connection with this contract shall be settled amicable by negotiation. In case of settlement can be reached through negotiation the case shall then be submitted to China International Economic & Trade Arbitration Commission. In Nanjing for arbitration in act with its sure of procedures. The arbitral award is final and binding upon both parties for setting the Dispute. The fee，for arbitration shall be borne by the losing party unless otherwise awarded.

　　THE SELLER：　　　　　　　　　　　　　　THE BUYER：

（二）

ISSUE OF DOCUMENTARY CREDIT

ISSUING BANK	METITABANKLED., JAPAN
DOC. CREDIT NUMBER	LTR0505457
DATE OF ISSUE	150727
EXPIRY	DATE 150908 PLACE NANJING, CHINA
APPLICANT	YAHALUCHI CO., LTD. 3-72, OHTAMACHI, NAKA-KU, YOKOHAMA, JAPAN231
BENEFICIARY	SHANXI HONGFA CO., LTD ROOM 2501, JIAFA MANSTION, BEIJING WEST ROAD, SHANXI
AMOUNT	CURRENCY USD AMOUNT 14 580.00
POS. /NEG. TOL. (%)	5/5
AVAILABLE WITH/BY	ANY BANK IN ADVISING COUNTRY BY NEGOTIATION
DRAFT AT···	DRAFTS AT SIGHT FOR FULL INVOICE VALUE
PARTIAL SHIPMENTS	ALLOWED
TRANSSHIPMENT	ALLOWED
LOADING IN CHARGE	TAIYUAN
FOR TRANSPORT TO	AKITA
SHIPMENT PERIOD	AT THE LATEST AUG. 30, 2014
DESCRIPT. OF GOODS	1 800 DOZS OF H6-59940BS GOLF CAPS, USD 8.10 PER DOZ AS PER SALES CONTRACT 03TG28711 DD 22，7，03 CIF AKITA
DOCUMENTS REQUIRED	*COMMERCIAL INVOICE 1 SIGNED ORIGINAL AND 5 COPIES *PACKING LIST IN 2 COPIES *FULL SET OF CLEAN ON BOARD, MARKED "FREIGHT PREPAID" AND NOTIFY APPLICANT (AS INDICATE ABOVE) *GSP CERTIFICATE OF ORIGIN FORM A, CERTIFYING GOODS OF ORIGIN IN CHINA, ISSUED BY COMPETENT AUTHORITIES *INSURANCE POLICY/CERTIFICATE COVERING F.P.A. OF PICC. INCLUDING WARWHOUSE TO WAREHOUSE CLAUSE UP TO FINAL DESTINATION AT AKITA, FOR AT LEAST 110 PCT OF CIF-VALUE. *SHIPPING ADVICES MUST BE SENT TO APPLICANT WITHIN 2 DAYS AFTER SHIPMENT ADVISING NUMBERE OF PACKAGES, GROSS & NET WEIGHT, VESSEL NAME, BILL OF LADING NO. AND DATE, CONTRACT NO., VALUE.
PRESENTATION PERIOD	21 DAYS AFTER ISSUANCE DATE OF SHIPPING DOCUMENT
CONFIRMATION	WITHOUT
INSTRUCTIONS	THE NEGOTIATION BANK MUST FORWARD THE DRAFTS AND ALL DOCUMENTS BY REGISTERED AIRMAIL.DIRECT TO US IN TWO CONSECUTIVE LOTS, UPON RECEIPT OF THE DRAFTS AND DOCUMENTS IN ORDER, WE WILL REMIT THE PROCEEDS AS INSTRUCTED BY THE NEGOTIATING BANK.

（三）

COMMERCIAL INVOICE

To:

From: _____

Letter of Credit No.: _____

Invoice No.: _____

Invoice Date: _____

S/C No.: _____

S/C Date: _____

To: _____

Issued By: _____

Marks and Numbers	Number and kind of package Description of goods	Quantity	Unit Price	Amount
	TOTAL:			

SAY TOTAL:

二、根据以下信用证内容，修改以下商业发票

DOC.CREDIT NUMBER：044 / 307587

APPLICANT：EEN CO.，VANCOUVER，CANADA

BENEFICIARY：GUANGDONG HUALIAN TRADING CORPORATION 60 HUHAI ROAD GUANGZHOU CHIN A

AMOUNT CURRENCY：USD 5 256.00

AVAILABLE WITH/BY：FREELY NEGOTIABLE AT ANY BANK BY NEGOTIATION

LADING IN CHARGE：CHINA

FOR TRANSPORT TO：VANCOUVER VIA HONGKONG

LATEST DATE OF SHIPMENT：150131

DESCRIPTION OF GOODS：2.920DS OF 100PCT COTTON DENIM-8 02-ROPE DYED INDIGO(CT-121)

DOUBLE P/SHRUNK RESIDUAL AHRINKAGE NOT MORE THAN 3-4PCT 82×50/14S×14S-WIDTH：58/59'AT USD 1.80/YD AS PER PURCHASE ORDER NO. FAB10-20030087/01-02，CIF VANCOUVER

DOCUMENTS REQUIRED：+SIGNED COMMERCIAL INVOICE IN TRIPLICATE.

COMMERCIAL INVOICE

TO MESSRS.：EEN CO.，VANCOUVER，CANADA	INVOICE NO.：SHE01/7203
L/C NO.：044/387587	DATE：JAN. 28，2015
SHIPPED FROM GUANGZHOU TO VANCOUVER	P. O. No.：FAB10 -20030087/0l -02

MARKS & NOS.	DESCRIPTION	QUANTITY	UNIT PRICE	AMOUNT
	GOLDTRON GARMENTS SDN BHD			
	PO NO. FAB10 – 20030087/01 – 02			
	COLOR：INDIGO			
	R/NO.：1-4，6-36			
	2 928 YARDS USD 1.80/YARD USD 5 256.00			
	100PCT COTTON DENIM-80Z- ROPE DYED INDIGO (CT- 121)			
	DOUBLE P/SHRUNK RESIDUAL AHRINKAGE NOT MORE THAN			
	3– 4PCT 82×50/14S×14S – WIDTH：58/59' AS PER PURCHASE ORDER NO.			
	FAB10-20030087/01 -02			
	TOTAL：US DOLLARS FIVE THOUSAND TWO HUNDRED FIFTY SIX ONLY			

GUANGDONG HUALIAN TRADING CORPORATION

张三

三、实务思考

1. 某年 3 月我工艺品公司向巴基斯坦 BICI 公司出口一批货物。6 月 5 日对方开来信用证有下列条款："...350 sets of dinner set，price：USD1351.00 per set，C&F Karachi，shipment from Qingdao to Karachi，shipping Mark to be 'BICI/381 and 451/ Karachi only I'"（350 套西餐具，价格每套 35 美元，C&F 卡拉奇。从青岛装运至卡拉奇，运输标志仅为"BICI/381 AND 451/KARACHI"）。

我工艺品出口公司装运后即议付交单，议付行就寄单索汇，单到，开证行审单后指出下列不符而拒付：①提单及发票等单据上表示的运输标志与信用证不符。信用证规定："BICI/381 AND 451/KARACHI"，寄来的发票等单据的运输标志为"BICI/381 & 451/KARACHI"。②信用证规定价格条款为"USD135100 per set C&F Karachi"，而发票上表示的价格条款为"USD135100 per set CFR Karachi"。③包装单上运输标志栏表示："As per invoice"漏列发票号码。

我方出口单位即回电反驳：①关于信用证规定的运输标志与我方交单内容不符问题，仅系"AND"与"&"之别，实际上两者并无差异，不能当作不符。②关于价格条款的"C&F"与"CFR"的不符问题，根据国际商会 600 出版物规定 C&F 术语已被 CFR 代替。所以，我方发票上才是正确的。③关于包装单上运输标志表示"As per invoice"，未列发票号码问题。本信用证项下的发票只有一个，再无其他发票，所以不予表示号码，并不是不符。

开证行接电后再次来电坚持认为单证不符而拒付：①关于运输标志问题，信用证中规定"shipping Mark to be 'BICI/381 and 451/ Karachi only I'"，其要求是指必须完全一致 (only) 内容才能接受。你方将"AND"改为"&"，当然属于不符。②关于贸易价格条件，根据《UCP 600》规定，银行只管单据是否与信用证表面上相符，"C&F"与"CFR"就是表面上不符。③关于单据上"As per invoice"，我们认为必须表示该发票的号码才能"有所依据"。

我工艺品出口公司与议付行共同研究认为，对方有些意见固属挑剔过分，但我方单据存在缺陷也是事实，后几经洽商，以我方让价 10% 而结案。

2. 不同付款方式下的两张发票案例。

(1) 2014 年 3 月，Nr 公司与 A 国 cL 公司签订合同。以每公斤 18 美元的价格从中国进口 10 吨价值 18 万美元的 CF 产品。L/C SIGHT 付款方式。cL 公司在开出信用证之后，提出为其提供两张商业发票的要求。原因是国际市场价格可能下降，这样货到报关时可以少纳税。其中，每公斤 18 美元的发票随提单、汇票等其他单证一起通过银行正常交单；另做一张价格为每公斤 10 美元的发票，直接邮递给进口商。

(2) 2014 年 8 月，NI 公司与 B 国 PP 公司签订合同，以每公斤 12 美元的价格，从中国进口 20 吨 SC 产品，付款方式是 D/P SIGHT 进口商提出要求做两张发票，原因是进口国政府对 SC 产品实际进口实行海关估价制，对于进口该产品的关税征税标准为：

FOB 进口价低于或等于每公斤 8 美元，按照 8 美元计价征纳关税；FOB 进口价高于每公斤 8 美元，按照实际成交的 FOB 价格征纳关税。过去，国际市场行情低于每公斤 8 美元时，进口商缴了很多关税，为了寻求平衡，需要出一张每公斤 8 美元的发票，直接快递进口商用于报关。至于实际进口货物付款，仍然按照合同签订的每公斤 12 美元执行。

实训项目24

缮制装箱单

一、操作练习

根据信用证及下列资料，制作装箱单，要求格式清楚、内容完整。

2014 年 8 月 12 日，福建昌达贸易公司填制装箱单。

商业发票编号为 2003SDT009，日期为 2014 年 8 月 12 日。

Package：240 CARTONS

G.W：19 KGS

N.W：17 KGS

Meas.：21.583 CBM

（一）

ISSUE OF DOCUMENTARY CREDIT

ISSUING BANK	METITABANKLED.，JAPAN
DOC. CREDIT NUMBER	LTR0505457
DATE OF ISSUE	140727
EXPIRY	DATE 140908 PLACE NANJING，CHINA
APPLICANT	EAST AGENT COMPANY
	3-72，OHTAMACHI，NAKA-KU，YOKOHAMA，JAPAN231
BENEFICIARY	FUJIAN CHANGDA CO.，LTD
	ROOM 2501，JIAFA MANSTION，BEIJING WEST ROAD，FUJIAN
AMOUNT	CURRENCY USD AMOUNT 14 580.00
POS. /NEG. TOL. (%)	5/5
AVAILABLE WITH/BY	ANY BANK IN ADVISING COUNTRY
	BY NEGOTIATION
DRAFT AT…	DRAFTS AT SIGHT FOR FULL INVOICE VALUE
PARTIAL SHIPMENTS	ALLOWED
TRANSSHIPMENT	ALLOWED
LOADING IN CHARGE	FUZHOU
FOR TRANSPORT TO	AKITA
SHIPMENT PERIOD	AT THE LATEST AUG. 30，2014
DESCRIPT. OF GOODS	1800 DOZS OF H6-59940BS GOLF CAPS，USD 8.10 PER DOZ AS PER
	SALES CONTRACT 03TG28711 DATED DEC. 22，2014 CIF AKITA
	SHIPPING MARKS：V.H / LAS PLAMS / C/NO.1-240
DOCUMENTS REQUIRED	*COMMERCIAL INVOICE 1 SIGNED ORIGINAL AND 5 COPIES
	*PACKING LIST IN 2 COPIES
	*FULL SET OF CLEAN ON BOARD，MARKED "FREIGHT PREPAID"
	AND NOTIFY APPLICANT (AS INDICATE ABOVE)
	*GSP CERTIFICATE OF ORIGIN FORM A，CERTIFYING GOODS OF
	ORIGIN IN CHINA，ISSUED BY COMPETENT AUTHORITIES
	*INSURANCE POLICY/CERTIFICATE COVERING F.P.A. OF PICC.
	INCLUDING WARWHOUSE TO WAREHOUSE CLAUSE UP TO FINAL
	DESTINATION AT AKITA，FOR AT LEAST 110 PCT OF CIF-VALUE.
	*SHIPPING ADVICES MUST BE SENT TO APPLICANT WITHIN 2
	DAYS AFTER SHIPMENT ADVISING NUMBERE OF PACKAGES，
	GROSS & NET WEIGHT，VESSEL NAME，BILL OF LADING NO.
	AND DATE，CONTRACT NO.，VALUE.
PRESENTATION PERIOD	21 DAYS AFTER ISSUANCE DATE OF SHIPPING DOCUMENT
CONFIRMATION	WITHOUT
INSTRUCTIONS	THE NEGOTIATION BANK MUST FORWARD THE DRAFTS AND
	ALL DOCUMENTS BY REGISTERED AIRMAIL.DIRECT TO US IN
	TWO CONSECUTIVE LOTS，UPON RECEIPT OF THE DRAFTS AND
	DOCUMENTS IN ORDER，WE WILL REMIT THE PROCEEDS AS
	INSTRUCTED BY THE NEGOTIATING BANK.

（二）

Marks and Numbers	Number and kind of package/Description of goods	Quantity	Package	G.W	N.W	Meas.

ISSUER

TO

装箱单
PACKING LIST

INVOICE NO.	DATE

TOTAL:

SAY TOTAL:

二、审单练习

Date of Issue：140120 Form of Doc. Credit：IRREVOCABLE

Doc. Credit Number：M20K2710NS00032

Expiry：Date 141215 Place IN BENEFICIARY'S COUNTRY

Applicant：SE BANG TRADING CO.，LTD.

        148 NAMCHEON- 2 DONG，SUYOUNG – KU PUSAN，KOREA

Beneficiary：GUANGZHOU ARTS & CRAFTS IMP. & EXP. CORP.

        628 GUAGNZHOU DADAO ZHONG ROAD，GUANGZHOU，CHINA

Partial Shipments：ALLOWED

Transshipment：ALLOWED

Loading in Charge：GUANGZHOU，CHINA

For Transport to...：PUSAN，KOREA

Latest Date of Ship：141105

Descript. of Goods：CHINA ORIGIN CIF PUSAN ARTIFICIAL FLOWERS

        AB – 06001 5，184DOZ @ USD2.50/DOZ

        AB – 07049 2，880DOZ @ USD2.50/DOZ

        AS PER S/C NO.11A/KF002A DATE OCT. 15，2013，ISSUED

        BY GUANGZHOU ARTS & CRAFTS IMPS & EXP. CORP.

Documents Required：PACKING LIST IN TRIPLICATE

Additional Cond.：ALL DOCUMENTS MUST INDICATE THIS CREDIT NUMBERS

        THE DETAILS SUCH AS ART NO. COLOR，Q'TY SHOULD BE

        MARKED ON THE EACH INNER BOX AND CARTON EXACTLY.

INV. NO.：11KF335

INV. DATE：OCT. 28，2014

B/L NO.：DSA11 -1102

SHIPPING MARKS：SE BANG/PUSAN

PACKING：AB-06001 36DOZ/CTN G. W.：23KGS/CTN N.W.：18KGS/CTN

        AB-07049 36DOZ/CTN G.W.：19KGS/CTN N.W.：13KGS/CTN

NAME OF STEAMER：SUI 301/NORASIA V. 49 -3 W/T HONGKONG

CONTAINER NO.：MSCU 4097560 (20')，MSCU 4097615 (40')

MEASUREMENT：(40×50×80) CM/CTN

```
┌─────────────────────────────────────────────────────────────────────────┐
│                            PACKING LIST                                   │
│ Exporter: GUANGZHOU ARTS & CRAFTS IMP.              ORIGINAL              │
│           AND EXP.CORP.                    DATE: OCT. 28，2014            │
│           628 GUANGZHOU DADAO ZHONG        INVOICE NO.: 11KF335          │
│           ROAD，GUANGZHOU，CHINA.          B/L NO.: OCT. 31，2014        │
│                                            S/C NO.: DSA11—1102          │
│                                            L/C NO.: M20K2710NS4)0032     │
│                                                     DSA11—1102          │
│ TRANSPORT DETAILS: FROM GUANGZHOU TO PUSAN                               │
│                    BY VESSEL                                             │
│                    224CTNS    3 632.00KGS    4 832.00KGS    35.84CBMS    │
│ TOTAL QUANTITY: 224CTNS                                                  │
│ TOTAL: TWO HUNDRED AND TWENTY-FOUR CARTONS ONLY                         │
│                                                                          │
│              GUANGZHOU ARTS & CRAFTS IMP.AND EXP.CORP.                   │
│         628 GUANGZHOU DADAO ZHONG ROAD，GUANGZHOU，CHINA                 │
│                         王丽丽                                           │
└─────────────────────────────────────────────────────────────────────────┘
```

三、实务思考

A company in Nanning，China chooses to make shipment in Guangzhou for its high-efficiency. They mailed the full set documents for declaration to the agent declaration company in Guangzhou on June 30，2015 and sent the contracted 1 000 cartons of products by truck 2 days later. When the products arrived in Guangzhou and ready for loading，they found that only 998 cartons can be shipped due to a miscalculation of volume. Under the request of the customhouse，the company immediately made a new set of shipping list and commercial invoice and drive to Guangzhou day and night and finally handed it to the customhouse before the ship set off.

Question: what's the mistake of the Nanning company?

Analyze: The figures on the packing list and commercial invoice must be the same with B/L. However，the number of products that will be actually loaded may be different with the predicted sometimes due to many reasons. Generally，the shipper should give the agent declaration company several empty and signed packing list forms and invoice forms with the ready-made ones. Once the number changes，the agent declaration company can use the empty forms and make the invoice and packing list with actual figures.

因为广州的通关效率很高，一家南宁公司选择在广州装运。他们在 2015 年 6 月 30 日把全套报关单据寄出至广州的报关公司，并于 2 天后把 1 000 纸箱合同项下的货物通过卡车运到广州。当货物到达广州并准备装运时，他们发现因为对体积的计算失误，租赁的舱位实际只能装运 998 纸箱。在海关的要求下，该公司立即制作一套新的装箱单和商业发票并日夜兼程赶到广州，终于在货物装运前将单据交给海关。

　　问题：这家南宁公司的失误在哪里？

　　分析：装箱单和商业发票上的数字必须与提单上的一致。然而，因为各种原因，有时候实际装运的数量与预期的不一致。一般来说，发货人向报关公司提供制作好的报关单据时，应同时提供空白、已签名的商业发票和装箱单若干份。万一装运数量有变化，报关公司可以使用空白签名的表格制作出与实际装运数量一致的单据。

实训项目25

填制一般原产地证书

一、操作练习

工厂资料: XUZHOU SHENGTONG FOODSTUFTS CO., LTD.

NO.15 HEPING ROAD, XUZHOU 221009, CHINA

TEL: 86-0516-3402323

FAX: 86-0516-3402330

商品海关编码: 2010.1011

根据信用证要求准备一般产地证。

（一）

ISSUER FUJIAN INTERNATIONAL IMPORT & EXPORT CORP. 8TH FLOOR，200 ZHANQIAN ROAD，FUZHOU，CHINA	商业发票 COMMERCIAL INVOICE		
TO NEO GENERAL TRADING CO. P. O. BOX 99552，RIYADH 22766，KSA TEL：00966-1-4659220 FAX：00966-1-4659213	NO. 2001SDT001		DATE Apr. 25，2015
TRANSPORT DETAILS SHIPMENT FROM SHANGHAI，CHINA TO DAMMAM，KSA BY SEA	S/C NO. NEO2001026		L/C NO. 0011LC123756
	TERMS OF PAYMENT L/C AT SIGHT		

Marks and Numbers	Number and kind of package Description of goods	Quantity	Unit Price	Amount USD
ROSE BRAND 178/2001 RIYADH				CFR DAMMAM
	ABOUT 1700 CARTONS CANNED MUSRHOOMS PIECES & STEMS 24 TINS × 425 GRAMS NET WEIGHT (D.W. 227 GRAMS)	1 700 CTNS	USD 7.80	USD 13 260.00
	Total：	1 700 CTNS		USD 13 260.00

SAY TOTAL：USD THIRTEEN THOUSAND TWO HUNDRED AND SIXTY ONLY.

BREAK DOWN OF THE AMOUNT AS FOLLOWS：
 FOB VALUE：USD 12 260.00
FREIGHT CHARGES：USD 1 000.00
TOTAL AMOUNT C AND F：USD 13 260.00

（出口商签字和盖单据章）

（二）

ORIGINAL	
1. Exporter	Certificate No.
2. Consignee	**CERTIFICATE OF ORIGIN** **OF** **THE PEOPLE'S REPUBLIC OF** **CHINA**
3. Means of transport and route	5. For certifying authority use only
4. Country / region of destination	

6. Marks and numbers	7. Number and kind of packages; description of goods	8. H. S. Code	9. Quantity	10. Number and date of invoices

11. Declaration by the exporter The undersigned hereby declares that the above details and statements are correct, that all the goods were produced in China and that they comply with the Rules of Origin of the People's Republic of China.	12.Certification It is hereby certified that the declaration by the exporter is correct.
Place and date, signature and stamp of authorized signatory	Place and date, signature and stamp of certifying authority

二、请根据以下资料进行审单练习

SELLER：GUANGDONG DONGFENG IMPORT AND EXPORT CORP.122 DONGFENG ROAD EAST，GUANGZHOU

BUYER：ANYEI HONG KONG 14/F．，KAISER ESTATE 1，MANYUE STREET，HUNG HOM，SYDNEY，AUSTRALIA

1. 2，400PCS (STAINLESS STEEL SPADE HEAD)

2. 12PCS/BUNDLE

3. SHIPPING DATE：DEC. 1ST，2014

Original					
1. Goods consigned from (Exporter's business name，address，country) CUANCDONG DONGFENG IMPORT AND EXPORT CORP. 122 DONGFENG ROAD EAST，GUANGZHOU			Reference NO.　　GZ9/12078/6311 **GENERALIZED SYSTEM OF PREFERENCES CERTIFICATE OF ORIGIN** (Combined declaration and certificate) FORM A		
2. Goods consigned to Consignee's name，address，country) SANYEI HONG KONG 14/F，．KAISER ESTATE 1，MANYUE STREET，HUNG HOM，SYDNEY			issued in THE PEOPLE'S REPUBLIC OF CHINA (COUNTRY) See Notes overleaf		
3. Means of transport an Route as far as known FROM GUANGZHOU TO SYDNEY BY VESSEL			4. For official use		
5. Item number I	6. Marks And numbers of packages KMART SYDNEY NO.1-200	7. Number and kind of packages； description of goods TWO THOUSAND FOUR HUNDRED (2 400) PCS OF STAINLESS STEELSPADE HEAD	8. Origin criterion (see Notes overleaf) "P"	9. Gross weight or other quantity 200 PCS	10. Number and date of invoice SMI9990I NOV.11，2014
11. Certification It is hereby certified，on the basis of control carried out，that the declaration by the exporter is correct. 　　　GUANGZHOU NOV. 21，2014 Place and date，signature and stamp of certifying authority			12. Declaration by the exporter The undersigned hereby declares that the above details and statements are correct；that all the goods were produced in 　　GUANGZHOU　(country) and that they comply with the origin requirements specified for those goods in the Generalized System of Preferences for goods exported to 　　SYDNEY　(importing country) 　GUANGZHOU NOV. 20，2014 Place and date，signature of authorized signature		

实训项目26
缮制普惠制产地证

一、操作练习

2015 年 3 月 20 日，北京纺织服装有限公司的货物顺利装船出运。根据信用证要求，3 月 22 日，北京公司将普惠制产地证及其他随附单据用 DHL 寄给开证人供其用于清关。一般原产地证书 (商会产地证) 和普惠制原产地证书都是一种证明商品的原产国别的一种证书。其中，普惠制原产地证书是当商品出口到给予普惠制的国家时所应提供的原产地证书。在我国一般原产地证书 (商会产地证) 是由中国国际贸易促进委员会 (China Council for the Promotion of International Trade，CCPIT－简称贸促会) 签发的。而普惠制原产地证书是由商检局签发的。

根据信用证要求准备普惠制产地证。

（一）

ISSUER BEIJING TEXTILE GARMENT CO.，LTD. HUARONG MANSION RM2901 NO.85 CHANGAN ROAD, BEIJING 100005，CHINA	商业发票 COMMERCIAL INVOICE		
TO FASHION FORCE CO.，LTD. P. O. BOX 8935 NEW TERMINAL，ALTA, VISTA OTTAWA，CANADA	NO. NT01FF004		DATE Mar. 9，2015
TRANSPORT DETAILS SHIPMENT FROM BEIJING，CHINA TO MONTREAL, CANADA BY VESSEL	S/C NO. F01LCB05127		L/C NO. 63211020049
	TERMS OF PAYMENT L/C AT SIGHT		
Marks and Numbers	Number and kind of package Description of goods	Quantity	Unit Price	Amount
			USD	
FASHION FORCE F01LCB05127 CTN NO. MONTREAL MADE IN CHINA				CIF MONTREAL
	LADIES COTTON BLAZER (100% COTTON，40S×20/140×60)	2 550 PCS	USD 12.80	USD 32 640.00
	Total:	2 550 PCS		USD 32 640.00

SAY TOTAL：USD THIRTY TWO THOUSAND SIX HUNDRED AND FORTY ONLY

SALES CONDITIONS：CIF MONTREAL/CANADA

           SALES CONTRACT NO. F01LCB05127

           LADIES COTTON BLAZER (100% COTTON，40S×20/140×60)

STYLE NO.	PO NO.	QTY/PCS	USD/PC
46-301A	10337	2 550	12.80

（出口商签字和盖单据章）

（二）

```
2015JAN31 15：23：46                          LOGICAL TERMINAL E102 MT S700
```

ISSUE OF A DOCUMENTARY CREDIT

```
                                              PAGE00001
                                              FUNC MSG70
                                              UMR06607642
```

MSGACK DWS765I AUTH OK，KEY B110106173BAOC53B，BKCHCNBJ BNPA**** RECORO

BASIC HEADER   F 01 BKCHCNBJA940 0542 725524

APPLICATION HEADER		0 700 1122 010129 BNPACAMMAXXX 4968 839712 010130 0028 N
		*BNP PARIBAS (CANADA)
		*MONTREAL
USER HEADER		SERVICE CODE 103：
		BANK. PRIORITY 113：
		MSG USER REF. 108：（银行盖信用证通知专用章）
		INFO. FROM CI 115：
SEQUENCE OF TOTAL	*27	1 / 1
FORM OF DOC. CREDIT	*40 A	IRREVOCABLE
DOC. CREDIT NUMBER	*20	63211020049
DATE OF ISSUE	31 C	150129
EXPIRY	*31 D	DATE 150410 PLACE IN BENEFICIARY'S COUNTRY
APPLICANT	*50	FASHION FORCE CO.，LTD
		P. O. BOX 8935 NEW TERMINAL，ALTA，VISTA OTTAWA，
		CANADA
BENEFICIARY	*59	BEIJING TEXTILE GARMENT CO.，LTD.
		HUARONG MANSION RM2901 NO.85 CHANGAN ROAD，
		BEIJING 100005，CHINA
AMOUNT	*32 B	CURRENCY USD AMOUNT 32640，
AVAILABLE WITH/BY	*41 D	ANY BANK BY NEGOTIATION
DRAFTS AT ...	42 C	SIGHT
DRAWEE	42 A	BNPACAMMXXX
		*BNP PARIBAS (CANADA)
		*MONTREAL
PARTIAL SHIPMTS	43 P	NOT ALLOWED
TRANSSHIPMENT	43 T	ALLOWED
LOADING ON CHARGE	44 A	CHINA
FOR TRANSPORT TO...	44 B	MONTREAL
LATEST DATE OF SHIP.	44 C	150325
DESCRIPT. OF GOODS	45 A	SALES CONDITIONS：CIF MONTREAL/CANADA
		SALES CONTRACT NO. F01LCB05127
		LADIES COTTON BLAZER (100% COTTON，40S×20/140×60)
		STYLE NO. PO NO. QTY/PCS USD/PC
		46-301A 10337 2 550 12.80
DOCUMENTS REQUIRED	46 A	+COMMERCIAL INVOICES IN 3 COPIES SIGNED BY
		BENEFICIARY'S REPRESENTATIVE.
		+CANADA CUSTOMS INVOICES IN 4 COPIES.

		+FULL SET OF ORIGINAL MARINE BILLS OF LADING CLEAN ON BOARD PLUS 2 NON NEGOTIABLE COPIES MADE OUT OR ENDORSED TO ORDER OF BNP PARIBAS (CANADA) MARKED FREIGHT PREPAID AND NOTIFY APPLICANT'S FULL NAME AND ADDRESS.
		+DETAILED PACKING LISTS IN 3 COPIES.
		+COPY OF CERTIFICATE OF ORIGIN FORM A.
		+COPY OF EXPORT LICENCE.
		+BENEFICIARY'S LETTER STATING THAT ORIGINAL CERTIFICATE OF ORIGIN FORM A，ORIGINAL EXPORT LICENCE，COPY OF COMMERCIAL INVOICE，DETAILED PACKING LISTS AND A COPY OF BILL OF LADING WERE SENT DIRECT TO APPLICANT BY COURIER WITHIN 5 DAYS AFTER SHIPMENT.THE RELEATIVE COURIER RECEIPT IS ALSO REQUIRED FOR PRESENTATION.
		+COPY OF APPLICANT'S FAX APPROVING PRODUCTION SAMPLES BEFORE SHIPMENT.
		+LETTER FROM SHIPPER ON THEIR LETTERHEAD INDICATING THEIR NAME OF COMPANY AND ADDRESS，BILL OF LADING NUMBER，CONTAINER NUMBER AND THAT SHIPMENT，INCLUDING ITS CONTAINER，DOES NOT CONTAIN ANY NON-MANUFACTURED WOODEN MATERIAL，DUNNAGE，BRACING MATERIAL，PALLETS，CRATING OR OTHER NON-MANUFACTURED WOODEN PACKING MATERIAL.
		+INSPECTION CERTIFICATE ORIGINAL SINGED AND ISSUED BY FASHION FORCE CO.，LTD STATING THE SAMPLES OF FOUR STYLE GARMENTS HAD BEEN APPROVED，WHICH SEND THROUGH DHL BEFORE 15 DAYS OF SHIPMENT.
		+INSURANCE POLICY OR CERTIFICATE IN 1 ORIGINAL AND 1 COPY ISSUED OR ENDORSED TO THE ORDER OF BNP PARIBAS (CANADA) FOR THE CIF INVOICE PLUS 10 PERCENT COVERING ALL RISKS，INSTITUTE STRIKES，INSTITUTE WAR CLAUSES AND CIVIL COMMOTIONS CLAUSES.
ADDITIONAL COND.	47 A	+IF DOCUMENTS PRESENTED ARE FOUND BY US NOT TO BE IN FULL COMPLIANCE WITH CREDIT TERMS.WE WILL ASSESS A CHARGE OF USD 55.00 PER SET OF DOCUMENTS.
		+ALL CHARGES IF ANY RELATED TO SETTLEMENTS ARE FOR ACCOUNT OF BENEFICIARY.
		+3 PCT MORE OR LESS IN AMOUNT AND QUANTITY IS ALLOWED.
		+ALL CERTIFICATES/LETTERS/STATEMENTS MUST BE SIGNED AND DATED

（续表）

		+FOR INFORMATION ONLY，PLEASE NOTE AS OF JANUARY 4，2015 THAT ALL SHIPMENTS FROM CHINA THAT ARE PACKED WITH UNTREATED WOOD WILL BE BANNED FROM CANADA DUE TO THE THREAT POSED BY THE ASIAN LONGNORNED BEETLE.
		+THE CANADIAN GOVERNMENT NOW INSIST THAT EVERY SHIPMENT ENTERING CANADA MUST HAVE THE ABOVE DOCUMENTATION WITH THE SHIPMENT.
		+BILL OF LADING AND COMMERCIAL INVOICE MUST CERTIFY THE FOLLOWING:
		THIS SHIPMENT，INCLUDING ITS CONTAINER DOES NOT CONTAIN ANY NON-MANUFACTURED WOODEN MATERIAL，DUNNAGE，BRACING MATERIAL PALLETS，CRATING OR OTHER NON MANUFACTURED WOODEN PACKING MATERIAL.
		+BENEFICIARY'S BANK ACCOUNT NO. 07773108201140121
CHARGES	71 B	OUTSIDE COUNTRY BANK CHARGES TO BE BORNE BY THE BENEFICIARY OPENING BANK CHARGES TO BE BORNE BY THE APPLICANT
CONFIRMATION	*49	WITHOUT
INSTRUCTIONS	78	+WE SHALL COVER THE NEGOTIATING BANK AS PER THEIR INSTRUCTIONS
		+FORWARD DOCUMENTS IN ONE LOT BY SPECIAL COURIER PREPAID TO BNP PARIBAS (CANADA) 1981 MCGILL COLLECE AVE.MONTREAL QC H3A 2W8 CANADA.
SEND. TO REC. INFO.	72	THIS CREDIT IS SUBJECT TO UCP FOR DOCUMENTARY CREDIT REVISION ICC PUBLICATION 600 AND IS THE OPERATIVE INSTRUMENT
TRAILER		ORDER IS <MAC：> <PAC：> <ENC：> <CHK：> <TNG：> <PDE：> MAC：F344CA36 CHK：AA6204FFDFC2

（三）

1. Goods consigned from (Exporter's business name，address，country)	Reference No.
	GENERALIZED SYSTEM OF PREFERENCES CERTIFICATE OF ORIGIN (Combined declaration and certificate) **FORM A** Issued in THE PEOPLE'S REPUBLIC OF CHINA (country) See Notes overleaf
2. Goods consigned to (Consignee's name，address，country)	

3. Means of transport and route (as far as known)	4. For official use

5.Item number	6. Marks and numbers of packages	7. Number and kind of packages；description of goods	8. Origin criterion (see Notes overleaf)	9. Gross weight or other quantity	10. Number and date of invoices

| 11. Certification
 It is hereby certified，on the basis of control carried out，that the declaration by the exporter is correct.

 Place and date，signature and stamp of certifying authority | 12. Declaration by the exporter
 The undersigned hereby declares that the above details and statements are correct，that all the goods were <br> produced in $\frac{\text{CHINA}}{\text{(country)}}$
 and that they comply with the origin requirements specified for those goods in the Generalized System of Preferences for goods exported to

 Place and date，signature and stamp of authorized signatory |

二、实务思考

Indian Company Can Not Get Tariff Deducted With C/O

An Indian trading company exported tools from India to China，and the production process of the exported tools were finished in India. They applied for a C/O before tools were being shipped 3 days ago. When these tools arrived in China，they apply for tariff deducted with C/O，but they get refused.

Case analysis：

The Bangkok Agreement is an initiative under the Economic and Social Commission for Asia and the Pacific (ESCAP) to exchange tariff concessions among countries in the ESCAP region. India，South Korea，Bangladesh and Sri Lanka were signatories to the Agreement since 1975，but China joined the Agreement in April，2001. As a result of China becoming a signatory to the Agreement，bilateral negotiations for exchange of tariff concessions between India and China were concluded in the year 2003.

Therefore，in this case，it is normal that the India trading company get refused for deducted tariff with C/O，they should apply for a FORM B instead of it.

印度公司持有原产地证书但未得到关税减免

一家印度贸易公司出口一批工具至中国，这批工具的最终生产环节在印度完成。工具装运前 3 天，该公司申请了原产地证书。当工具到达中国时，他们申请关税减免但遭到拒绝。

案例分析：《曼谷协定》是亚洲及太平洋经济社会委员会 (ESCAP) 为了让亚洲及太平洋区域内的国家能相互享受关税减让而采用的初步措施。印度、韩国、孟加拉和斯里兰卡于 1975 年成为该协议的签约国，中国 2001 年 4 月才加入该协定。2003 年印度与中国达成关于双边关税减让的双边谈判。因此，在此案中，印度贸易公司持原产地证书被拒绝关税减让是正常的。要获得这个待遇，他们应该使用 FORM B 表格。

实训项目27

缮制受益人证明书

操作练习

2015年3月20日，广州纺织服装有限公司的货物顺利装船出运。根据信用证的规定，唐朝公司所准备的议付单据中，必须要出具一份受益人证明："证明装运后5天内，将普惠制产地证正本、输加拿大纺织出口许可证正本、商业发票副本、明细装箱单副本、正本提单的复印件已经由快递方式直接寄送给开证人，并附快件回执。"

根据信用证要求准备议付单据之一"受益人证明书"。

（一）

ISSUER GUANGZHOU TEXTILE GARMENT CO.，LTD. HUARONG MANSION RM2901 NO.85 GUANJIAQIAO，GUANGZHOU 210005，CHINA	商业发票 COMMERCIAL INVOICE	
TO FASHION FORCE CO.，LTD P. O. BOX 8935 NEW TERMINAL，ALTA， VISTA OTTAWA，CANADA	NO. NT01FF004	DATE Mar. 9，2015
TRANSPORT DETAILS SHIPMENT FROM GUANGZHOU，CHINA TO MONTREAL，CANADA BY VESSEL	S/C NO. F01LCB05127	L/C NO. 63211020049
	TERMS OF PAYMENT L/C AT SIGHT	

Marks and Numbers	Number and kind of package Description of goods	Quantity	Unit Price	Amount
				USD
FASHION FORCE F01LCB05127 CTN NO. MONTREAL MADE IN CHINA	CIF MONTREAL LADIES COTTON BLAZER (100% COTTON，40S×20/140×60)	2 550 PCS	USD 12.80	USD 32 640.00
	Total:	2 550 PCS		USD 32 640.00

SAY TOTAL：USD THIRTY TWO THOUSAND SIX HUNDRED AND FORTY ONLY

SALES CONDITIONS：CIF MONTREAL/CANADA
          SALES CONTRACT NO. F01LCB05127
          LADIES COTTON BLAZER (100% COTTON，40S×20/140×60)

STYLE NO.	PO NO.	QTY/PCS	USD/PC
46-301A	10337	2 550	12.80

（出口商签字和盖单据章）

（二）

ISSUE OF A DOCUMENTARY CREDIT

MSGACK　DWS765I AUTH OK，KEY B110106173BAOC53B，BKCHCNBJ BNPA**** RECORO

BASIC HEADER	F 01 BKCHCNBJA940 0542 725524
APPLICATION HEADER	0 700 1122 010129 BNPACAMMAXXX 4968 839712 010130 0028 N
	*BNP PARIBAS (CANADA)
	*MONTREAL
USER HEADER	SERVICE CODE 103：
	BANK. PRIORITY 113：
	MSG USER REF. 108： （银行盖信用证通知专用章）
	INFO. FROM CI 115：

SEQUENCE OF TOTAL　*27 1／1

FORM OF DOC. CREDIT　*40 IRREVOCABLE

DOC. CREDIT NUMBER　*20 63211020049

DATE OF ISSUE　31 C 150129

EXPIRY　*31 D DATE 150410 PLACE IN BENEFICIARY'S COUNTRY

APPLICANT　*50 FASHION FORCE CO.，LTD
　　　　　　　　P. O. BOX 8935 NEW TERMINAL，ALTA，VISTA OTTAWA，CANADA

BENEFICIARY　*59 GUANGZHOU TEXTILE GARMENT CO.，LTD.
　　　　　　　HUARONG MANSION RM2901 NO.85 GUANJIAQIAO，GUANGZHOU 210005，CHINA

AMOUNT　*32 B CURRENCY USD AMOUNT 32640，

AVAILABLE WITH/BY　*41 D ANY BANK BY NEGOTIATION

DRAFTS AT ...　42 C SIGHT

DRAWEE　42 A BNPACAMMXXX
　　　　　　*BNP PARIBAS (CANADA)
　　　　　　*MONTREAL

PARTIAL SHIPMTS　43 P NOT ALLOWED

TRANSSHIPMENT　43 T ALLOWED

LOADING ON CHARGE　44 A CHINA

FOR TRANSPORT TO...　44 B MONTREAL

LATEST DATE OF SHIP.　44 C 150325

DESCRIPT. OF GOODS　45 A SALES CONDITIONS：CIF MONTREAL/CANADA
　　　　　　SALES CONTRACT NO. F01LCB05127
　　　　　　LADIES COTTON BLAZER (100% COTTON，$40S \times 20/140 \times 60$)

STYLE NO.	PO NO.	QTY/PCS	USD/PC
46-301A	10337	2 550	12.80

DOCUMENTS REQUIRED 46A　+COMMERCIAL INVOICES IN 3 COPIES SIGNED BY
　　　　　　　　　BENEFICIARY'S REPRESENTATIVE.

（续表）

		+CANADA CUSTOMS INVOICES IN 4 COPIES. +FULL SET OF ORIGINAL MARINE BILLS OF LADING CLEAN ON BOARD PLUS 2 NON NEGOTIABLE COPIES MADE OUT OR ENDORSED TO ORDER OF BNP PARIBAS (CANADA) MARKED FREIGHT PREPAID AND NOTIFY APPLICANT'S FULL NAME AND ADDRESS. +DETAILED PACKING LISTS IN 3 COPIES. +COPY OF CERTIFICATE OF ORIGIN FORM A. +COPY OF EXPORT LICENCE. +BENEFICIARY'S LETTER STATING THAT ORIGINAL CERTIFICATE OF ORIGIN FORM A, ORIGINAL EXPORT LICENCE, COPY OF COMMERCIAL INVOICE, DETAILED PACKING LISTS AND A COPY OF BILL OF LADING WERE SENT DIRECT TO APPLICANT BY COURIER WITHIN 5 DAYS AFTER SHIPMENT.THE RELEATIVE COURIER RECEIPT IS ALSO REQUIRED FOR PRESENTATION. +COPY OF APPLICANT'S FAX APPROVING PRODUCTION SAMPLES BEFORE SHIPMENT. +LETTER FROM SHIPPER ON THEIR LETTERHEAD INDICATING THEIR NAME OF COMPANY AND ADDRESS, BILL OF LADING NUMBER, CONTAINER NUMBER AND THAT SHIPMENT, INCLUDING ITS CONTAINER, DOES NOT CONTAIN ANY NON-MANUFACTURED WOODEN MATERIAL, DUNNAGE, BRACING MATERIAL, PALLETS, CRATING OR OTHER NON-MANUFACTURED WOODEN PACKING MATERIAL. +INSPECTION CERTIFICATE ORIGINAL SINGED AND ISSUED BY FASHION FORCE CO., LTD STATING THE SAMPLES OF FOUR STYLE GARMENTS HAD BEEN APPROVED, WHICH SEND THROUGH DHL BEFORE 15 DAYS OF SHIPMENT. +INSURANCE POLICY OR CERTIFICATE IN 1 ORIGINAL AND 1 COPY ISSUED OR ENDORSED TO THE ORDER OF BNP PARIBAS (CANADA) FOR THE CIF INVOICE PLUS 10 PERCENT COVERING ALL RISKS, INSTITUTE STRIKES, INSTITUTE WAR CLAUSES AND CIVIL COMMOTIONS CLAUSES.
ADDITIONAL COND.	47 A	+IF DOCUMENTS PRESENTED ARE FOUND BY US NOT TO BE IN FULL COMPLIANCE WITH CREDIT TERMS. WE WILL ASSESS A CHARGE OF USD 55.00 PER SET OF DOCUMENTS. +ALL CHARGES IF ANY RELATED TO SETTLEMENTS ARE FOR ACCOUNT OF BENEFICIARY. +3 PCT MORE OR LESS IN AMOUNT AND QUANTITY IS ALLOWED. +ALL CERTIFICATES/LETTERS/STATEMENTS MUST BE SIGNED AND DATED

（续表）

		+FOR INFORMATION ONLY，PLEASE NOTE AS OF JANUARY 4，2015 THAT ALL SHIPMENTS FROM CHINA THAT ARE PACKED WITH UNTREATED WOOD WILL BE BANNED FROM CANADA DUE TO THE THREAT POSED BY THE ASIAN LONGNORNED BEETLE. +THE CANADIAN GOVERNMENT NOW INSIST THAT EVERY SHIPMENT ENTERING CANADA MUST HAVE THE ABOVE DOCUMENTATION WITH THE SHIPMENT. +BILL OF LADING AND COMMERCIAL INVOICE MUST CERTIFY THE FOLLOWING：THIS SHIPMENT，INCLUDING ITS CONTAINER DOES NOT CONTAIN ANY NON-MANUFACTURED WOODEN MATERIAL，DUNNAGE，BRACING MATERIAL PALLETS，CRATING OR OTHER NON MANUFACTURED WOODEN PACKING MATERIAL. +ENEFICIARY'S BANK ACCOUNT NO. 07773108201140121
CHARGES	71 B	OUTSIDE COUNTRY BANK CHARGES TO BE BORNE BY THE BENEFICIARY OPENING BANK CHARGES TO BE BORNE BY THE APPLICANT
CONFIRMATION	*49	WITHOUT
INSTRUCTIONS	78	+WE SHALL COVER THE NEGOTIATING BANK AS PER THEIR INSTRUCTIONS +FORWARD DOCUMENTS IN ONE LOT BY SPECIAL COURIER PREPAID TO BNP PARIBAS (CANADA) 1981 MCGILL COLLECE AVE.MONTREAL QC H3A 2W8 CANADA.
SEND. TO REC. INFO.	72	THIS CREDIT IS SUBJECT TO UCP FOR DOCUMENTARY CREDIT 2007 REVISION ICC PUBLICATION 600 AND IS THE OPERATIVE INSTRUMENT
TRAILER		ORDER IS <MAC：><PAC：><ENC：><CHK：><TNG：><PDE：> MAC：F344CA36 CHK：AA6204FFDFC2

（三）

GUANGZHOU TEXTILE GARMENT CO.，LTD.

HUARONG MANSION RM2901 NO.85 GUANJIAQIAO，GUANGZHOU CHINA

CERTIFICATE

To：		Invoice No.：	
		Date：	

实训项目28

缮制商业汇票

一、操作练习

根据信用证条款的内容，制作一份信用证项下的商业汇票。

（一）

NATIONAL PARIS BANK

24 MARSHALL AVE DONCASTER MONTREAL，CANADA

WE ISSUE OUR IRREVOCABLE DOCUMENTARY CREDIT NUMBER：TH2003

IN FAVOUR OF：GUANGZHOU KNITWEAR AND MANUFACTURED GOODS IMPORT AND EXPORT TRADE CORPORATION 321，ZHOUGSHAN ROAD GUANGZHOU，CHINA

BY ORDER OF：YI YANG TRADING CORPORATION

88 MARSHALL AVE DONCASTER VIC 3108 CANADA

FOR AN AMOUNT OF USD 89 705.50

DATE OF EXPIRY：15NOV14

PLACE：IN BENEFICIARY'S COUNTRY

    AVAILABLE WITH ANY BANK BY NEGOTIATION OF BENEFICIARY'S DRAFT DRAWN ON US AT SIGHT IN MONTREAL.THIS CREDIT IS TRANSFERABLE AGAINST DELIVERY OF THE FOLLOWING DOCUMENTS

    +COMMERCIAL INVOICES IN 5 COPIES

    +CANADA CUSTOMS INVOICES IN 6 COPIES

    +FULL SET OF NEGOTIABLE INSURANCE POLICY OR CERTIFICATE BLANK ENDORSED FOR 110 PERCENT OF INVOICE VALUE COVERING ALL RESKS

    +FULL SET OF ORIGINAL MARINE BILLS OF LADING CLEAN ON BOARD PLUS 2 NON-NEGOTIABLE COPIES MADE OUT OR ENDORSED TO ORDER OF NATIONAL PARIS BANK 24 MARSHALL VEDONCASTER MONTREAL，CANADA.

    +SPECIFICATION LIST OF WEIGHTS AND MEASURESIN 4 COPIES COVERING SHIPMENT OF COTTON TEATOWELS AS PER S/C ST303.

    FOR 1-300 SIZE 10 INCHES * 10 INCHES 16000 DOZ. AT USD 1.31/DOZ. 301-600 SIZE 20 INCHES * 20 INCHES 6000 DOZ. AT USD 2.51/DOZ. AND 601-900 SIZE 30 INCHES * 30 INCHES 11350 DOZ. AT USD 4.73/DOZ. CIF MONTREAL FROM SHANGHAI PORT TO MONTREAL PORT NOT LATER THAN 31，OCT.14

PARTIAL SHIPMENTS: ALLOWED

TRANSHIPMENT: ALLOWED

    SPECIAL INSTRUCTIONS

    +ALL CHARGES IF ANY RELATED TO SETTLEMENTS ARE FOR ACCOUNT OF BENEFICIARY

    +IN CASE OF PRESENTATION OF DOCUMENTS WITH DISCREPANCY (IES) A CHARGE OF USD 55.00

    THIS CREDIT IS SUBJECT TO UCP FOR DOCUMENTARY CREDITS 2007 REVISION ICC PUBLICATION 600 AND IS THE OPERATIVE INSTRUMENT

（二）

BILL OF EXCHANGE

凭 Drawn Under _____		不可撤销信用证 Irrevocable L/C No.
日期 Date	支取 Payable With interest @ % 按 息 付款	
号码 No.	汇票金额 Exchange for	广州 Guangzhou

见票　日后(本汇票之副本未付)付交

at _____sight of this FIRST of Exchange （Second of Exchange Being unpaid)

Pay to the order of

金额
the sum of

此致
To

二、请根据以下信用证进行审单练习

（一）

TO：BANK OF CHINA，GUANGDONG

FROM：ARAB NATIONAL BANK

P. O. BOX 18745 JEDDAH SAUDI ARABIA

DEAR SIRS，

KINDLY ADVISE BENEFICIARY'S M/S GUANGDONG METALS AND MINERALS I/E CORP. 5 TIANHE ROAD，GUANGZHOU，CHINA OF OUR OPENING WITH YOU AN IRREVOCABLE DOCUMENTARY CREDIT DATED 10 MARCH，2015 IN THEIR FAVOUR ON BEHALF OF M/S MIGHWLLI STEEL PRODUCTS CO. P. O. BOX 18741 JEDDAH SAUDI ARABIA FOR AMOUNT ABOUT USD 75 683.00 VALID IN CHINA UNTILL 20 MAY 2015，AVAILABLE WITH YOU BY PAYMENT AGAINST PRESENTATION OF BENEFICIARYS' DRAFT(S) AT 30 DAYS AFTER B/L DATE DRAWN ON OURSELVES AND MARKED "DRAWN UNDER ARAB NATIONAL BANK CREDIT NO.254LK254".5% COMMISSION MUST BE DEDUCTED FROM DRAWINGS UNDER THIS CREDIT.

（二）

BILL OF EXCHANGE

NO.　　　　　　　　　　　　　　DATE　JAN. 10，2015

DRAWN UNDER ARAB NATIONAL BANK

EXCHANGE FOR USD 14 200. 00

AT ×××　DAYS AFTER SIGHT OF THIS FIRST OF EXCHANGE (SECOND OF EXCHANGE BEING UNPAID)

PAY TO THE ORDER OF　BANK OF CHINA，GUANGZHOU BRANCH

THE SUM OF　US DOLLARS FOURTEEN THOUSAND TWO HUNDRED ONLY

TO　HONGKONG ABC CO.

　　3/F GUANGTEX BUILDING TAIKOKTSUI

　　KOWLOON，HONGKONG

　　　　　　GUANGDONG HUADA FOOD CO.，LTD.

　　　　　　　　　　张三

三、实务思考

"调包计"以假换真窃取真汇票

某年 1 月 8 日，某石油公司业务员约翰逊持某银行 A 支行金额分别为 100 万元、200 万元的两张银行汇票 (未写兑付地) 和某银行 B 支行 350 万元的一张汇票，去美国东北部购买石油。1 月 11 日，前来联系业务的布朗提出让供货方看款项证明的要求，约翰逊毫无警觉，便提供给布朗 3 张金额为 650 万元的银行汇票复印件。1 月 15 日，趁约翰逊不备，布朗 (诈骗犯罪嫌疑人) 以"调包计"的手法，用伪造的假汇票换取了真汇票，并以联系业务为由，稳住约翰逊，前往某行作案。石油公司约翰逊购石油不成，于 1 月 26 日返回住地，1 月 27 日向 A 行退票时，才发现自己拿的是假汇票，即向法院报案，并发了停止支付通知书，1 月 28 日通过 A 行电传全行系统。但为时已晚，1 月 24 日，某商业银行珍妮 (布朗同伙罪犯) 手持约翰逊的假身份证，将 300 万元银行汇票在 A 行系统办理处兑付，其中 200 万元转存到 B 行，100 万元于 1 月 27 日存入该所信用卡部某职员的个人卡上，并在 4 天内分 5 次将 100 万元全部提取现金。其中，该犯又将存在 B 行某支行的 200 万元分别转入两个商业银行。截至 2 月 3 日，除 80 万元被警方冻结外，120 万美元又分 5 次全部以现金提取。

请分析这起汇票诈骗案件发生的主要原因和我们应该吸取的教训。

实训项目29

缮制托收汇票

操作练习

根据下列信息出具托收汇票。

已知发票金额为 $ 738 000.00，发票号码为 81609D3030。

ISSUING BANK：BANK OF CHINA SHANDONG BRANCH

L/C NO.：810080000797 DATED 2014-11-07

EXPIRY DATE：2015-01-08 PLACE KOREA

APPLICANT：QINGHE LIGHT IND. PROD. IMP. & EXP. CORP

　　　　　　　NO.55 SHANDONG RD.，QINGDAO，CHINA

BENEFICIARY：SUNKUONG LINITED

　　　　　　　(HSRO) C. P. O. BOX 1780，SEOUL，KOREA

AMOUNT：USD 738 000.00

COMMODITY：1 000 CTNS SHOES

AVAILABLE WITH/BY：BKCHKRSE BANK OF CHINA SEOUL BRANCH SEOUL

　　　　　　　　　BY NEGOTIATION

DAFTS AT：120 DAYS AFTER THE DATE OF SHIPMENT FOR 100 PCT OF THE

　　　　　　INVOICE VALUE

DRAWEE：BKCHCNBJ810

　　　　　BANK OF CHINA QINGDAO (SHANDONG BRANCH)

　　　　　QUANTITY 5 PCT MORE OR LESS ARE ALLOWED.

　　　　　LATEST SHIPMENT：2014-12-23

BILL OF EXCHANGE

Drawn under   L/C NO.

Dated   Payable with interest@   %

NO.   Exchange for   shanghai   (Date)

At   Of this FIRST of Exchange (Second of Exchange being

Unpaid) Pay to the order of

Value received

To:

(Authorized Signature)

实训项目30

缮制出口货物许可证

操作练习

根据信用证有关内容缮制出口许可证一份，有关唛头、件数等内容应与该信用证的要求相符。

单位中文名称：福州毛织品进出口贸易公司

单位编码：195762654

出口许可证编码：2002122433

商品中文名称：全棉抹布

商品编码：888.666

（一）

NATIONAL PARIS BANK
24 MARSHALL AVE DONCASTER MONTREAL，CANADA

WE ISSUE OUR IRREVOCABLE DOCUMENTARY CREDIT NUMBER：TH2003

IN FAVOUR OF：FUZHOU KNITWEAR AND MANUFACTURED GOODS IMPORT AND EXPORT
　　　　　　TRADE CORPORATION 321，ZHOUGSHAN ROAD FUZHOU，CHINA

BY ORDER OF：YI YANG TRADING CORPORATION
　　　　　　88 MARSHALL AVE
　　　　　　DONCASTER VIC 3108 CANADA
　　　　　　FOR AN AMOUNT OF USD 89 705.50

DATE OF EXPIRY：15NOV14

PLACE：IN BENEFICIARY'S COUNTRY
　　　　AVAILABLE WITH ANY BANK
　　　　BY NEGOTIATION OF BENEFICIARY'S DRAFT DRAWN ON US
　　　　AT SIGHT IN MONTREAL
　　　　THIS CREDIT IS TRANSFERABLE
　　　　AGAINST DELIVERY OF THE FOLLOWING DOCUMENTS
　　　　+COMMERCIAL INVOICES IN 5 COPIES
　　　　+CANADA CUSTOMS INVOICES IN 6 COPIES
　　　　+FULL SET OF NEGOTIABLE INSURANCE POLICY OR CERTIFICATE BLANK
　　　　　ENDORSED FOR 110 PERCENT OF INVOICE VALUE COVERING ALL RISKS
　　　　+FULL SET OF ORIGINAL MARINE BILLS OF LADING CLEAN ON BOARD PLUS 2 NON-
　　　　　NEGOTIABLE COPIES MADE OUT OR ENDORSED TO ORDER OF NATIONAL PARIS
　　　　　BANK 24 MARSHALL VEDONCASTER MONTREAL，CANADA.
　　　　+SPECIFICATION LIST OF WEIGHTS AND MEASURESIN 4 COPIES COVERING
　　　　　SHIPMENT OF COTTON TEATOWELS AS PER S/C ST303.
　　　　FOR 1-300 SIZE 10 INCHES * 10 INCHES 16000 DOZ. AT USD 1.31/DOZ. 301-600 SIZE 20
　　　　INCHES * 20 INCHES 6000 DOZ. AT USD 2.51/DOZ. AND 601-900 SIZE 30 INCHES * 30
　　　　INCHES 11350 DOZ. AT USD 4.73/DOZ.
　　　　CIF MONTREAL
　　　　FROM FUZHOU PORT TO MONTREAL PORT
　　　　NOT LATER THAN 31，OCT.14

PARTIAL SHIPMENTS：ALLOWED

TRANSHIPMENT：ALLOWED
　　　　　　　SPECIAL INSTRUCTIONS
　　　　　　　+ALL CHARGES IF ANY RELATED TO SETTLEMENTS ARE FOR ACCOUNT OF
　　　　　　　　BENEFICIARY
　　　　　　　+IN CASE OF PRESENTATION OF DOCUMENTS WITH DISCREPANCY (IES) A
　　　　　　　　CHARGE OF USD 55.00

THIS CREDIT IS SUBJECT TO UCP FOR DOCUMENTARY CREDITS 2007 REVISION ICC
PUBLICATION 600 AND IS THE OPERATIVE INSTRUMENT

（二）

中华人民共和国出口货物许可证
EXPORT LICENCE THE PEOPLE'S REPUBLIC OF CHINA　A 类

申领许可证单位　　编码 Exporter	出口许可证编号 Licence No.
发货单位 Consignee	许可证有效期 Validity
贸易方式 Terms of	输往国家（地区） Country of destination
合同号 Contract No.	收款方式 Terms of payment
出运口岸 Port of shipment	运输方式 Means of transport

唛头——包装件数 Marks & numbers ——number of packages					
商品名称 Desertification of commodity			商品编码 Commodity No.		
商品规格、型号 Specification	单位 Unit	数量 Quantity	单价 Unit price	总值 Amount	总值折美元 Amount in USD
总计 Total					
备注 Supplementary details		发证机关盖章 Issuing Authority's Stamp 发证日期 Signature Date			

商务部监制　　　　　　　　　　　　　　　　　　　　　　　本证不得涂改，不得转让。

实训项目31

缮制输加拿大纺织出口许可证

操作练习

根据信用证和商业发票，填制"输加拿大纺织出口许可证"送交外经贸委申请出口配额。

向与我国订有纺织品贸易协定的国家出口纺织品时，应按贸易协定的要求提供不同的单证，其中纺织品出口许可证是政府机关批准配额纺织品出口的证明文件。其作用是出口商凭此办理出口报关和进口商凭此申领进口许可证并办理进口报关手续。因此，2015年3月9日，福建公司向外经贸委申领纺织品配额。拿到签发的输加拿大纺织出口许可证后，方可凭此办理出口报关手续。

许可证相关栏位填写如下：

No：141252

Category number：15

Supplementary details：若无附注，此栏可空白不填。

Competent authority：DEPARTMENT OF FOREIGN TRADE AND ECONOMIC
                    COOPERATION，JIANGSU PROVINCIAL GOVERNMENT，
                    29 EAST BEIJING ROAD，NANJING JIANGSU，CHINA

（一）

ISSUER FUJIAN TEXTILE GARMENT CO.，LTD. HUARONG MANSION RM2901 NO.85 GUANJIAQIAO， FUZHOU 110005，CHINA	商业发票 **COMMERCIAL INVOICE**		
TO FASHION FORCE CO.，LTD P. O. BOX 8935 NEW TERMINAL，ALTA， VISTA OTTAWA，CANADA	NO. NT01FF004	DATE Mar.9，2015	
TRANSPORT DETAILS SHIPMENT FROM FUZHOU，CHINA TO MONTREAL， CANADA BY VESSEL	S/C NO. F01LCB05127 TERMS OF PAYMENT L/C AT SIGHT	L/C NO. 63211020049	
Marks and Numbers	Number and kind of package Description of goods	Quantity	Unit Price	Amount USD
FASHION FORCE F01LCB05127 CTN NO. MONTREAL MADE IN CHINA	LADIES COTTON BLAZER (100% COTTON，40S×20/140×60)	2 550 PCS	USD 12.80	CIF MONTREAL USD 32 640.00
	Total:	2 550 PCS		USD 32 640.00

SAY TOTAL：USD THIRTY TWO THOUSAND SIX HUNDRED AND FORTY ONLY

SALES CONDITIONS：CIF MONTREAL/CANADA

        SALES CONTRACT NO. F01LCB05127

        LADIES COTTON BLAZER (100% COTTON，40S×20/140×60)

STYLE NO.	PO NO.	QTY/PCS	USD/PC
46-301A	10337	2 550	12.80

（出口商签字和盖单据章）

（二）

```
2015JAN31 15：23：46        LOGICAL TERMINALE102 MT S700
                    ISSUE OF A DOCUMENTARY CREDIT          PAGE    00001
                                                          FUNC   MSG700
                                                          UMR    06607642
```

MSGACK DWS765I AUTH OK，KEY B110106173BAOC53B，BKCHCNBJ BNPA**** RECORO

BASIC HEADER F 01 BKCHCNBJA940 0542 725524

APPLICATION HEADER		0700 1122 010129 BNPACAMMAXXX 4968 839712 010130 0028 N
		*BNP PARIBAS (CANADA)
		*MONTREAL
USER HEADER		SERVICE CODE 103：
		BANK. PRIORITY 113：
		MSG USER REF. 108： （银行盖信用证通知专用章）
		INFO. FROM CI 115：
SEQUENCE OF TOTAL*	27	1 / 1
FORM OF DOC. CREDIT*	40 A	IRREVOCABLE
DOC. CREDIT NUMBER*	20	63211020049
DATE OF ISSUE	31 C	150129
EXPIRY*	31 D	DATE 150410 PLACE IN BENEFICIARY'S COUNTRY
APPLICANT*	50	FASHION FORCE CO.，LTD
		P. O. BOX 8935 NEW TERMINAL，ALTA，VISTA OTTAWA，
		CANADA
BENEFICIARY*	59	FUJIAN TEXTILE GARMENT CO.，LTD.
		HUARONG MANSION RM2901 NO.85 GUANJIAQIAO，
		FUZHOU 110005，CHINA
AMOUNT*	32 B	CURRENCY USD AMOUNT 32640，
AVAILABLE WITH/BY*	41 D	ANY BANK BY NEGOTIATION
DRAFTS AT ...	42 C	SIGHT
DRAWEE	42 A	BNPACAMMXXX
		*BNP PARIBAS (CANADA)
		*MONTREAL
PARTIAL SHIPMTS	43 P	NOT ALLOWED
TRANSSHIPMENT	43 T	
ALLOWED LOADING ON		
CHARGE	44 A	CHINA
FOR TRANSPORT TO...	44 B	MONTREAL
LATEST DATE OF SHIP.	44 C	150325
DESCRIPT OF GOODS	45 A	SALES CONDITIONS：
		CIF MONTREAL/CANADA
		SALES CONTRACT NO. F01LCB05127
		LADIES COTTON BLAZER (100% COTTON，40S×20/140×60)

```
                          STYLE NO.      PO NO.              QTY/PCS    USD/PC
                          46-301A        10337                2 550     12.80
```

DOCUMENTS REQUIRED	46 A	+COMMERCIAL INVOICES IN 3 COPIES SIGNED BY
		BENEFICIARY'S REPRESENTATIVE.
		+CANADA CUSTOMS INVOICES IN 4 COPIES.

		+FULL SET OF ORIGINAL MARINE BILLS OF LADING CLEAN ON BOARD PLUS 2 NON NEGOTIABLE COPIES MADE OUT OR ENDORSED TO ORDER OF BNP PARIBAS (CANADA) MARKED FREIGHT PREPAID AND NOTIFY APPLICANT'S FULL NAME AND ADDRESS.
		+DETAILED PACKING LISTS IN 3 COPIES.
		+COPY OF CERTIFICATE OF ORIGIN FORM A.
		+COPY OF EXPORT LICENCE.
		+BENEFICIARY'S LETTER STATING THAT ORIGINAL CERTIFICATE OF ORIGIN FORM A, ORIGINAL EXPORT LICENCE, COPY OF COMMERCIAL INVOICE, DETAILED PACKING LISTS AND A COPY OF BILL OF LADING WERE SENT DIRECT TO APPLICANT BY COURIER WITHIN 5 DAYS AFTER SHIPMENT. THE RELATIVE COURIER RECEIPT IS ALSO REQUIRED FOR PRESENTATION.
		+COPY OF APPLICANT'S FAX APPROVING PRODUCTION SAMPLES BEFORE SHIPMENT.
		+LETTER FROM SHIPPER ON THEIR LETTERHEAD INDICATING THEIR NAME OF COMPANY AND ADDRESS, BILL OF LADING NUMBER, CONTAINER NUMBER AND THAT THIS SHIPMENT, INCLUDING ITS CONTAINER, DOES NOT CONTAIN ANY NON-MANUFACTURED WOODEN MATERIAL, DUNNAGE, BRACING MATERIAL, PALLETS, CRATING OR OTHER NON-MANUFACTURED WOODEN PACKING MATERIAL.
		+INSPECTION CERTIFICATE ORIGINAL SIGNED AND ISSUED BY FASHION FORCE CO., LTD STATING THE SAMPLES OF FOUR STYLE GARMENTS HAD BEEN APPROVED, WHICH SEND THROUGH DHL BEFORE 15DAYS OF SHIPMENT.
		+INSURANCE POLICY OR CERTIFICATE IN 1 ORIGINAL AND 1 COPY ISSUED OR ENDORSED TO THE ORDER OF BNP PARIBAS (CANADA) FOR THE CIF INVOICE PLUS 10 PERCENT COVERING ALL RISKS, INSTITUTE STRIKES, INSTITUTE WAR CLAUSES AND CIVIL COMMOTIONS CLAUSES.
ADDITIONAL COND.	47 A	+IF DOCUMENTS PRESENTED ARE FOUND BY US NOT TO BE IN FULL COMPLIANCE WITH CREDIT TERMS. WE WILL ASSESS A CHARGE OF USD 55.00 PER SET OF DOCUMENTS.
		+ALL CHARGES IF ANY RELATED TO SETTLEMENTS ARE FOR ACCOUNT OF BENEFICIARY.
		+3 PCT MORE OR LESS IN AMOUNT AND QUANTITY IS ALLOWED.
		+ALL CERTIFICATES/LETTERS/STATEMENTS MUST BE SIGNED AND DATED

（续表）

		+FOR INFORMATION ONLY，PLEASE NOTE AS OF JANUARY 4，2015 THAT ALL SHIPMENTS FROM CHINA THAT ARE PACKED WITH UNTREATED WOOD WILL BE BANNED FROM CANADA DUE TO THE THREAT POSED BY THE ASIAN LONGNORNED BEETLE.
		+THE CANADIAN GOVERNMENT NOW INSIST THAT EVERY SHIPMENT ENTERING CANADA MUST HAVE THE ABOVE DOCUMENTATION WITH THE SHIPMENT.
		+BILL OF LADING AND COMMERCIAL INVOICE MUST CERTIFY THE FOLLOWING: THIS SHIPMENT, INCLUDING ITS CONTAINER DOES NOT CONTAIN ANY NON-MANUFACTURED WOODEN MATERIAL，DUNNAGE，BRACING MATERIAL PALLETS，CRATING OR OTHER NON MANUFACTURED WOODEN PACKING MATERIAL.
		+ENEFICIARY'S BANK ACCOUNT NO. 07773108201140121 WITHOUT
CONFIRMATION*	49	
INSTRUCTIONS	78	+WE SHALL COVER THE NEGOTIATING BANK AS PER THEIR INSTRUCTIONS
		+FORWARD DOCUMENTS IN ONE LOT BY SPECIAL COURIER PREPAID TO BNP PARIBAS (CANADA) 1981 MCGILL COLLECE AVE.MONTREAL QC H3A 2W8 CANADA. SEND. TO REC. INFO.72: THIS CREDIT IS SUBJECT TO UCP FOR DOCUMENTARY CREDIT 2007 REVISION ICC PUBLICATION 600 AND IS THE OPERATIVE INSTRUMENT TRAILER ORDER IS <MAC: > <PAC: > <ENC: > <CHK: > <TNG: > <PDE: >MAC: F344CA36CHK: AA6204FFDFC2

（三）

输加拿大纺织品出口许可证		
1. Exporter (EID. Name，full address，country)	2. No. ORIGINAL	
	3. Quota year	4. Category number
5. Consignee (name，full address，country)	**EXPORT LICENCE** (Textile products)	
	6. Country of origin	7. Country of destination
8. Place and date of shipment – Means of transport	9. Supplementary details	
10. Marks and numbers – Number and kind of packages – DESCRIPTION OF GOODS	11. Quantity	12. FOB Value
13. CERTIFICATION BY THE COMPETENT AUTHORITY I，the undersigned，certify that the goods described above have been charged against the quantitative limit established for the year shown in box No 3 in respect of the category shown in box No 4 by the provisions regulating trade in textile products with CANADA.		
14.Competent authority (name，full address，country)	At-A ___ on ___	

实训项目32

缮制加拿大海关发票

操作练习

根据下列资料填制加拿大海关发票。

2015年3月20日，山东纺织服装有限公司的货物顺利装船出运。根据信用证要求，3月22日，山东公司将加拿大海关发票及其他随附单据用DHL寄给开证人供其用于清关。

各国的海关发票格式不同，不能混用。

海关发票的内容必须与商业发票的有关内容完全一致。

加拿大海关发票中的每一栏都必须填满，若某栏没有所要填的内容，则必须填上N/A(Not Applicable)字样，不得空白。

（一）

1. Shipper Insert Name，Address and Phone SHANDONG TEXTILE GARMENT CO.，LTD. HUARONG MANSION RM2901 NO.85 GUANJIAQIAO，QINGDAO 110005，CHINA	B/L No. COS6314203208 中远集装箱运输有限公司 COSCO CONTAINER LINES TLX：33057 COSCO CN FAX：+86(021) 6545 8984 ORIGINAL

| 2. Consignee Insert Name，Address and Phone
TO THE ORDER OF BNP PARIBAS
(CANADA) | Port-to-Port or Combined Transport
BILL OF LADING |

3. Notify Party Insert Name，Address and Phone
 (It is agreed that no responsibility shall attach to
the Carrier or his agents for failure to notify)
FASHION FORCE CO.，LTD
P. O. BOX 8935 NEW TERMINAL，ALTA，
VISTA OTTAWA，CANADA

RECEIVED in external apparent good order and condition except as otherwise noted. The total number of packages or units stuffed in the container，The description of the goods and the weights shown in this Bill of Lading are furnished by the Merchants，and which the carrier has no reasonable means of checking and is not a part of this Bill of Lading contract. The carrier has Issued the number of Bills of Lading stated below，all of this tenor and date，One of the original Bills of Lading must be surrendered and endorsed or signed against the delivery of the shipment and whereupon any other original Bills of Lading shall be void. The Merchants agree to be bound by the terms And conditions of this Bill of Lading as if each had personally signed this Bill of Lading.See clause 4 on the back of this Bill of Lading (Terms continued on the back hereof，please read carefully).
*Applicable Only When Document Used as a Combined Transport Bill of Lading.

4. Combined Transport * Pre – carriage by	5. Combined Transport* Place of Receiptt
6. Ocean Vessel Voy. No. HUA CHANG V.09981	7. Port of Loading QINGDAO，CHINA
8. Port of Discharge MONTREAL，CANADA	9. Combined Transport *Place of Delivery MONTREAL，CANADA

Marks & Nos. Container / Seal No.	No. of Containers or Packages	Description of Goods (If Dangerous Goods，See Clause 20)	Gross Weight Kgs	Measurement
		Description of Contents for Shipper's Use Only (Not part of this B/L contract)		

10. Total Number of containers and/or packages (in words) SAY TWO HUNDRED AND ONE CARTONS ONLY

| Subject to Clause 7 Limitation | |

11. Freight & Charges Declared Value Charge	Revenue Tons	Rate	Per	Prepaid	Collect
Ex. Rate：	Prepaid at	Payable at		Place and date of issue QINGDAO，CHINA MAR. 20，2015	
	Total Prepaid	No. of Original B(s)/L THREE		Signed for the Carrier， COSCO CONTAINER LINES	

LADEN ON BOARD THE VESSEL

| DATE：MAR. 20，2015 | BY |

（二）

ISSUER SHANDONG TEXTILE GARMENT CO., LTD. HUARONG MANSION RM2901 NO.85 GUANJIAQIAO， QINGDAO 110005，CHINA	商业发票 COMMERCIAL INVOICE		
TO FASHION FORCE CO.，LTD P. O. BOX 8935 NEW TERMINAL，ALTA， VISTA OTTAWA，CANADA	NO. NT01FF004		DATE Mar.9，2015
TRANSPORT DETAILS SHIPMENT FROM QINGDAO，CHINA TO MONTREAL，CANADA BY VESSEL	S/C NO. F01LCB05127		L/C NO. 63211020049
	TERMS OF PAYMENT L/C AT SIGHT		

Marks and Numbers	Number and kind of package Description of goods	Quantity	Unit Price	Amount USD
FASHION FORCE F01LCB05127 CTN NO. MONTREAL MADE IN CHINA				CIF MONTREAL
	LADIES COTTON BLAZER (100% COTTON，40S×20/140×60)	2 550 PCS	USD 12.80	USD 32 640.00
	Total：	2 550 PCS		USD 32 640.00

SAY TOTAL：USD THIRTY TWO THOUSAND SIX HUNDRED AND FORTY ONLY

SALES CONDITIONS：CIF MONTREAL/CANADA

     SALES CONTRACT NO. F01LCB05127

     LADIES COTTON BLAZER (100% COTTON，40S×20/140×60)

STYLE NO.	PO NO.	QTY/PCS	USD/PC
46-301A	10337	2 550	12.80

（出口商签字和盖单据章）

（三）

2015JAN31 15：23：46		LOGICAL TERMINAL　E102
MT S700	**ISSUE OF A DOCUMENTARY CREDIT**	PAGE　00001
		FUNC　MSG700
		UMR　06607642

MSGACK　DWS765I AUTH OK，KEY B110106173BAOC53B，BKCHCNBJ BNPA**** RECORO

BASIC HEADER		F 01　BKCHCNBJA940 0542 725524
APPLICATION HEADER		0 7001122 010129 BNPACAMMAXXX 4968 839712 010130 0028 N
		*BNP PARIBAS (CANADA)
		*MONTREAL
USER HEADER		SERVICE CODE　103：
		BANK. PRIORITY 113：
		MSG USER REF.　108：　（银行盖信用证通知专用章）
		INFO. FROM CI　115：
SEQUENCE OF TOTAL	*27	1／1
FORM OF DOC. CREDIT	*40 A	IRREVOCABLE
DOC. CREDIT NUMBER	*20	63211020049
DATE OF ISSUE	31 C	150129
EXPIRY	*31 D	DATE 150410 PLACE IN BENEFICIARY'S COUNTRY
APPLICANT	*50	FASHION FORCE CO.，LTD
		P. O. BOX 8935 NEW TERMINAL，ALTA，VISTA OTTAWA，CANADA
BENEFICIARY	*59	SHANDONG TEXTILE GARMENT CO.，LTD.
		HUARONG MANSION RM2901 NO.85 GUANJIAQIAO，QINGDAO 210005，CHINA
AMOUNT	*32 B	CURRENCY USD AMOUNT 32640，
AVAILABLE WITH/BY	*41 D	ANY BANK BY NEGOTIATION
DRAFTS AT ...	42 C	SIGHT
DRAWEE	42 A	BNPACAMMXXX
		*BNP PARIBAS (CANADA)
		*MONTREAL
PARTIAL SHIPMTS	43 P	NOT ALLOWED
TRANSSHIPMENT	43 T	ALLOWED
LOADING ON CHARGE	44 A	CHINA
FOR TRANSPORT TO...	44 B	MONTREAL
LATEST DATE OF SHIP.	44 C	150325
DESCRIPT. OF GOODS	45 A	SALES CONDITIONS: CIF MONTREAL/CANADA
		SALES CONTRACT NO. F01LCB05127
		LADIES COTTON BLAZER (100% COTTON，40S×20/140×60)

STYLENO.	PO NO.	QTY/PCS	USD/PC
46-301A	10337	2 550	12.80

（续表）

DOCUMENTS REQUIRED	46 A	+COMMERCIAL INVOICES IN 3 COPIES SIGNED BY BENEFICIARY'S REPRESENTATIVE. +CANADA CUSTOMS INVOICES IN 4 COPIES. +FULL SET OF ORIGINAL MARINE BILLS OF LADING CLEAN ON BOARD PLUS 2 NON NEGOTIABLE COPIES MADE OUT OR ENDORSED TO ORDER OF BNP PARIBAS (CANADA) MARKED FREIGHT PREPAID AND NOTIFY APPLICANT'S FULL NAME AND ADDRESS. +DETAILED PACKING LISTS IN 3 COPIES. +COPY OF CERTIFICATE OF ORIGIN FORM A. +COPY OF EXPORT LICENCE. +BENEFICIARY'S LETTER STATING THAT ORIGINAL CERTIFICATE OF ORIGIN FORM A, ORIGINAL EXPORT LICENCE, COPY OF COMMERCIAL INVOICE, DETAILED PACKING LISTS AND A COPY OF BILL OF LADING WERE SENT DIRECT TO APPLICANT BY COURIER WITHIN 5 DAYS AFTER SHIPMENT.THE RELEATIVE COURIER RECEIPT IS ALSO REQUIRED FOR PRESENTATION. +COPY OF APPLICANT'S FAX APPROVING PRODUCTION SAMPLES BEFORE SHIPMENT. +LETTER FROM SHIPPER ON THEIR LETTERHEAD INDICATING THEIR NAME OF COMPANY AND ADDRESS, BILL OF LADING NUMBER, CONTAINER NUMBER AND THAT SHIPMENT, INCLUDING ITS CONTAINER, DOES NOT CONTAIN ANY NON-MANUFACTURED WOODEN MATERIAL, DUNNAGE, BRACING MATERIAL, PALLETS, CRATING OR OTHER NON-MANUFACTURED WOODEN PACKING MATERIAL. +INSPECTION CERTIFICATE ORIGINAL SINGED AND ISSUED BY FASHION FORCE CO., LTD STATING THE SAMPLES OF FOUR STYLE GARMENTS HAD BEEN APPROVED, WHICH SEND THROUGH DHL BEFORE 15DAYS OF SHIPMENT. +INSURANCE POLICY OR CERTIFICATE IN 1 ORIGINAL AND 1 COPY ISSUED OR ENDORSED TO THE ORDER OF BNP PARIBAS (CANADA) FOR THE CIF INVOICE PLUS 10 PERCENT COVERING ALL RISKS, INSTITUTE STRIKES, INSTITUTE WAR CLAUSES AND CIVIL COMMOTIONS CLAUSES.
ADDITIONAL COND.	47 A	+IF DOCUMENTS PRESENTED ARE FOUND BY US NOT TO BE IN FULL COMPLIANCE WITH CREDIT TERMS. WE WILL ASSESS A CHARGE OF USD 55.00 PER SET OF DOCUMENTS.

（续表）

		+ALL CHARGES IF ANY RELATED TO SETTLEMENTS ARE FOR ACCOUNT OF BENEFICIARY. +3 PCT MORE OR LESS IN AMOUNT AND QUANTITY IS ALLOWED. +ALL CERTIFICATES/LETTERS/STATEMENTS MUST BE SIGNED AND DATED +FOR INFORMATION ONLY，PLEASE NOTE AS OF JANUARY 4，2015 THAT ALL SHIPMENTS FROM CHINA THAT ARE PACKED WITH UNTREATED WOOD WILL BE BANNED FROM CANADA DUE TO THE THREAT POSED BY THE ASIAN LONGNORNED BEETLE. +THE CANADIAN GOVERNMENT NOW INSIST THAT EVERY SHIPMENT ENTERING CANADA MUST HAVE THE ABOVE DOCUMENTATION WITH THE SHIPMENT. +BILL OF LADING AND COMMERCIAL INVOICE MUST CERTIFY THE FOLLOWING: THIS SHIPMENT，INCLUDING ITS CONTAINER DOES NOT CONTAIN ANY NON-MANUFACTURED WOODEN MATERIAL，DUNNAGE，BRACING MATERIAL PALLETS，CRATING OR OTHER NON MANUFACTURED WOODEN PACKING MATERIAL. +BENEFICIARY'S BANK ACCOUNT NO. 07773108201140121
CHARGES	71 B	OUTSIDE COUNTRY BANK CHARGES TO BE BORNE BY THE BENEFICIARY OPENING BANK CHARGES TO BE BORNE BY THE APPLICANT
CONFIRMATION	*49	WITHOUT
INSTRUCTIONS	78	+WE SHALL COVER THE NEGOTIATING BANK AS PER THEIR INSTRUCTIONS +FORWARD DOCUMENTS IN ONE LOT BY SPECIAL COURIER PREPAID TO BNP PARIBAS (CANADA) 1981 MCGILL COLLECE AVE.MONTREAL QC H3A 2W8 CANADA.
SEND. TO REC. INFO.	72	THIS CREDIT IS SUBJECT TO UCP FOR DOCUMENTARY CREDIT 2007 REVISION ICC PUBLICATION 600 AND IS THE OPERATIVE INSTRUMENT TRAILER ORDER IS <MAC：> <PAC：> <ENC：> <CHK：> <TNG：> <PDE：> MAC：F344CA36 CHK：AA6204FFDFC2

（四）

山东纺织服装有限公司
SHANDONG TEXTILE GARMENT CO.，LTD.
DEAILED PACKING LIST

TO:			INVOICE NO.:	NT01FF004
FASHION FORCE CO.，LTD			INVOICE DATE：	MAR. 9，2015
P. O. BOX 8935 NEW TERMINAL，ALTA，			S/C NO.：	F01LCB05127
VISTA OTTAWA，CANADA			S/C DATE：	DEC. 26，2014

FROM:	SHANGHAI		TO:	MONTREAL
Letter of Credit No.:	63211020049		Date of Shipment：	APR. 20，2015

CTN NO	CTNS	DESIGNS/ COLORS	STYLE NO	SIZE ASSORTMENT PER CARTON						PCS/ CNT	TOTAL PCS/ CNTS	G.W./ CTN	N.W./ CTN	MEAS./ CTN	CBM/ CTN
				10	12	14	16	18	20						
1/18	18	BLACK	46-301A	14						14	252	15	10	97×72×12	0.084
19/56	38	BLACK			14					14	532				
57/106	50	BLACK				13				13	650			98×76×12	0.089
107/149	43	BLACK					12			12	516				
150/175	25	BLACK						12		12	300			99×80×11	0.087
176/194	19	BLACK							12	12	228				
196	1	WHITE		11						11	11				0.084
197	1	WHITE			9	3				12	12				
198	1	WHITE				13				13	13				0.089
199	1	WHITE				3	9			12	12				
200	3	WHITE						4		4	12				0.087
201	1	WHITE						2	10	12	12				
1/201ex															
TOTAL	201										2 550	3 015	2 010		17.51

SHIPPING MARKS: FASHION FORCE

F01LCB05127

CTN NO.

MONTREAL

MADE IN CHINA

SALES CONDITIONS: CIF MONTREAL/CANADA

SALES CONTRACT NO. F01LCB05127

LADIES COTTON BLAZER (100% COTTON，40S×20/140×60)

STYLE NO.	PO NO.	QTY/PCS	USD/PC
46-301A	10337	2 550	12.80

（续表）

Revenue Canada Customs and Excise	Revenue Canada Douanes et accise	CANADA CUSTOMS INVOICE FACTURE DES DOUANES CANADIENNES	Page of de	
1. Vendor (Name and Address) *Vender (Nom et adresse)*		2. Date of Direct Shipment to Canada/*Date d' expedition directe vers ie Canade*		
		3.Other References (include Purchaser's，Order No.) *Autres references(include ie n de command de Í acheteur)*		
4. Consignee (Name and Address) Destinataire (Nom et adresse)		5. Purchaser's Name and Address(if other than Consignee) *Nom et adresse de Í acheteur(S'll differe du destinataire)*		
		6. Country of Transhipment/Pays de transbordement		
		7. Country of Origin of Goods *pays d' origine des merchandises*	IF SHIPMENT INCLUDES GOODS OF DIFFERENT ORIGINS ENTER ORIGINS AGAINST ITEM A IN12 *SIL' EXPEDON COMPREND DES MARCHANDISES D' ORIGINES* DIFFERENTES PRECISER LEUR PROVENANCE EN12	
8. Transportation Give Mode and Place of Direct Shipment to Canada *Transport Preciser mode et point d' expedition directe verste vers ie Canada*		9. Conditions of Sale and Terms of Payment (i.e Saie. Consignment Shipment，Leased Goods，etd.) Conditions de vente et modalities de pavement (*P.ex vente，expedition en consignation，location，de merchandises，etc*)		
		10. Currency of Settlement/Devises du pavement		
11. No. of Pkgs Nore de colis	12. Specification of Commodities (Kind of Packages，Marks，and Numbers，General Description and Characteristics，ie Grade，Quality) Designation des articles (Nature des colis，marques et numeros，description ger erale et caracteristiques，Pex classe，quality)	13. Quantity (State Unit) Quantite (Preciser Í unite)	Selling Price/*Prix de vente*	
			14. Unit Price Prix unitaire	15. Total
18. if any Of fields 1 to 17 are included on an attached commercial invoice，check this box *si tout renseignement relatlvement aux zones 1e 17 ligure sur une ou des tactures commerciaies ci-attachees cocher cette case* commercial invoice No. 1 N de la factre commerciaie		16. Total Weight/*Poids Total*		17. Invoice Total Total de la facture
		Net	Gross/*Brut*	
19. Exporter's Name and Address(if other than Vendor) *Nom et adresse de Í exportateur(s'll differe du vendeur)*		20. Originator (Name and Address)/*Expediteur d'origine(Nom et adresse)*		

（续表）

21. Departmental Rulikg(if applicable)/Decision du Ministere(S' lly a lieu)	22. If fields 23 to 25 are not applicable，check this box Si ies zones 23 e 25 sont sans objet，cocher cette case	
23.if included in field 7 indicate amount Si compris dans ie total a ia zone 17，preciser (I)Transportation charges，expenese and insurance from the place of direct shipment to Canada *Les frais de transport，depenses et assurances a partir du point of expedition directe vers is Canada.* (II) Costs for const: action，erection and assembly incurred atter importation into Canada *Les couts de construction，d'erection etd' assemblage，pres imporaation au.Canada* (III) Export packing Le cout de Í emballage d' exportation	24.If not included in field 17 indicate amount *Si non compris dans le total a ie zone 17，Dreciser* (I)Transportation charges，expense and insurance to the place of direct shipment to Canada *Les frais de transport，depenses et assurances Iusqu' au point d'of expedition directd vers ie Canada* (II) Amounts for commissions other than buying commissions Les commissions autres que celles verses Pour Í achat _____ _____ (III) Export packing Le cout de Í emballage d' exportation	25.Check (if applicable)Cochet (s'lly a liso) (I)Royalty payments or subsequent proceede are paid or payable by the purchaser *Des redevances ou prodults ont ete ou seront Verses par Í acheteur* (II) The purchaser has supplied goods or services for use in the production of these goods *L'acheteur a fouml des merchandises ou des Services pour ia production des merchandises*

实训项目33

缮制装船通知

一、操作练习

根据海运提单和商业发票制作装船通知。

2015 年 3 月 20 日，广西纺织服装有限公司的货物装上由北海港开往加拿大蒙特利尔港的"HUA CHANG"轮第 09981 船次并出运。在拿到了船公司的海运提单后，广西纺织有限公司即于 3 月 21 日缮制装船通知书给客户。

（一）

1. Shipper Insert Name，Address and Phone GUANGXI TEXTILE GARMENT CO.，LTD. HUARONG MANSION RM2901 NO.85 GUANQIAO，BEIHAI 540005，CHINA	B/L No. COS6314203208
2. Consignee Insert Name，Address and Phone TO THE ORDER OF BNP PARIBAS (CANADA)	中远集装箱运输有限公司 COSCO CONTAINER LINES TLX：33057 COSCO CN FAX：+86(021) 6545 8984
3. Notify Party Insert Name，Address and Phone (It is agreed that no responsibility shall attach to the Carrier or his agents for failure to notify) FASHION FORCE CO.，LTD. P. O. BOX 8935 NEW TERMINAL，ALTA，VISTA OTTAWA，CANADA	ORIGINAL Port-to-Port or Combined Transport BILL OF LADING

4. Combined Transport * Pre – carriage by	5. Combined Transport* Place of Receipt	RECEIVED in external apparent good order and condition except as otherwise noted. The total number of packages or units stuffed in the container, The description of the goods and the weights shown in this Bill of Lading are furnished by the Merchants，and which the carrier has no reasonable means of checking and is not a part of this Bill of Lading contract. The carrier has Issued the number of Bills of Lading stated below，all of this tenor and date，One of the original Bills of Lading must be surrendered and endorsed or signed against the delivery of the shipment and whereupon any other original Bills of Lading shall be void. The Merchants agree to be bound by the terms And conditions of this Bill of Lading as if each had personally signed this Bill of Lading. See clause 4 on the back of this Bill of Lading (Terms continued on the back hereof，please read carefully). *Applicable Only When Document Used as a Combined Transport Bill of Lading. Combined Transport
6. Ocean Vessel Voy. No. HUA CHANG V.09981	7. Port of Loading BEIHAI，CHINA	
8. Port of Discharge MONTREAL， CANADA	9. Place of Delivery MONTREAL，CANADA	

Marks & Nos. Container / Seal No.	No. of Containers or Packages	Description of Goods (If Dangerous Goods, See Clause 20)	Gross Weight Kgs	Measurement
FASHION FORCE F01LCB05127 CTN NO. MONTREAL MADE IN CHINA MSKU2612114 / 1681316 20'	CARTONS	SHIPPER'S LOAD&COUNT&SEAL SAID TO CONTAINER ONLY SALES CONDITIONS：CIF MONTREAL/CANADA SALES CONTRACT NO F01LCB05127. LADIES COTTON BLAZER(100% COTTON， (40S×20/140×60) STYLE NO. PONO. QTY/ PCSUSD/PC 46-301A 10337 2550 12.80 1×20' GP FCLS CY-CY CLEAN ON BOARD FREIGHT PREPAID	3 015.000 KGS	17.51M^3

		Description of Contents for Shipper's Use Only (Not part of This B/L Contract)		

10. Total Number of containers and/or packages (in words)

Subject to Clause 7 Limitation SAY TWO HUNDRED AND ONE CARTONS ONLY

11. Freight & Charges		Revenue Tons	Rate	Per	Prepaid	Collect
Declared Value Charge						
Ex. Rate:		Prepaid at	Payable at	Place and date of issue		
				BEIHAI，CHINA MAR. 20，2015		
		Total Prepaid	No. of Original B(s)/L THREE	Signed for the Carrier，COSCO CONTAINER LINES		
LADEN ON BOARD THE VESSEL DATE MAR. 20，2015			BY			

（二）

ISSUER GUANGXI TEXTILE GARMENT CO., LTD. HUARONG MANSION RM2901 NO.85 GUANQIAO, BEIHAI 540005, CHINA		商业发票 COMMERCIAL INVOICE		
TO FASHION FORCE CO., LTD P. O. BOX 8935 NEW TERMINAL, ALTA, VISTA OTTAWA, CANADA		NO. NT01FF004		DATE MAR. 9, 2015
TRANSPORT DETAILS SHIPMENT FROM BEIHAI, CHINA TO MONTREAL, CANADA BY VESSEL		S/C NO. F01LCB05127		L/C NO. 63211020049
		TERMS OF PAYMENT L/C AT SIGHT		
Marks and Numbers	Number and kind of package Description of goods	Quantity	Unit Price	Amount
				USD
FASHION FORCE F01LCB05127 CTN NO. MONTREAL MADE IN CHINA				CIF MONTREAL
	LADIES COTTON BLAZER (100% COTTON, 40S×20/140×60)	2 550 PCS	USD 12.80	USD 32 640.00
	Total:	2 550 PCS		USD 32 640.00

SAY TOTAL: USD THIRTY TWO THOUSAND SIX HUNDRED AND FORTY ONLY

SALES CONDITIONS: CIF MONTREAL/CANADA

        SALES CONTRACT NO. F01LCB05127

        LADIES COTTON BLAZER (100% COTTON, 40S×20/140×60)

STYLE NO.	PO NO.	QTY/PCS	USD/PC
46-301A	10337	2 550	12.80

（出口商签字和盖单据章）

（三）

GUANGXI TEXTILE GARMENT CO.，LTD.
HUARONG MANSION RM2901 NO.85 GUANQIAO，
BEIHAI 540005，CHINA

SHIPPING ADVICE

TO：

ISSUE DATE：
OUR REF. DATE：

Dear Sir or Madam，

We are Pleased to advise you that the following mentioned goods have been shipped out，full details were shown as follows:

Invoice Number：

Bill of loading Number：

Ocean Vessel：

Port of Loading：

Date of shipment：

Port of Destination：

Estimated date of arrival：

Containers/Seals Number：

Description of goods：

Shipping Marks：

Quantity：

Gross Weight：

Net Weight：

Total Value：

Thank you for your patronage. We look forward to the pleasure of receiving your valuable repeat orders.

Sincerely yours

二、实务思考

2015 年，我国某进出口公司按 CFR 术语与德国一进口商签订一批棉布出口合同，价值 30 万美元，即期付款交单。货物于 8 月 15 日上午装船完毕，业务员因当天工作比较忙忘记向买方发出装船通知，16 日上班时才想起并发出装船通知。德商收到装船通知向当地保险公司投保时，该保险公司已获悉装载该批货物的轮船已于 16 日凌晨在海上遇难而拒绝承保。德商立即来电称："由于你方晚发装船通知，以至我方无法完成投保，因货轮已遇难，货物损失应由你方负担并赔偿我方利润及费用损失 10 000 美元。"不久我进出口公司通过托收银行寄去的全套货运单证被退回。请问：德商的要求合理吗？出口商该不该赔偿？

实训项目34

缮制议付单证

一、操作练习

上海工具制造有限公司于 2015 年 6 月 29 日将货物装运后，即准备议付单据向交通银行上海分行交单。根据提供的信用证的内容制作信用证指定的议付单证。

有关缮制议付单证的要求如下：

合同号：MOU0210S03

合同日期：2015 年 4 月 21 日

商业发票号：SHE021845

装运港口：上海

货物包装：50 PCS/DRUM，净重 2 000 KGS，毛重 2 200 KGS，体积 2.610 CBM

运费：USD 0.08/KG

海运提单号：SCOISG7564

船名：JENNY/03

集装箱号 / 铅封号：UXXU4240250/0169255

40'集装箱，CFS/CFS

（一）

LETTER OF CREDIT

SEQUENCE OF TOTAL	*27	1 / 1
FORM OF DOC. CREDIT	*40 A	IRREVOCABLE
DOC. CREDIT NUMBER	*20 A	4028D223
DATE OF ISSUE	31 C	20150104
EXPIRY	*31 D	DATE 20150720 PLACE CHINA
APPLICANT	*50 D	AYU IMPORT & EXPORT TRADE COPORATION
		564-8，SUNAM-DONG，NAM-KU ULSAN KOREA.
		TEL：(052)288-5300
BENEFICIARY	*59	SHANGHAI TOOLS MANUFACTURE CO.，LTD.
		NO.3188 JINZHANG ROAD，SHANGHAI，CHINA
AMOUNT	*32 B	CURRENCY USD AMOUNT 13608.00
AVAILABLE WITH/BY	*41	D ANY BANK IN CHINA，BY NEGOTIATION
DRAFTS AT...	42 C	AT SIGHT
DRAWEE	42 A	PUSBKR2PXXX
		*PUSAN BANK *PUSAN
PARTIAL SHIPMTS	43	P NOT ALLOWED
TRANSSHIPMENT	43 T	NOT ALLOWED
LOADING IN CHARGE	44 A	SHANGHAI PORT，CHINA
FOR TRANSPORT TO⋯	44 B	PUSAN PORT，KOREA
LATEST SHIPMENT	44 C	20150710
GOODS DESCRIPT.	45 A	ORIGIN CHINA CIF PUSAN PORT
		DOUBLE OPEN AND SPANER
		SAME AS THE SAMPLE9 5600PCS AT USD2.43 USD13608.00
DOCS REQUIRED	46 A	+SIGNED COMMERCIAL INVOICE IN 3 COPIES
		+PACKING LIST IN 3 COPIES
		+FULL SET OF CLEAN ON BOARD OCEAN BILLS OF LADING MADE OUT TO THE ORDER OF PUSAN BANK MARKED FREIGHT PREPAID AND NOTIFY APPLICANT
		+INSURANCE POLICY OR CERTIFICATE IN DUPLICATE ENDORSED IN BLANK FOR 110 PERCENT OF THE INVOICE VALUE. INSURANCE POLICIES OR CERTIFICATES MUST EXPRESSLY STIPULATE THAT CLAIMS ARE PAYABLE IN THE CURRENCY OF THE DRAFT AND MUST ALSO INSURANCE MUST INCLUDE: INSTITUTE CARGO CLAUSE ALL RISK
ADDITIONAL COND	*47A	THIS IS THE OPERATIVE INSTRUMENT SUBJECT TO THE UCP 600(2007 REVISON).THE AMOUNT OF EACH DRAFT MUST BE ENDORSED ON THE REVERSE OF THIS ADVICE BY NEGOTIATING BANK.A DISCREPANCY FEE OF USD 50.00 AND CABLE CHARGE USD 50.00(OR EQUIVALENT) WILL BE DEDUCTED FROM THE PROCEEDS IF DOCUMENTS ARE PRESENTED WITH DISCREPANCIES FOR PAYMENTS/ REIMBURSEMENT IS SUBJECT TO ICCURR525
DETAILS OF CHARGES	71 B	ALL BANKING CHARGES，INCLUDING REIMBURSING BANK'S CHARGE OUTSIDE KOREA ARE FOR ACCOUNT OF BENEFICIARY DOCUMENTS MUST BE PRESENTED FOR NEGOTIATION WITHIN 10 DAYS AFTER THE DATE OF SHIPMENT

（二）

SHANGHAI TOOLS MANUFACTURE CO.，LTD.

NO.3188 JINZHANG ROAD，SHANGHAI，CHINA

PACKING LIST

Invoice No.: _____

Invoice Date：_____

S/C No.: _____

S/C Date：_____

To:

From: _____ To: _____

Letter of Credit No.: _____ Date of Shipment：_____

Marks and Numbers	Number and kind of package Description of goods	Quantity	Package	G.W	N.W	Meas.
	TOTAL:					

SAY TOTAL:

1. Shipper Insert Name，Address and Phone			B/L No.		
2. Consignee Insert Name，Address and Phone			中远集装箱运输有限公司 **COSCO CONTAINER LINES** TLX：33057 COSCO CN FAX：+86(021) 6545 8984 ORIGINAL Port-to-Port or Combined Transport		
3. Notify Party Insert Name，Address and Phone (It is agreed that no responsibility shall attach to the Carrier or his agents for failure to notify)			**BILL OF LADING**		
4. Combined Transport * Pre – carriage by	5. Combined Transport* Place of Receipt		RECEIVED in external apparent good order and condition except as otherwise noted. The total number of packages or units stuffed in the container，The description of the goods and the weights shown in this Bill of Lading are furnished by the Merchants，and which the carrier has no reasonable means of checking and is not a part of this Bill of Lading contract. The carrier has Issued the number of Bills of Lading stated below，all of this tenor and date，One of the original Bills of Lading must be surrendered and endorsed or signed against the delivery of the shipment and whereupon any other original Bills of Lading shall be void. The Merchants agree to be bound by the terms And conditions of this Bill of Lading as if each had personally signed this Bill of Lading. See clause 4 on the back of this Bill of Lading (Terms continued on the back hereof，please read carefully). *Applicable Only When Document Used as a Combined Transport Bill of Lading. Combined Transport		
6. Ocean Vessel Voy. No.	7. Port of Loading				
8. Port of Discharge	9. Place of Delivery				
Marks & Nos. Container / Seal No.	No. of Containers or Packages	Description of Goods (If Dangerous Goods，See Clause 20)		Gross Weight Kgs	Measurement
Description of Contents for Shipper's Use Only (Not part of This B/L Contract)					
10. Total Number of containers and/or packages (in words) Subject to Clause 7 Limitation					
11. Freight & Charges Declared Value Charge	Revenue Tons	Rate	Per	Prepaid	Collect
Ex. Rate：	Prepaid at	Payable at	Place and date of issue		
	Total Prepaid	No. of Original B(s)/L	Signed for the Carrier， COSCO CONTAINER LINES		
LADEN ON BOARD THE VESSEL					
DATE		BY			

BILL OF EXCHANGE

凭 Drawn Under	不可撤销信用证 Irrevocable L/C No.

支取 Payable With interest   @   %   按   息   付款

| 号码
No. | 汇票金额
Exchange for | | 南京
Nanjing |

见票
at

日后（本汇票之副本未付）付交
sight of this First of Exchange （Second of Exchange

Being unpaid) Pay to the order of

金额
the sum of

此致
To

二、实务思考

卖方挫败买方与开证行相互勾结拒付货款的阴谋

河北省某进出口公司于 2015 年 2 月 14 日与新加坡某公司以传真方式成交一笔价值 26 597.50 美元的毛浴巾的出口合同，该客户于 2015 年 2 月 20 日开立了相同数量与金额的信用证。业务员审证时发现，合同中规定尺寸为 13″×30″，而信用证却描述为 13″×39″，电告开证人要求修改，客户声称此错误为银行笔误所致，无须修改，当时考虑到该客户为老客户，故并未再坚持要求修改。在货物于装运期内顺利出运后，即以表提方式将所有单据送交银行。开证行于 3 月 25 日、4 月 25 日和 5 月 8 日连续发出传真要求该公司"速洽客赎单"，该公司业务员多次传真买方要求其马上赎单，外商以质量有问题为由，要求货物降价处理。请问：我方公司应该如何处理？

实训项目35

缮制全套议付单据

操作练习

货名	数量	单价	毛重 (KGS)	净重 (KGS)
TRANSMISISION BELT 100MM×4P×350	60PACKAGES /120ROLLS	USD 201.92	55@ROLL	54@ROLL
TRANSMISSION BELT 125MM×4P×350	15PACKAGES /30ROLLS	USD 227.89	74@ROLL	73.2@ROLL

唛头：N/M

体积：20CBM

FOB 价：USD 24 493.10

运费：USD 6 574.00

船名：GUANG HANG V.312

开航日期：March 19，2015

H. S. Code：：4010.2564

商业发票、汇票号码：SHE021845

根据信用证内容填制上海化工公司的全套单据。

（一）

SSUE OF DOCUMENTARY CREDIT

TO：BANK OF CHINA，SHANGHAI BRANCH，CHINA

ATTN：L/C DEPT

FROM：COMMERCIAL BANK OF ETHIOPIA，ADDIS ABABA，ETHIOPIA

DATE：15-01-2015

WE HEREBY OPEN OUR IRREVOCABLE DOCUMENTARY LETTER OF CREDIT NO.LC/78563 FAVOURING M/S SHANGHAI CHEMICALS IMPORT AND EXPORT CORPORATION 16 JIANG YAN LU SHANGHAI CHINA BY ORDER OF MAGIC INTERNATIONAL PLC DEBRE ZEIT ROAD ADDIS ABABA ETHIOPIA TO THE EXTENT OF USD 31067.10 CFR ASSAB AVAILABLE BY NEGOTIATION WITH ANY BANK AGAINST THE DOCUMENTS DETAILED HEREIN AND BENEFICIARY'S DRAFTS AT 60 DAYS AFTER B/L DATE DRAWN ON OURSELVES FOR 100% OF THE INVOICE VALUE.

1. SIGNED COMMERCIAL INVOICES IN FIVE COPIES CERTIFYING FOB ABABA AND FREIGHT CHARGES AND ALL COPIES CERTIFIED BY THE CHINA COUNCIL FOR THE PROMOTION OF INTERNATIONAL TRADE INDICATING EXCHANGE CONTROL LICENCE NO.749/000066 JANJUARY 02，2015

2. PACKING LIST IN FIVE COPIES INDICATING GROSS AND NET WEIGHT OF EACH ROLL

3. FULL SET OF CLEAN ON BOARD OCEAN BILLS OF LADING AND ONE NON-NEGOTIABLE COPY MADE OUT TO ORDER OF COMMERCIAL BANK OF ETHIOPIA AND NOTIFYING MAGIC INTERNATIONAL PLC MARKED FREIGHT PREPAID

4. CERTIFICATE OF ORIGIN ISSUED BY THE CHINA COUNCIL FOR THE PROMOTION OF INTERNATIONAL TRADE IN TWO COPIES

COVERING SHIPMENT OF 120 ROLLS 100MM×4P×350 AND 30 ROLLS 125MMx4Px350 TRANSMISSION BELT AS PER CONTRACT NO.03PI/421/122 DATED DEC 26 20009

TERMS CFR ASSAB

INSURANCE COVERED LOCALLY BY BUYER

THE EXPIRY PLACE OF THE CREDIT IS CHINA

PARTIAL SHIPMENTS ARE NOT PERMITTED

TRANSHIPMENT ARE PERMITTED

SHIPMENT FROM SHANGHAI TO ASSAB NOT LATER THAN 21ST MARCH 2015

THIS CREDIT IS VALID FOR NEGOTIATION NOT LATER THAN 5TH APRIL，2015

ALL BANKING CHARGES OUTSIDE ETHIOPOA ARE FOR ACCOUNT OF THE BENEFICIARY

IPROVIDED THAT ALL TERMS AND CONDITIONS OF THE LETTER OF CREDIT HAVE BEEN COMPLIED WITH，WE UNDERTAKE TO HONOUR YOUR CLAIMS IN ACCORDANCE WITH YOUR INSTRUCTIONS VALUE THREE BUSINESS DAYS FROM THE DATE OF RECEIPT OF THE SHIPPING DOCUMENTS AT OUR COUNTERS

PLEASE FORWARD THE ORIGINAL AND DUPLICATE SETS OF SHIPPING DOCUMENTS IN TWO SEPARATETHIS LETTER OF CREDIT IS SUBJECT TO UCP FOR DOCUMENTARY CREDITS (REVISION 2007)I.C.C，PUBLICATION NO.600

PLEASE TREAT THIS MESSAGE AS AN OPERATIVE CREDIT INSTRUMENT AND NO MAIL CONFIRMATION WILL FOLLOW

PLEASE ADVISE THE BENEFICIARY LOTS TO US BY DHL COURIER SERVICE

（二）

商业发票
COMMERCIAL INVOICE

To

日期
Date

发票号
Invoice No.

合约号
Contract No.

信用证号
L/C No. _____

| 装　由 | | 开船日期 | |
| Shipped per _____ | | Sailing about _____ | |

出
From _____

至
To _____

唛头 SHIPPING MARK	货 名 数 量 QUANTITIES AND DESCRIPTIONS	单价 UNIT PRICE	金额 AMOUNET

（三）

装箱单
PACKING LIST

发票号码
Invoice No. _____

日期
Date _____

SHIPPING MARK 标志及箱号	NAME OF COMMODITY & SPECIFICATION 品名及规格	QUANTITY 数量	PACKAGE 件数	G.W. 毛重	N.W. 净重	MEASUREMENT 尺码
	TOTAL:					

Shipper	B/L NO.
	PIL
Consignee	**PACIFIC INTERNATIONAL LINES (PTE) LTD** (Incorporated in Singapore) **COMBINED TRANSPORT BILL OF LADING**
	Received in apparent good order and condition except as otherwise noted the total number of container or other packages or units enumerated below for transportation from the place of receipt to the place of delivery subject to the terms hereof. One of the signed Bills of Lading must be surrendered duly endorsed in exchange for the Goods or delivery order. On presentation of this document (duly) Endorsed to the Carrier by or on behalf of the Holder, the rights and liabilities arising in accordance with the terms hereof shall (without prejudice to any rule of common law or statute rendering them binding on the Merchant) become binding in all respects between the Carrier and the Holder as though the contract evidenced hereby had been made between them.
Notify Party	
	SEE TERMS ON ORIGINAL B/L

Vessel and Voyage Number	Port of Loading	Port of Discharge
Place of Receipt	Place of Delivery	Number of Original Bs/L

PARTICULARS AS DECLARED BY SHIPPER – CARRIER NOT RESPONSIBLE

Container Nos/Seal Nos. Marks and/Numbers	No. of Container / Packages / Description of Goods	Gross Weight (Kilos)	Measurement (cu-metres)

FREIGHT & CHARGES	Number of Containers/Packages (in words)
	Shipped on Board Date:
	Place and Date of Issue:
	In Witness Whereof this number of Original Bills of Lading stated Above all of the tenor and date one of which being accomplished the others to stand void. for **PACIFIC INTERNATIONAL LINES (PTE) LTD** as Carrier

（四）

ORIGINAL	
1. Exporter	Certificate No.
2. Consignee	**CERTIFICATE OF ORIGIN** **OF** **THE PEOPLE'S REPUBLIC OF** **CHINA**
3. Means of transport and route	5. For certifying authority use only
4. Country / region of destination	

6. Marks and numbers	7. Number and kind of packages; description of goods	8. H. S. Code	9. Quantity	10. Number and date of invoices

11. Declaration by the exporter	12. Certification
The undersigned hereby declares that the above details and statements are correct，that all the goods were produced in China and that they comply with the Rules of Origin of the People's Republic of China.	It is hereby certified that the declaration by the exporter is correct.
--	--
Place and date，signature and stamp of authorized signatory	Place and date，signature and stamp of certifying authority

（五）

BILL OF EXCHANGE

凭 Drawn Under		不可撤销信用证 Irrevocable L/C No.

日期　　　　　　　　　　支 取 Payable With　　@　　%　按　息　付款
Date　　　　　　　　　　interest

号码 No.	汇票金额 Exchange for	南京 Nanjing

见票　　　日后(本汇票之副本未付)付交
At_____ sight of this First of Exchange (Second of Exchange Being unpaid) Pay to
the order of

金额
the sum of

此致
To

实训项目36

填制出口收汇核销单

操作练习

根据信用证要求填写出口收汇核销单。

出口单位：江苏毛织品进出口贸易公司

单位编码：195762654

商品中文名称：全棉抹布

商品总包装数量：367 捆

（一）

NATIONAL PARIS BANK

24 MARSHALL AVE DONCASTER MONTREAL，CANADA

WE ISSUE OUR IRREVOCABLE DOCUMENT ARY CREDIT NUMBER：TH2003

IN FAVOUR OF：JIANGSU KNITWEAR AND MANUFACTURED GOODS IMPORT AND EXPORT

TRADE CORPORATION

321，ZHOUGSHAN ROAD SUZHOU，CHINA

BY ORDER OF：YI YANG TRADING CORPORATION

88 MARSHALL AVE

DONCASTER VIC 3108 CANADA

FOR AN AMOUNT OF USD 89 705.50

DATE OF EXPIRY：15NOV14

PLACE：IN BENEFICIARY'S COUNTRY

AVAILABLE WITH ANY BANK

BY NEGOTIATION OF BENEFICIARY'S DRAFT DRAWN ON US

AT SIGHT IN MONTREAL

THIS CREDIT IS TRANSFERABLE

AGAINST DELIVERY OF THE FOLLOWING DOCUMENTS

+COMMERCIAL INVOICES IN 5 COPIES

+CANADA CUSTOMS INVOICES IN 6 COPIES

+FULL SET OF NEGOTIABLE INSURANCE POLICY OR CERTIFICATE BLANK ENDORSED FOR
  110 PERCENT OF INVOICE VALUE COVERING ALL RESKS

+FULL SET OF ORIGINAL MARINE BILLS OF LADING CLEAN ON BOARD PLUS 2 NON-
  NEGOTIABLE COPIES MADE OUT OR ENDORSED TO ORDER OF NATIONAL PARIS BANK 24
  MARSHALL VEDONCASTER MONTREAL，CANADA.

+SPECIFICATION LIST OF WEIGHTS AND MEASURES IN 4 COPIES COVERING SHIPMENT OF
  COTTON TEATOWELS AS PER S/C ST303.

FOR 1-300 SIZE 10 INCHES * 10 INCHES 16000 DOZ. AT USD 1.31/DOZ. 301-600 SIZE 20 INCHES

6000 DOZ. AT USD 2.51/DOZ. AND 601-900 SIZE 30 INCHES * 30 INCHES 11350 DOZ. AT USD 4.73/

DOZ.CIF MONTREAL

FROM CHINESE PORT TO MONTREAL PORT

NOT LATER THAN 31，OCT. 14

PARTIAL SHIPMENTS：ALLOWED

TRANSHIPMENT：ALLOWED

SPECIAL INSTRUCTIONS

+ALL CHARGES IF ANY RELATED TO SETTLEMENTS ARE FOR ACCOUNT OF BENEFICIARY

+IN CASE OF PRESENTATION OF DOCUMENTS WITH DISCREPANCY (IES) A CHARGE OF USD
  55.00

THIS CREDIT IS SUBJECT TO UCP FOR DOCUMENTARY CREDITS 2007 RECISION ICC

PUBLICATION 600 AND IS THE OPERATIVE INSTRUMENT

未经核销此联不得撕开

（二）

出口收汇核销单
监制章

（沪）编号：

出口单位：
江苏毛织品进出口贸易公司

单位编码：195762654

货物名称	数量	币种总价
全棉抹布	367 捆	USD 89 705.50

报关单编号：

（出口单位盖章）

外汇局签注栏：

年　月　日（盖章）

出口收汇核销单
监制章

（沪）编号：

出口单位：
江苏毛织品进出口贸易公司

单位编码：195762654

银行签注栏	类别	币种金额	日期	盖章

海关签注栏：

（出口单位盖章）

外汇局签注栏：

年　月　日（盖章）

出口收汇核销单
存根

（沪）编号：

出口单位：
江苏毛织品进出口贸易公司

单位编码：195762654

出口币种总价：USD 89 705.50

收汇方式：L/C

预计收款日期：2014 年 10 月 26 日

报关日期：2014 年 10 月 18 日

备注：

此单报关有效期截止到

实训项目37

缮制出口收汇核销单送审登记表

一、操作练习

根据核销单内容填制出口收汇核销单送审登记表。

核销单编号	发票编号	结算方式
36D562123	JS03125	D/P

国别地区：加拿大

贸易方式：一般贸易

送审日期：2015 年 12 月 24 日

出口单位填表人：李华

未经核销此联不得撕开

（一）

出口收汇核销单
存根

（苏）编号：36D562123

出口单位：
华强（上海）手套有限公司

单位编码：14255643

出口币种总价：FOB USD 50 536.00

收汇方式：D/P

预计收款日期：2014.11.16

报关日期：2014.10.28

备注：

此单报关有效期截止到

外汇局签注栏

出口收汇核销单
监制章

（苏）编号：36D562123

出口单位：
华强（上海）手套有限公司

单位编码：14255643

银行签注栏	类别	币种金额	日期	盖章

（出口单位盖章）

海关签注栏：

外汇局签注栏

年　月　日（盖章）

出口收汇核销单
监制章

（苏）编号：36D562123

出口单位：
华强（上海）手套有限公司

单位编码：14255643

货物名称	数量	币种总价
劳保手套		USD 50 536.00

报关单编号：
523552149

（出口单位盖章）

外汇局签注栏

年　月　日（盖章）

第 一 联 外 汇 局 留 存

出口收汇核销单送审登记表

（二）

出口单位：

送审日期：　　　　　　　　　　年　月　日

核销单编号	发票编号	商品大类	国别地区	贸易方式	结算方式	报关日期	货款			收汇核销金额
							币别	报关金额	FOB 金额	

出口单位填表人　　　　　　　　　　　　　　　　　　　　　　　外汇局审核人

二、实务思考

2015 年 3 月 5 日，星鑫家具厂有一批家具需出口到迪拜，但该厂没有进出口权，不能向外汇管理局申领核销单，因此向联兴进出口公司买了一份核销单报关出口，货物出口后联兴进出口公司一直对该核销单未能按时收汇核销。请问：此例属于什么现象？联兴进出口公司卖出核销单的做法对吗？应如何处理？

实训项目38

缮制进口订舱委托书

操作练习

根据下列资料，制作进口订舱委托书，要求格式清楚、内容完整。

2014 年 12 月 13 日，广州朗明商贸有限公司填制编号为 CT8514895 的进口订舱委托书，从日本进口空调。

1. 发货人

广州明朗商贸有限公司

广州市天河路 267 号

电话：021-58693215

联系人：王贤

2. 其他

合同号：03TG28711

品名：AIR CONDITIONER

数量：500 台

包装：纸箱

重量：13kg/ 台

总体积：43m³

装运港：大阪

目的港：广州

装运要求：2015 年 2 月 28 日前，不准分批装运和转运。

进口订舱委托书

编号：   日期：　年　月　日

货　名 （英文）			
重　量		尺　码	
合　同　号		包　装	
装　卸　港		交　货　期	
装货条款			
发　货　人 名称地址			
发　货　人 电　挂			
订妥船名		预抵港口	
备注		委托单位	

① 危险品须注明性能，重大物件注明每件重量及尺码。

② 装货条款须详细注明。

实训项目39

缮制进口货物许可证

操作练习

根据下列资料，制作进口货物许可证，要求格式清楚、内容完整。

2014年12月1日，广州明朗商贸有限公司(单位编码：52304125596)申请签发编号为CT88661125839的进口货物许可证，从日本进口空调。

品名：空调

规格型号：制冷量≤4千大卡/时分体式空调

商品编码：84151021

单价：200美元FOB广州

数量：500台

包装：每台装一纸箱

总价：100 000美元

唛头：EAST

　　　GUANGZHOU

　　　NOSI-500

　　　MADE IN JAPAN

商品用途：外贸自营内销

装运港：大阪

目的港：广州

外汇来源：购汇

许可证有效期：2015年2月

中华人民共和国进口货物许可证 IMPORT LICENCE THE PEOPLE'S REPUBLIC OF CHINA					
1. 我国对外成交单位　　　编码 Importer			3. 进口许可证编号 License No.		
2. 收货单位 Consignee			4. 许可证有效期 Validity		
5. 贸易方式 Terms of trade			8. 进口国家（地区） Country whence consigned		
6. 外汇来源 Terms of foreign exchange			9. 商品原产地 Country of origin		
7. 到货口岸 Port of destination			10. 商品用途 Use of commodity		
11. 唛头——包装件数 Marks & numbers—number of packages					
12. 商品名称 Description of commodity			商品编码 Commodity No.		
13. 商品规格、型号 Specification	14. 单位 Unit	15. 数量 Quantity	16. 单价 Unit Price	17. 总值 Amount	18. 总值折美元 Amount in USD
19. 总计 Total					
20. 备注 Supplementary details			21. 发证机关盖章 **Issuing authority's stamp** 发证日期 **Signature Date**		

商务部监制　　　　　　　　　　　　　　　　　　　　　　本证不得涂改，不得转让

实训项目40

缮制进口付汇核销单

操作练习

根据下列资料，制作进口付汇核销单，要求格式清楚、内容完整。

2014年12月16日，北京德鑫贸易公司(单位代码：13438589-8)从日本进口空调后，填制编号为00492425的进口付汇核销单，向省外汇局申请付汇核销，付款银行为中行北京分行。此次付汇金额为1 728 600.00日元，全部以购汇方式支付，属正常付汇。

印单局代码：320000

合同号：DS1032E

进口批件号：20313768

预计到货日期：14/12/30

结算方式：即期信用证

付汇日期：14/12/12

贸易进口付汇核销单（代申报单）

印单局代码：　　　　　　　　　　　　　　　　　　　　核销单编号：

单位代码	单位名称	所在地外汇局名称
付汇银行名称	收汇人国别	交易编码□□□□
收款人是否在保税区：是□　否□	交易附言	

对外付汇币种　　　　　　　　　对外付汇总额
其中：购汇金额　　　　　　　　现汇金额　　　　　　　　　　　其他方式金额
　　　人民币账号　　　　　　　外汇账号

付汇性质

□正常付汇
□不在名录　　　　　　□90天以上信用证　　　□90天以上托收　　　□异地付汇
□90天以上到货　　　　□转口贸易
备案表编号

预计到货日期　／／	进口批件号	合同/发票号

结算方式

信用证　90天以内□　　　　90天以上□　　　承兑日期　／／　　付汇日期　／／　　期限　天

托收　90天以内□　　　　90天以上□　　　承兑日期　／／　　付汇日期　／／　　期限　天

	预付货款□　货到付汇（凭报关单付汇）□ 付汇日期　／／
汇	报关单号　报关日期　／／　报关单币种　　金额
	报关单号　报关日期　／／　报关单币种　　金额
	报关单号　报关日期　／／　报关单币种　　金额
	报关单号　报关日期　／／　报关单币种　　金额
款	报关单号　报关日期　／／　报关单币种　　金额
	（若报关单填写不完，可另附纸。）

其他□　　　　　　　　　　付汇日期　　／／

以下由付汇银行填写
申报号码：□□□□□□　□□□□　□□　□□□□□□　□□□□□

业务编号：　　　　审核日期：　／／　　（付汇银行签章）

进口单位签章

实训项目41
缮制进口货物运输预约保险合同

操作练习

根据下列资料，制作进口货物运输预约保险合同，要求格式清楚、内容完整。

2014年12月17日，上海朗明商贸有限公司的负责人王明与中国人民保险公司上海分公司的负责人张平签订了编号为TT080156的进口货物运输预约保险合同。本次投保货物为分体式空调，海运运输，按发票金额加一成投保一切险和战争险。合同于当日开始生效。

进口货物运输预约保险合同

合同号　　　　年　　月　　日

甲方：

乙方：中国人民保险公司

分公司

双方就进口货物的运输预约保险拟定各条以资共同遵守：

一、保险范围

甲方从国外进口全部货物，不论运输方式，凡贸易条件规定由买方办理保险的，都属于本合同范围之内。甲方应根据本合同规定，向乙方办理投保手续并支付保险费。

乙方对上述保险范围内的货物，负有自动承保的责任，在发生本合同规定范围内的损失时，均按本合同的规定，负责赔偿。

二、保险金额

保险金额以货物的到岸价格 (CIF) 即货价加运费加保险费为准 (运费可用实际运费，亦可由双方协定一个平均运费率计算)。

三、保险险别和费率

各种货物需要投保的险别由甲方选定并在投保单中填明。乙方根据不同的险别规定不同的费率。现暂定如下：

货物种类	运输方式	保险险别	保险费率

四、保险责任

各种险别的责任范围，按照所属乙方制定的"海洋货物运输保险条款"、"海洋运输货物战争险条款"、"海运进口货物国内转运期间保险责任扩展条款"、"航空运输一切险条款"和其他有关条款的规定为准。

五、投保手续

甲方一经掌握货物发运情况，即应向乙方寄送起运通知书，办理投保。通知书一式五份，由保险公司签认后，退回一份。如不办理投保，货物发生损失，乙方不予理赔。

六、保险费

乙方按照甲方寄送的起运通知书照前列相应的费率逐笔计收保费，甲方应及时付费。

七、索赔手续和期限

本合同所保货物发生保险责任范围内的损失时，乙方应按制定的"关于海运进口保险货物残损检验的赔款给付方法"和"进口货物施救整理费用支付方法"迅速处理。甲方应尽力采取防止货物扩大受损的措施，对已遭受损失的货物必须积极抢救，尽量减少货物的损失。向乙方办理索赔的有效期限，以保险货物卸离海港之日起满一年终止。如有特殊需要可向乙方提出延长索赔期。

八、合同期限

本合同自　　年　　月　　日起开始生效。

　　　　　　　　甲方　　　　　　　　　　　　　　　　乙方

实训项目42

缮制入境货物报检单

一、操作练习

根据下列资料，制作入境货物报检单，要求格式清楚、内容完整。

2014年8月12日，上海朗明商贸有限公司(单位登记号：52304125596)填制入境货物报检单，随附合同、发票、装箱单、许可证、提单等申请报检。

卖方：EAST AGENT COMPANY(东方代理公司)

买方：SHANGHAI LANGMING TRADING CO.，LTD.(上海朗明商贸有限公司)

　　　(电话：021-58693215，联系人：王明)

合同号：03TG28711

提单号：SOCO02596

进口许可证号：CT88661125839

品名：H6-59940BS GOLF CAPS(高尔夫球帽)

H. S. 编码：59019091

数量：1 800 打

包装：每50打装一纸箱

总价：14 580.00 美元

唛头：V.H

　　　SHANGHAI

　　　C/NO.1-36

　　　MADE IN JAPAN

商品用途：外贸自营内销

装运港：大阪

目的港：上海

船名：Volendam

航次：Voy. 8080

到货日期：2014年8月9日

卸货日期：2014年8月13日

索赔时效：两年

货物存放地点：上海市康元街119号

中华人民共和国出入境检验检疫
入境货物报检单

报检单位（加盖公章）：   *编号

报检单位登记号：   联系人：   电话：   报检日期：

收货人	（中文）		企业性质（划"√"）	□合资□合□外资
	（外文）			
发货人	（中文）			
	（外文）			

货物名称(中/外文)	H.S.编码	原产国（地区）	数/重量	货物总值	包装种类及数量

运输工具名称号码			合同号	
贸易方式		贸易国别（地区）	提单/运单号	
到货日期		启运国家（地区）	许可证/审批号	
卸货日期		启运口岸	入境口岸	
索赔有效期至		经停口岸	目的地	

集装箱规格、数量及号码	

合同、信用证订立的检验检疫条款或特殊要求		货物存放地点	
		用途	

随附单据（划"√"或补）	标记及号码	*外商投资资产（划"√"）	□是□否

□合同 □发票	□到货通知		*检验检疫费	
□提/运单	□装箱单		总金额（人民币元）	
□兽医卫生证书	□质保书			
□植物检疫证书	□理货清单			
□动物检疫证书	□磅码单		计费人	
□卫生证书	□验收报告			
□原产地证	□		收费人	
□许可/审批文件	□			

报检人郑重声明：	领取证单	
1.本人被授权报检。	日期	
2.上列填写内容正确属实。		
签名：_____	签名	

注：有"*"号栏由出入境检验检疫机关填写。   ◆国家出入境检验检疫局制

二、实务思考

受益人签发检验证书引起的纠纷案

F贸易进出口公司向E国际贸易公司出口一批蚕豆。在货物装运后，单证员向商品检验局申请出具品质检验证书时，据商品检验局查对，发现该批货物并未申请报验，所以不能出具品质检验证书。单证员经核对各项手续和资料，证实国外开来信用证规定要求出具"inspection certificate of quality in duplicate"（品质检验证书一式两份）。但业务部通知储运部的委托书上有关申请报验和出具检验证书栏漏填项目，使报验人员认为不需要报验，而且该商品又是属于非法定检验商品，合同也没有规定出具品质检验证书，所以未办理申请检验就装运了。

开证行根据《UCP600》关于出单人不明确的规定：信用证项下应提交的任何单据，如果对其出单人不明确时，只要所提交的单据表面与信用证其他条款相符，并且非由受益人出具单据表面上与信用证其他条款相符，并且非由受益人出具，银行将照予接受。所以受益人出具的品质检验证书不能生效。开证行通知我方F贸易进出口公司：经联系申请人不同意接受单据。单据暂代保管，速告单据处理意见。

E国际贸易公司也提出异议：第×××号合同项下货物的品质检验证书无法通关因系出口公司自己出具。我地当局规定该商品必须提供品质检验证书通关，而且规定出口商自己出具的证书无效。速补寄检验机关出具的证书。

请问：我方F公司应如何处理此事？为什么？

实训项目43

缮制进口货物报关单

一、操作练习

根据发票及下列资料，制作进口货物报关单，要求格式清楚、内容完整。

江苏纺织服装有限公司从加拿大进口的货物 2015 年 4 月 17 日抵达上海港，公司于 4 月 19 日填制进口货物报关单，随附发票、箱单等向海关进行申报。

江苏纺织服装有限公司

地址：南京市管桥 85 号华荣大厦 2901 室

邮编：210005

联系电话：025-4715004

经办人：李平

公司经营单位编码：5230412559

税务登记号码：320102134773852

海关预录入编号：DS9110006

船名：Volendam

航次：Voy. 7524

提单号：782-02458690

进口许可证号：CT88661182569

商品编号：62043200.90

数量：2 550 件

包装：每 30 件装一纸箱

商品用途：外贸自营内销

运费 600 美元，保费 50 美元，杂费 20

集装箱号：COSC51246

（一）

中华人民共和国海关进口货物报关单

预录入编号：   海关编号：

进口口岸	备案号		进口日期	申报日期
经营单位	运输方式		运输工具名称	提运单号
发货单位	贸易方式		征免性质	结汇方式
许可证号	运抵国（地区）		指运港	境内货源地
批准文号	成交方式	运费	保费	杂费
合同协议号	件数	包装种类	毛重（公斤）	净重（公斤）
集装箱号	随附单据		生产厂家	

标记唛码及备注

项号	商品编号	商品名称、规格型号	数量及单位	最终目的国（地区）	单价	总价	币制	征免

税费征收情况

录入员　　录入单位 兹声明以上申报无讹并承担法律责任 报关员　　　　申报单位（签章） 单位 地址 邮编　　　电话　　　　填制日期	海关审单批注及放行日期（签章） 审单　　　　　审价 征税　　　　　统计 查验　　　　　放行

（二）

ISSUER FASHION FORCE CO., LTD. P. O. BOX 8935 NEW TERMINAL, ALTA, VISTA OTTAWA, CANADA	商业发票 COMMERCIAL INVOICE		
TO JIANGSU TEXTILE GARMENT CO., LTD. HUARONG MANSION RM2901 NO.85 GUANQIAO, NANJING 210005, CHINA	NO. NT01FF004	DATE Mar.9, 2015	
TRANSPORT DETAILS SHIPMENT FROM MONTREAL, CANADA TO SHANGHAI, CHINA BY VESSEL	S/C NO. F01LCB05127	L/C NO. 63211020049	
	TERMS OF PAYMENT L/C AT SIGHT		

Marks and Numbers	Number and kind of package Description of goods	Quantity	Unit Price	Amount
				USD
FASHION FORCE F01LCB05127 CTN NO. SHANGHAI MADE IN CANADA				CIF SHANGHAI
	LADIES COTTON BLAZER (100% COTTON, 40S×20/140×60)	2 550 PCS	USD 12.80	USD 32 640.00
	Total:	2 550 PCS		USD 32 640.00

SAY TOTAL: USD THIRTY TWO THOUSAND SIX HUNDRED AND FORTY ONLY

SALES CONDITIONS: CIF SHANGHAI
SALES CONTRACT NO. F01LCB05127
LADIES COTTON BLAZER (100% COTTON, 40S×20/140×60)

STYLE NO.	PO NO.	QTY/PCS	USD/PC
46-301A	10337	2 550	12.80

PAKAGE	N. W.	G. W.
85 CARTONS	17 KGS	19 KGS

TOTAL PACKAGE: 85 CARTONS
TOTAL MEAS: 21.583 CBM

FASHION FORCE CO., LTD

Andy Burns

二、实务思考

海南三环公司 (4601137432) 签订合同从海口海关报关出口一批雨伞 (法定计量单位：把) 到印度尼西亚泗水 (苏腊巴亚)。该批货物内海南文昌宝宜公司 (4690160359) 生产，于 2014 年 9 月 18 日备妥并用汽车运抵海口港海关监管区，三环公司已办理相关托运和投保手续，并支付国际运杂费共 4 000 美元，运输保险费共 500 美元，该批货物计划于 9 月 21 日装运离境。三环公司将相关单据交由永佳报关行代理报关。

（一）

海南三环进出口贸易有限公司
HAINAN SANHUAN IMP. & EXP. TRADING GO.，LTD
Room 605，No. 397，Longkun Road，Haikou City，Hainan Province，China
TEL：+86-898-66745678

INVOICE

SOLD TO：

CV. UNIVERSAL ACTUF

JL，GUBERNUR SUR YO B-34 GBESIK，INDONESIA

PAYMENT TERM: T/T

SHIPPED PER：

INVOICE NO.: SH1109001

S/C NO. SH11230

DATE: SEP. 18，2014

FROM Haikou To Surabaya，Indonesia

Mark & Nos	Description of Goods	Size	Quantity	Unit Price	CIF Surabaya	Amount
N/M	UNBRELLA 直骨伞 UMBRELLA 折叠伞	21	3000DOZ 35928PCS	USD 9.10 USD 1.70 TOTAL：		USD 27 300.00 USD 61 077.60 USD 88 377.60
		HAINAN SANHUAN IMP. & EXP. TRADING CO.，LTD(公章)				

（二）

海南三环进出口贸易有限公司
HAINAN SANHUAN IMP. & EXP. TRADING GO.，LTD
Room 605，No. 397，Longkun Road，Haikou City，Hainan Province，China
TEL：+86-898-66745678

PACKING LIST

NO.: SH1109001

CONSIGNEE：

CV. UNIVERSAL ACTIF INDONESIA

FROM Haikou To Surabaya，Indonesia

SHIPPING MARKS：N/M

Carton No.	Packing No.	Description of Goods	Quantity	Net Weight	Gross Weight	Measurement
1-682 683-1176	682 CTNS 494 CTNS	UNBRELLA 直骨伞 UMBRELLA 折叠伞	3 000 DOZ 35 928 PCS	16 152.50 KGS 8 812.30 KGS	16 834.50 KGS 9 306.30 KGS	
				24 964.80 KGS	26 140.80 KGS	52.00 CBM
TOTAL：	1 176 CTNS			HAINAN SANHUAN IMP. & EXP. TRADING CO.，LTD(公章)		

集装箱货物货单

Shipper（发货人） HAINAN SANHUAN IMP. & EXP. TRADING CO.，LTD ROOM 605，NO397，LONGKUN ROAD，HAIKOU CITY， HAINAM PROVINCE，CHINA	D/R No.（编号） APLU050741869
Consignee（收货人） CV. UNIVERSAL JL. GUBERNUR SUR YO B-34 GBESIK， INDONESIA	集装箱货物托运单 场站收据副本 （第五联）
Notify Party（通知人） SAME AS CONSIGNEE	
Pre-carriage by（前程运输）Place of Receipt（收货地点） HAIKOU，CHINA	
Ocean Vessel（船名）Voy No.（航次）Port of Loading（装货港） APL REBY V.031 HAIKOU，CHINA	

Port of Discharge（卸货港） SURABAYA	Place of Delivery（交货地点） SURABAYA	Final Destination（目的地） SURABAYA

Marks & No. （标记与 号码） N/M	Container No （集装箱号） Seal No.（封志号） CNTR NO.： TOLL3635199/40' GP Seal No.：9422074	Containers or Description of Goods Kind of Packages； （箱数或件数、包装种类与货名） 1176GTNS UMBRELLA 伞	Gross Weight （毛重/千克） 26 140.80 KGS	Measurement （尺码/立方米） 52.000 GBM
Total Number of Containers or Packages (IN WORDS) 集装箱数或件数合计（大写）			SAY TOTAL：ONE FORTY FT. GP CONTAINER ONLY	

Freight & Charges （运费与附加费）	Revenue Tons （运费吨）	Rate （运费率）	Per （每）	Prepaid（运费预付） FREIGHT PREPAID	Collect （运费到付）

Ex Tate （兑换率）	Prepaid at（预付地点） HAIKOL，CHINA		Payable at （到付地点）	Place of Issue（签发地点） HAIKOU，CHINA
	Total Prepaid（预付总额）		No. of Original B(S)/L	（正本提单份数）THREE(3)

Service Type on Receiving □—CY □—CFS □—DOOR	Service Type on Delivery □—CY □—CFS □—DOOR	Reefer-Temperature Required （冷藏温度）	°F	°C

Type of Goods （种类）	□ Ordinary, □ Reefer, □ Dangerous □ Auto. （普通） （冷藏） （危险品） （裸装车辆） □ Liquid, □ Live Animal, □ Bulk （液体） （活动物） （散货）	危险品	Class: Property: IMDG Code Page: UN No.

可否转船 ALLOWED	可否分批 ALLOWED
装期	有效期
金额	
制单日期	

永佳报关行根据以上资料填写出口货物报关单，请选择下列栏目正确选项：

1. "备案号" 栏填 (　　)。

A. 此栏为空

B. 4601137432

C. 4690160359

D. SHll09001

2. "出口日期" 栏填 (　　)。

A. 20110918

B. 20110921

C. 110921

D. 此栏为空

3. "运输方式" 栏填 (　　)。

A. 公路运输

B. 铁路运输

C. 水路运输

D. 其他运输

4. "经营单位" 栏填 (　　)。

A. 海南三环公司 (4601137432)

B. 海南三环公司

C. 文昌宝宜公司 (4690160359)

D. 永佳报关行

5. "发货单位" 栏填 (　　)。

A. 海南三环公司 (4601137432)

B. 海南三环公司

C. 文昌宝宜公司 (4690160359)

D. 文昌宝宜公司

6. "结汇方式" 栏填 (　　)。

A. D/P　　　　B. D/A

C. T/T　　　　D. L/C

7. "成交方式" 栏填 (　　)。

A. 1　　　　B. 2

C. 3　　　　D. 4

8. "运报国 (地区)" 栏填 (　　)。

A. 中国

B. 印度尼西亚

C. 泗水

D. 海口

9. "运费" 栏填 (　　)。

A. 502/4000/3

B. 4000

C. 502/4000/2

D. 此栏为空

10. "件数" 栏填 (　　)。

A. 38928　　　　B. 1176

C. 71928　　　　D. 1

11. "包装种类" 栏填 (　　)。

A. 纸箱　　　　B. 集装箱

C. 其他　　　　D. 此栏为空

12. "集装箱号" 栏填 (　　)。

A. TOLU3635199

B. 9422074/40/××××

C. ToLL3635199/40/××××

D. 0

13. "随附单据" 栏填 (　　)。

A. 发票、装箱单、提货单

B. SHll09001

C. APLUD50741869

D. 此栏为空

14."数量及单位"栏填（　　）。

A. 第一项：36 000 把（第一行），3 000 打（第三行）

第二项：35 928 把

B. 第一项：3 000 打

第二项：35 928 把

C. 第一项：36 000 把

第二项：35 928 把

D. 第一项：3 000 打

第二项：2 994 打

15."征免"栏填（　　）。

A. 一般征税　　　　B. 全免　　　　C. 全额退税　　　　D. 照章征税

议付单据审核1

一、操作练习

根据信用证内容审核全套结汇单据，指出单据中的不符点并改正。

发票号码：WHC-05Y2988

发票日期：2014.08.15

FORM A 号码：GZ7/80067/0158

船名：SUISU/SENTOR V.001

产品原材料情况：完全自产品

集装箱号码：TEXU3730336/20'

装运港：NANJING

毛重：40.7KGS/PAPERSACK

净重：40KGS/PAPERSACK

总尺码：24CBM

提单号码：GSG05-723858

提单日期：2014.09.01

唛头：H&L

HAMBUGR

NO.1-200

包装：200 PAPERSACK

（一）

1. Shipper Insert Name，Address and Phone JIANGSU DECHUANGWEIYE IMPORT & EXPORT CO.，LTD. HONGWU ROAD 16#，NANJING 210004 P. R. CHINA			B/L No. GSG05-723858
2. Consignee Insert Name，Address and Phone TO ORDER			中远集装箱运输有限公司 COSCO CONTAINER LINES TLX：33057 COSCO CN FAX：+86(021) 6545 8984 ORIGINAL
3. Notify Party Insert Name，Address and Phone（It is agreed that no responsibility shall attach to the Carrier or his agents for failure to notify） INTERCOM IMPORT & EXPORT CO.，LTD. 123 FRIEDRICH-EBERT STREET，HAMBURG			Port-to-Port or Combined Transport BILL OF LADING RECEIVED in external apparent good order and condition except as otherwise noted. The total number of packages or units stuffed in the container，The description of the goods and the weights shown in this Bill of Lading are furnished by the Merchants，and which the carrier has no reasonable means of checking and is not a part of this Bill of Lading contract. The carrier has Issued the number of Bills of Lading stated below，all of this tenor and date，One of the original Bills of Lading must be surrendered and endorsed or signed against the delivery of the shipment and whereupon any other original Bills of Lading shall be void. The Merchants agree to be bound by the terms And conditions of this Bill of Lading as if each had personally signed this Bill of Lading. See clause 4 on the back of this Bill of Lading（Terms continued on the back hereof，please read carefully).*Applicable Only When Document Used as a Combined Transport Bill of Lading.
4. Combined Transport * Pre - carriage by	5. Combined Transport *Place of Receipt		
6. Ocean Vessel Voy. No. SUISU/SENTOR V.001	7. Port of Loading NANJING，CHINA		
8. Port of Discharge HAMBURG	9. Combined Transport *Place of Delivery		

Marks & Nos. Container / Seal No.	No. of Containers or Packages	Description of Goods (If Dangerous Goods，See Clause 20)	Gross Weight Kgs	Measurement
H&L HAMBUGR NO.1-200	200 PAPERSACKS	4439 CHINA BLACK TEA FREIGHT PREPAID TOTOAL TWO HUNDRED PAPERSACKS ONLY	8 140 KGS	24 CBM
		Description of Contents for Shipper's Use Only (Not part of This B/L Contract)		

10. Total Number of containers and/or packages (in words)				
Subject to Clause 7 Limitation SAY：FORTY DRUMS ONLY				

11. Freight & Charges	Revenue Tons	Rate	Per	Prepaid	Collect
Declared Value Charge					
Ex. Rate：	Prepaid at	Payable at	Place and date of issue		
			NANJING，CHINA		
	Total Prepaid	No. of Original B(s)/L TWO	Signed for the Carrier，COSCO CONTAINER LINES		
LADEN ON BOARD THE VESSEL					
DATE			BY		

（二）

ORIGINAL	
1. Goods consigned from (Exporter's business name，address，country) JIANGSU DECHUANGWEIYE IMPORT & EXPORT CO., LTD. HONGWU ROAD 16#，NANJING 210004 P. R. CHINA	Reference No. GZ7/80067/0158 ## GENERALIZED SYSTEM OF PREFERENCES ### CERTIFICATE OF ORIGIN (Combined declaration and certificate) ## FORM A
2. Goods consigned to (Consignee's name，address，country) INTERCOM IMPORT & EXPORT CO.，LTD. 123 FRIEDRICH-EBERT STREET，HAMBURG	Issued in ### THE PEOPLE'S REPUBLIC OF CHINA (country) <div align="right">See Notes overleaf</div>
3. Means of transport and route (as far as known) ON/AFTER AUGST 15，2005 FROM NANJING，CHINA TO HAMBURG BY VESSEL	4. For official use

5. Item number	6. Marks and numbers of packages	7. Number and kind of packages；description of goods	8. Origin criterion (see notes overleaf)	9. Gross weight or other quantity	10. Number and date of invoices
1	H&L HAMBUGR NO.1-200	(8000)EIGHT THOUSAND KGS OF 4439 CHINA BLACK TEA ***************************	"P" ******* TOTAL:	8 140 KGS ********* 2 550 KGS	WHC-05Y2988 AUG 15，2014

| 11. Certification
It is hereby certified，on the basis of control carried out，that the declaration by the exporter is correct.

NANJING，JIANGSU AUG.20，2014

Place and date，signature and stamp of certifying authority | 12. Declaration by the exporter
The undersigned hereby declares that the above details and statements are correct，that all the goods were produced in
CHINA
(country)
and that they comply with the origin requirements specified for those goods in the Generalized System of Preferences for goods exported to
GERMANY
NANJING，JIANGSU AUG.20，2010

Place and date，signature and stamp of authorized signatory |

（三）

江苏德创伟业进出口有限公司
Jiangsu Dechuangweiye Import & Export Co.，ltd
Hongwu Road 16#，Nanjing 210004 P.R.China

COMMERCIAL INVOICE

Date 2014.08.15
Invoice No. WHC-05Y2988
S/C No.：BT7095

Messrs：	Intercom Import & Export Co.，ltd
	123 FRIEDRICH-EBERT STREET，HAMBURG

Terms of Payment：L/C AT SIGHT

Marks and Numbers	Description & Quantity	Quantity	Unit Price	Amount
H&L HAMBUGR NO.1-200	4 439 CHINA BLACK TEA	8 000 KGS	CIF USD 4.05	HAMBURG USD 32 400.00
	TOTAL：	8 000 KGS		USD 31 428.00

TOTAL QUANTITY：8 000 KGS

PACKING：200 PAPERSACKS

TOTAL WEIGHT：8 000 KGS N.W.：8 000 KGS G.W.：8 140 KGS

TOTAL：US DOLLARS THIRTY ONE THOUSAND FOUR HUNDRED AND TWENTY EIGHT ONLY.

PACKING：IN PAPERSACKS，PALLETIZED AND CUNTAINERIZED INTO 1×20' FCL.

（四）

| 2014AUG01 | | LOGICAL TERMINALE102MT S700 |

ISSUE OF A DOCUMENTARY CREDIT

PAGE 00001
FUNC JSRVPR1

USER HEADER		SERVICE CODE	103：	（银行盖信用证通知专用章）
		BANK. PRIORITY	113：	
		MSG USER REF.	108：	
		INFO. FROM CI	115：	

SEQUENCE OF TOTAL	*27	1 / 1
FORM OF DOC. CREDIT	*40 A	IRREVOCABLE
DOC. CREDIT NUMBER	*20	4006LC129336
DATE OF ISSUE	31 C	140801
EXPIRY	*31 D	DATE 141005 PLACE CHINA
APPLICANT	*50	INTERCOM IMPOTR & EXPORT CO.，LTD.
		123 FRIEDRICH-EBERT STREET，HAMBURG
BENEFICIARY	*59	JIANGSU DECHUANGWEIYE IMPORT & EXPORT CO.，LTD.
		HONGWU ROAD 16#，NANJING 210004 P.R.CHINA
		AMOUNT *32 B CURRENCY USD AMOUNT 31428
POS./NEG.TOL.(%)	39 A	03/03
AVAILABLE WITH/BY	*41 D	ANY BANK IN CHINA，BY NEGOTIATION AGAINST THE DOCUMENTS DETAILED HEREIN AND BENEFICIARY'S DRAFT AT 30 DAYS SIGHT DRAWN ON US UNDER L/C NO. 4006LC129336 FOR 100P.C.OF THE INVOICE VALUE.
DRAWEE	42 A	THE CHARTERED BANK AG HAMBURG
PARTIAL SHIPMTS	43 P	NOT ALLOWED
TRANSSHIPMENT	43 T	NOT ALLOWED
LOADING IN CHARGE	44 A	CHINA FORT
FOR TRANSPIRT TO···	44 B	HAMBURG
LATEST SHIPMENT	44 C	AT THE LATEST SEPT.10，2014
GOODS DESCRIPT.	45 A	4439 CHINA BLACK TEA BAT.8000KGS @ USD4.05/KG CIF3% HAMBURG (1x20' FCL/200 PAPERSACKS)PACKED IN PAPERSACKS. PALLETIZED AND CUNTAINERIZED AS PER THE SALES CONFIRMATION NO.BT7095 THE PRICE IS TO BE UNDERSTOOD PER KILO NET SHIPPED WEIGHT CIF HAMBURG LESS 3 PERCENT COMISSION.
DOCS REQUIRED	46 A	+ SIGNED COMMERCIAL INVOICE IN 4-FOLD.
		+ FULL SET OF CLEAN ON BOARD MARINE BILL OF LADING MADE OUT TO THE ORDER，MARKED FREIGHT PREPAID AND NOTIFY APPLICANT.
		+ CERTIFICATE OF WEIGHT IN 4-FOLD.
		+ GSP CERTIFICATE OF ORIGIN FORM A，CERTIFYING GOODS OF ORIGIN IN CHINA，ISSUED BY COMPETENT AUTHORITIES.
		+INSURANCE POLICY OR CERTIFICATE COVERING ALL RISKS AND WAR RISK，INCLUDING WAREHOUSE TO WAREHOUSE CLAUSE，ISSUED FOR AT LEAST 110 % OF CIF-VALUE.

（续表）

ADDITIONAL CONDITION	47 A	IF BILL OF LADING ARE REQUIRED ABOVE，PLEASE FORWARD DOCUMENT IN TWO MAILS，ORIGINALS SEND BY COURIER AND DUPLICATES BY REGISTERED AIRMAIL.
DETAILS OF CHARGES	71 B	BANK CHARGES EXCLUDING ISSUING BANKS ARE FOR ACCOUNT OF BENEFICIARY.
PRESENTATION PERIOD	48	DOCUMENTS TO BE PRESENTED WITHIN 15 DAYS FROM SHIPMENT DATE
CONFIRMATION	*49	WITHOUT
INSTRUCTIONS	78	DISCREPANT DOCUMENTS，IF ACCEPTABLE，WILL BE SUBJECT TO A DISCREPANCY HANDLING FEE OF USD 50.00 OR EQUIVALENT WHICH WILL BE FOR ACCOUNT OF BENEFICIARY.
		SPECIAL NOTE: ISSUING BANK WILL DISCOUNT ACCEPTANCES ON REQUEST，FOR A/C OF BENEFICIARY (UNLESS OTHERWISE STATED)AT APPROPRIATE LIBOR RATE PLUS 1.00PER CENT MARGIN.
SEND. TO REC. INFO.	72	THIS CREDIT IS ISSUED SUBJECT TO 2007 REVISION，I.C.C.PUBLICATIONS NO.600

TRAILER ORDER IS <MAC：> <PAC：> <ENC：> <CHK：> <TNG：> <PDE：>MAC：E55927A4 CHK：7B505952829A

（五）

江苏德创伟业进出口有限公司

Jiangsu Dechuangweiye Import & Export Co.，ltd

Hongwu Road 16#，Nanjing 210004 P.R.China

CERTIFICATE OF WEIGHT

DATE：2014.08.15

INVOICE NO.：WHC-05Y2988

LOADING PORT			
S/C No.：	BT7095	L/C NO.：	4006LC129336

Shipping Marks	Descriptions of Goods	Quantity	G.W	N.W
H&L HAMBUGR NO.1-200	4439 CHINA BLACK TEA 200 PAPERSACKS	8 000 KGS	40.7 KGS/PAPERSACK	40 KGS/PAPERSACK
	TOTAL:	8 000 KGS	8 140 KGS	8 000 KGS

SAY TOTAL:	EIGHT THOUSAND KGS ONLY.

（六）

单据审核结果

二、实务思考

某食品进出口公司向国外某公司出口一批野禽。3 月 9 日，接到买方开来一张电开信用证，证中关于商品条款规定"100m/tons of frozen partridge，packing：in cartons，each containing 20-24 brace"（100 吨冷冻鹧鸪，纸箱包装，每箱 20-24 对）。某食品进出口公司根据对方开来的信用证要求，于 3 月 13 日进行装运，14 日备妥所有单据向议付行交单办理议付。但 3 月 29 日开证行提出拒付，指出：卖方发票有不符点，未表明商品规格"Fresh feathers-on，neat and intact，with viscera，without distinction as to sex，a grade，0.5Kg，per brace"（新鲜、羽毛整洁、带内脏、不分雌雄。一级，每对净重 0.5 公斤以上）。开证申请人不接受上述单据。某食品进出口公司查对留底单据与信用证，没有规定商品规格，随即发电反驳：你 3 月 9 日开立的信用证条款并没有规定有上述规格，因此我方是相符交单。开证行答复："关于商品规格事，我 3 月 9 日电开信用证注明'证实书后寄'，后于 3 月 10 日邮寄证实书，在证实书中规定了上述商品规格。"并提出根据 UCP 600，"如电开信用证中声明'详情后告'或声明以邮寄证实书为有效信用证，则电讯不应视为有效信用证，应以规定有商品规格的证实书为有效信用证，所以你方是不符交单"。请问：我方公司应如何处理此事？

议付单据审核2

一、操作练习

根据信用证内容审核全套结汇单据，指出单据中的不符点并改正。

发票号码：H2455683

发票日期：MARCH 20.2015

商品毛重：15 KGS/CARTON

商品净重：10 KGS/CARTON

商品总尺码：3.40CBM

（一）

中华人民共和国出入境检验检疫 出境货物报检单						
报检单位（加盖公章） 上海对外贸易公司					*编号	
报检单位登记号		联系人	电话 66835158	报检日期 2014 年 12 月 4 日		
发货人	（中文）	上海对外贸易公司				
	（外文）	SHANGHAI FOREIGN TRADE CORP.				
收货人	（中文）					
	（外文）	MOUN NO.，LTD.				

货物名称（中 / 外文）	H. S. 编码	产地	数 / 重量	货物总值	包装种类及数量
男式羽绒夹克 MENS NYLON DOWN JACKETS	6201.9310	上海	1 800 PCS	USD 37 800.00	150 CARTONS

运输工具名称号码	海运	贸易方式	一般贸易	货物存放地点	工厂仓库
合同号	33745	信用证号	329898875457	用途	其他
发货日期	2014-12-07	输往国家（地区） 泰国	许可证 / 审批号		
启运地	南京	到达口岸 曼谷	生产单位注册号		

集装箱规格、数量及号码	1×40'/APLU5833259		
合同、信用证订立的检验检疫条款或特殊要求	标记及号码	随附单据（划"√"或补填）	
	MOUN BANGKOK C/NO.1-150 MADE IN CHINA	☑合同 ☑信用证 ☑发票 □换证凭单 ☑装箱单 □厂检单	□包装性能结果单 □许可 / 审批文件 □ □ □ □

需要证单名称（划"√"或补填）			*检验检疫费	
☑品质证书 __ 正 __ 副 □重量证书 __ 正 __ 副 ☑数量证书 __ 正 __ 副 □兽医卫生证书 __ 正 __ 副 □健康证书 __ 正 __ 副 □卫生证书 __ 正 __ 副 □动物卫生证书 __ 正 __ 副		□植物检疫证书 □熏蒸 / 消毒证书 □出境货物换证凭单 ☑出境货物通关单 □ □ □	__ 正 __ 副 __ 正 __ 副 __ 正 __ 副	总金额 （人民币元） 计费人 收费人

报检人郑重声明： 1. 本人被授权报检。 2. 上列填写内容正确属实，货物无伪造或冒用他人的厂名、标志、认证标志，并承担货物质量责任。 签名：_____	领取证单
	日期
	签名

注：有"*"号栏由出入境检验检疫机关填写。　　　　　　◆国家出入境检验检疫局制

（二）

中华人民共和国海关出口货物报关单

预录入编号：2250866　　　　　　　　　海关编号：

出口口岸 SHANGHAI PORT		备案号		出口日期 2014-12-07	申报日期 2014-12-01
经营单位　3201003830 SHANGHAI FOREIGN TRADE CORP.		运输方式 江海运输	运输工具名称 DAFENG	提运单号 LU0148R52698	
发货单位		贸易方式 一般贸易		征免性质 一般征免	结汇方式 L/C
许可证号	运抵国（地区） 泰国		指运港 曼谷	境内货源地 上海	
批准文号	成交方式 CFR		运费 USD 160.00	保费	杂费
合同协议号 33745	件数 150		包装种类箱	毛重（公斤） 2 200.00 KGS	净重（公斤） 2 000.00 KGS
集装箱号 APLU5833259	随附单据			生产厂家	

标记唛码及备注
MOUN
BANGKOK
C/NO.1-150
MADE IN CHINA

项号	商品编号	商品名称、规格型号	数量及单位	最终目的国（地区）	单价	总价	币制	征免
1	6201.9300	MENS NYLON DOWN JACKETS	1 800 件	泰国	8.92/KG	37 800.00	USD	照章
		Total：1 800 件				USD 37 800.00		

税费征收情况

录入员　　　录入单位	兹声明以上申报无讹并承担法律责任	海关审单批注及放行日期 （签章）	
		审单	审价
报关员	申报单位（签章）	征税	统计
单位地址　　上海对外贸易公司			
邮编	电话 86-21-66835158　填制日期 2014-12-01	查验	放行

（三）

出口货物明细单

2014 年 12 月 1 日

开证银行		BANGKOK BANK PUBLIC COMPANY LIMITED, BANGKOK	信用证号	329898871232			
经营单位（装船人）		SHANGHAI FOREIGN TRADE CORP. 1288 ZHONG SHAN ROAD, SHANGHAI, CHINA TEL: 86-21-66835158	银行编号			外运编号	
			核销单号	327656960		许可证号	
提单或承运收据	抬头人	TO THE ORDER OF MOUN NO., LTD.	货物性质			贸易国别	THAILAND
	通知人	MOUN NO., LTD. NO.443, 249, ROAD, BANGKOK, THAILAND	出口口岸	SHANGHAI		目的港	BANGKOK
			可否转运	Y		可否分批	Y
	运费	FREIGHT PREPAID	装运期限	2014-12-10		有效期限	2010-12-30

标记唛头	货名规格及货号	包装件数	数量或尺码	毛重	净重	价格（成交条件） 单价	总价
						CFR BANGKOK，THAILAND	
MOUN BANGKOK C/NO.1-150 MADE IN CHINA	MENS NYLON DOWN JACKETS	150 CTNS	1 800 PCS	16 200 KGS	14 400 KGS	USD 21.00	USD 37 800.00
TOTAL:		150 CTNS	1 800 PCS	16 200 KGS	14 400 KGS		USD 37 800.00

SAY TOTAL: ONE HUNDRED AND FIFTY CARTONS ONLY.

外运外轮注意事项		总体积	25M^3
		船名	
		装货单号	
		海关编号	

（四）

未经核销此联不得撕开

出口收汇核销单
出口退税专用

（苏）编号：32765960

出口单位：上海对外贸易公司		
单位代码：		
货物名称	数　量	币种总价
男式羽绒夹克	1 800 件	USD 37 800.00

报关编号：

（出口单位盖章）

（海关盖章）

外汇局签注栏：

年　月　日（盖章）

出口收汇核销单

（苏）编号：32765960

3 2 7 6 5 6 9 6 0

出口单位：上海对外贸易公司				
单位代码：				
类别	币种金额	日期	盖章	

银行签注栏

海关签注栏：

外汇局签注栏：

年　月　日（盖章）

（出口单位盖章）

出口收汇核销单
存根

（苏）编号：32765960

出口单位：上海对外贸易公司

单位代码：

出口币种总价：USD 37 800.00

收汇方式：L/C AT SIGHT

预计收款日期：20141230

报关日期：20141204

备注：

此单报关有效期截止到　　年　月　日（盖章）

（五）

BILL OF EXCHANGE

| 凭
Drawn Under | BANGKOK BANK PUBLIC COMPANY LIMITED, BANGKOK | 不可撤销信用证
Irrevocable L/C No. | 32989871232 |

| 日期
Date | NOV. 15, 2014 | 支取 Payable With interest | @ % 按 息 付款 |

| 号码
No. | 9005 |

汇票金额
Exchange for   US$37810.00   上海   DEC.15, 2000
                               Shanghai

见票 _____ 日后（本汇票之副本未付）付交
at   sight of this FIRST of Exchange (Second of Exchange

Being unpaid) Pay to the order of   BANK OF COMMUNICATIONS, SHANGHAI

金额
the sum of   U.S.DOLLARS THIRTY SEVEN THOUSAND EIGHT HUNDRED ONLY.

此致   MOUN NO., LTD.
To   NO.443, 249, ROAD, BANGKOK, THAILAND

                                     SHANGHAI FOREIGN TRADE CORP.

（六）

SHANGHAI FOREIGN TRADE CORP. 1288 ZHONG SHAN ROAD，SHANGHAI，CHINA **COMMERCIAL INVOICE**				

Invoice No.: 2000FT011			Date：DEC. 3，2014	

Seller：
SHANGHAI FOREIGN TRADE CORP.
1288 ZHONG SHAN ROAD，SHANGHAI，CHINA

Buyer：
MOUN NO.，LTD.
NO.443，249，ROAD，BANGKOK，THAILAND

L/C No.:	329898871		Contract No.		33745
From	SHANGHAI，CHINA		To	BANGKOK，THAILAND	
Marks and No.	Description of goods	Quantity	Unit Price	Amount	
MOUN BANGKOK C/NO.1-150 MADE IN CHINA				FOB SHANGHAI	
	MENS NYLON DOWN JACKETS	1 800 PCS	USD 21.00	USD 37 800.00	
	TOTAL:	1 800 PCS		USD 37 800.00	

SAY TOTAL:	U.S. DOLLARS THIRTY SEVEN THOUSAND EIGHT HUNDRED ONLY

（七）

SHANGHAI FOREIGN TRADE CORP.

1288 ZHONG SHAN ROAD，SHANGHAI，CHINA

PACKING LIST

Invoice No.：2000FT011   Date：DEC. 3，2014

Seller：

SHANGHAI FOREIGN TRADE CORP.

1288 ZHONG SHAN ROAD，SHANGHAI，CHINA

Buyer：

MOUN NO.，LTD.

NO.443，249，ROAD，BANGKOK，THAILAND

From SHANGHAI，CHINA   To BANGKOK，THAILAND

Marks and No.	Description of goods	Quantity	Package	G.W	N.W	Meas.
MOUN BANGKOK C/NO.1-150 MADE IN CHINA	MENS NYLON DOWN JACKETS	1 800 PCS	150CTNS	16 100 KGS	14 400 KGS	25M^3
	TOTAL：	1 800 PCS	150 CARTONS	16 200 KGS	14 400 KGS	25M^3

SAY TOTAL：U. S. DOLLARS THIRTY SEVEN THOUSAND EIGHT HUNDRED ONLY

（八）
单据审核结果

（九）

LETTER OF CREDIT	
RCVD *	FIN/Session/OSN: F01　430429526
RCVD *	Own AddressCOMMCNSELXXXX BANK OF COMMUNICATIONS
RCVD *	SHANGHAI
RCVD *	(HEAD OFFICE)
RCVD *	Output Message Type: 700 ISSUE OF A DOCUMENTARY CREDIT
RCVD *	Input Time: 1322
RCVD *	MIR: 001115BKKBTHBKBXXX51958227342
RCVD *	Send by: BKKBTHBKBXXX BANGKOK BANK PUBLIC COMPANY LIMITED
RCVD *	BANGKOK
RCVD *	Output Date/Time：101115/1422
RCVD *	Priority：Normal
RCVD *	27 A /SEQUENCE OF TOTAL1/1
RCVD *	40 A /FORM OF DOCUMENTARY CREDIT IRREVOCABLE
RCVD *	20/ DOCUMENTARY CREDIT NUMBER329898871232
RCVD *	31 C /DATE OF ISSUE141115
RCVD *	31 D /DATE AND PLACE OF EXPIRY 141230 BENEFICIARIES' COUNTRY
RCVD *	50/ A PPLICANT MOUN NO.，LTD.
RCVD *	NO.443，249，ROAD，BANGKOK THAILAND
RCVD *	59/ B ENEFICIARY SHANGHAI FOREIGN TRADE CORP.
RCVD *	1288 ZHONG SHAN ROAD，SHANGHAI，CHINA
RCVD *	TEL：86-21-66835158
RCVD *	32/ C URRENCY CODE AMOUNT USD 37 800.00
RCVD *	41 D /AVAILABLE WITH…BY…-NAME/ADDR
RCVD *	ANY BANK IN CHINA
RCVD *	BY NEGOTIATION
RCVD *	42 C /DRAFTS AT…SIGHT
RCVD *	42 D /DRAWEE-NAME AND ADDRESS
RCVD *	ISSUING BANK
RCVD *	43 P /PARITIAL SHIPMENTS NOT ALLOWED
RCVD *	43 T /TRANSSHIPMENT ALLOWED
RCVD *	44 A /ON BOARD/DISP/TAKING CHARGE SHANGHAI，CHINA
RCVD *	44 B /FOR TRANSPORTATION TO BANGKOK，THAILAND
RCVD *	44 C /LATEST DATE OF SHIPMENT141210 DEC-10-2014
RCVD *	45 A /DESC OF GOODS AND/OR SERVICES
RCVD *	1 800 PCS OF MENS NYLON DOWN JACKETS
RCVD *	HS NO. 6201.9310
RCVD *	AT USD21.00 PER PC.CFR BANGKOK，THAILAND
RCVD *	PACKING IN 150 CARTONS
RCVD *	G.W.: 16 200 KGS，N.W.: 14 400 KGS，MEASUREMENT: 25M^3

（续表）

RCVD *		SHIPPING MARK：MOUN
		BANGKOK
		C/NO.1-150
		MADE IN CHINA
RCVD *	46 A	(DETAILS AS PER SALES CONFIRMATION NO.33745)
RCVD *		/DOCUMENTS REQUIRED
RCVD *		+ORIGINAL SIGNED COMMERCIAL INVOICE IN DUPLICATE
RCVD *		+ORIGINAL PAKCING LIST IN DUPLICATE
RCVD *		+FULL SET CLEAN ON BOARD MARINE BILL OF LADING
RCVD *		CONSIGNED TO THE ORDER OF BANGKOK BANK PUBLIC COMPANY LIMITED，BANGKOK MARKED PREPAID AND NOTIFY APPLICANT NAME OF SHIPPING AGENT IN BANGKOK WITH FULL ADDRESS AND TELEPHONE NUMBER，INDICATING THIS L/C NUMBER.
RCVD *	47 A	/ADDITIONAL CONDITIONS
RCVD */		DRAFTS IN DUPLICATE AT 120 DAYS AFTER SHIPMENT DATE, INTEREST/DISCOUNT AND INDICATING THIS L/C NUMBER
RCVD *		A DISCREPANCY FEE OF USD50.00 WILL BE IMPOSED ON EACH SET OF DOCUMENTS PRESENTED FOR NEGOTIATION UNDER THIS L/C WITH DISCREPANCY. THE FEE WILL BE DEDUCTED FROM THE BILL AMOUNT.
RCVD *	47 B	/CHARGES
RCVD *		ALL BANK CHARGES OUTSIDE THAILAND INCLUDING REIMBURSING BANK COMMISSION AND DISCREPANCY FEE(IF ANY) ARE FOR BENEFICIARIES' ACCOUNT
RCVD *	49	/CONFIREMATION INSTRUCTIONS
RCVD *		WITHOUT
RCVD *	53 D	/REIMBURSING BANK-NAME/ADDRESS
RCVD *		BANGKOK BANK PUBLIC COMPANY LIMITED，NEW YORK BRANCH
RCVD *		AT MATURITY
RCVD *	78	/INSTRUCS TO PAY/ACCPT/NEGOT BANK
RCVD *		DOCUMENTS TO BE DISPATCHED IN ONE SET BY COURIER
RCVD *		ALL CORRESPONDENCE TO BE SENT TO BANGOKOK BANK PUBLIC COMPANY LIMITED HEAD OFFICE，333 SILOM ROAD，BANGKOK 10500，AHAILAND.
RCVD *		ATTN: L/C MP/1011027792163 IMPORT L/C SECTION 6.

二、实务思考

1. 我国 B 公司与法国 C 公司签订合同出口货物到法国，采用信用证方式结算货款，公司通过其开证行 BANK I 巴黎分行申请开立了非保兑信用证，通知行为中国银行江苏分行，信用证规定"DATE AND PLACE OF EXPIRY: 111105 FRANCE, AVAILABIE WITH ISSUING BANK BY PAYMENT，LATEST DATE 0F SHIPMENT: 111102, PRESENTATIONPERIOD: WITHIN l5 DAYS AFTER THE DATE OF SHIPMENT"。B 公司于 2014 年 11 月 1 日将货物装船，并于 2014 年 11 月 5 日将信用证要求的全套单据提交中国银行江苏分行，中国银行江苏分行立即于当日使用 DHL 将单据寄往法国的开证行，收到单据后，开证银行 BANK I 巴黎分行以信用证已过期为由拒付。请问：BANK I 巴黎分行的拒付理由是否成立？为什么？

2. 某公司接到国外开来的信用证，规定"于或约于 5 月 15 日装船"。该公司于 5 月 8 日装船，并向银行提交了一份 5 月 8 日签发的提单，但却遭到银行拒绝付款。请问这是为什么？

3. 某公司接到一份经 B 银行保兑的不可撤销信用证。当该公司按信用证规定办完装运手续后，向 B 银行提交符合信用证各项要求的单据要求付款时，B 银行却声称：该公司应先要求开证行付款，如果开证行无力偿付时，再由其保证付款。请问 B 银行的要求是否合理？

4. 某开证行按照自己所开出信用证的规定，对受益人提交的，经审查符合要求的单据已履行了付款责任。但在进口商向开证行赎单后发现单据中提单是倒签的，于是进口商立即要求开证行退回贷款并赔偿其他损失。请问进口商的要求合理吗？

实训项目46

议付单据审核3

操作练习

根据信用证内容就上海对外贸易公司进口男式羽绒夹克审核全套结汇单据，指出单据中的不符点并改正。

（一）

THE ROYAL BANK OF CANADA

BRITISH COLUMBIA INTERNATION CENTRE

1055 WEST GEORGIA STREET, VANCOUVER, B.C. V6E 3P3 CANADA

☐ CONFIRMATION OF TELEX/CABLE PER-ADVISED

TELEX NO. 4720688 CA

DATE: APR 8, 2015

PLACE: VANCOUVER

IRREVOCABLE DOCUMENTARY CREDIT	CREDIT NUMBER: 01/0501-FCT	ADVISING BANK'S REF. NO.
ADVISING BANK: SHANGHAI A J FINANCE CORPORATION 59 HONGKONG ROAD NANJING 210002, CHINA	APPLICANT: NEO GENERAL TRADING CO. #362 JALAN STREET, VANCOUVER, CANADA	
BENEFICIARY: SHANGHAI FOREIGN TRADING CO., LTD. ROOM 2501, JIAFA MANSION, BEIJING WEST ROAD, SHANGHAI 110005, P.R.CHINA	AMOUNT: USD 35 229.00 (US DOLLARS THIRTY FIVE THOUSAND TWO HUNDRED AND TWENTY NINE ONLY)	
EXPIRY DATE: MAY 15, 2015	FOR NEGOTIATION IN BENEFICIARY'S COUNTRY	

GENTLEMEN:

WE HEREBY OPEN OUR IRREVOCABLE LETTER OF CREDIT IN YOUR FAVOR WHICH IS AVAILABLE BY YOUR DRAFTS AT SIGHT FOR FULL INVOICE VALUE ON US ACCOMPANIED BY THE FOLLOWING DOCUMENTS:

+SIGNED COMMERCIAL INVOICE AND 3 COPIES.

+PACKING LIST AND 3 COPIES, SHOWING THE INDIVIDUAL WEIGHT AND MEASUREMENT OF EACH ITEM.

+ORIGINAL CERTIFICATE OF ORIGIN AND 3 COPIES ISSUED BY THE CHAMBER OF COMMERCE.

+FULL SET CLEAN ON BOARD OCEAN BILLS OF LADING SHOWING FREIGHT PREPAID CONSIGNED TO ORDER OF THE ROYAL BANK OF CANADA INDICATING THE ACTUAL DATE OF THE GOODS ON BOARD AND NOTIFY THE APPLICANT WITH FULL ADDRESS AND PHONE NO. 77009910.

+INSURANCE POLICY OR CERTIFICATE FOR 110 PERCENT OF INVOICE VALUE COVERING: INSURANCE CARGO CLAUSES (A) AS PER I.C.C. DATED 1/1/1982.

COVERING SHIPMENT OF: 4 ITEMS TERMS OF CHINESE CERAMIC DINNERWARE INCLUDING:

30-PIECE DINNERWARE AND TEA SET, 544 SETS, USD 17.50/SET, 1 260 KGS(G.W.), 1 010 KGS(N.W.), 19M^3

20-PIECE DINNERWARE SET, 800 SETS, USD 15.00/SET, 1590 KGS (G.W.), 1 320 KGS (N.W.), 27.8M^3

45-PIECE DINNERWARE SET, 443 SETS, USD 19.00/SET, 950 KGS (G.W.), 780 KGS (N.W.), 17.8M^3

95-PIECE DINNERWARE SET, 245 SETS, USD 21.60/SET, 920 KGS (G.W.), 790 KGS (N.W.), 17.3M^3

N/M, PACKAGE: ONE SET PER CARTON

DETAILS IN ACCORDANCE WITH SALES CONTRACT NO. HSDS03027 DATED APR. 3, 2015.

[ ] FOB / [ ]CFR / [X] CIF/ [ ]FAX VANCOUVER CANADA

SHIPMENT FROM SHANGHAI	TO VANCOUVER	LATEST APRIL 30, 2015	PARTIAL SHIPMENTS PROHIBITED	TRANSSHIPMENT PROHIBITED

DRAFT AT SIGHT TO BE PRESENTED FOR NEGOTIATION WITHIN 15 DAYS AFTER SHIPMENT, BUT WITHIN THE VALIDITY OF CREDIT. ALL DOCUMENTS TO BE FORWARDED IN ONE COVER, BY AIRMAIL, UNLESS OTHERWISE STATED UNDER SPECIAL INSTRUCTIONS.

SPECIAL INSTRUCTIONS: ALL BANKING CHARGES OUTSIDE CANADA ARE FOR ACCOUNT OF BENEFICIARY.

+ALL GOODS MUST BE SHIPPED IN ONE 20' CY TO CY CONTAINER AND B/L SHOWING THE SAME.

+THE VALUE OF FREIGHT PREP AID HAS TO BE SHOWN ON BILLS OF LADING.

+DOCUMENTS WHICH FAIL TO COMPLY WITH THE TERMS AND CONDITIONS IN THE LETTER OF CREDIT SUBJECT TO A SPECIAL DISCREPANCY HANDLING FEE OF US$35.00 TO BE DEDUCTED FROM ANY PROCEEDS.

DRAFT MUST BE MARKED AS BEING DRAWN UNDER THIS CREDIT AND BEAR ITS NUMBER; THE AMOUNTS ARE TO BE ENDORSED ON THE REVERSE HERE OF BY NEG. BANK. WE HEREBY AGREE WITH THE DRAWERS, ENDORSERS AND FIDE HOLDER THAT ALL DRAFTS DRAWN UNDER AND IN COMPLIANCE WITH THE TERMS OF THIS CREDIT SHALL BE DULY HONORED UPON PRESENTATION.THIS CREDIT IS SUBJECT TO THE UNIFORM CUSTOMS AND PRACTICE FOR DOCUMENTARY CREDITS (2007 REVISION) BY THE INTERNATIONAL CHAMBER OF COMMERCE PUBLICATION NO. 600.　　　Yours Very Truly,

David Jone　　　　　　　Joanne Hsan

AUTHORIZED SIGNATURE　　　AUTHORIZED SIGNATURE

（二）

Shipper SHANGHAI FOREIGN TRADE CO., LTD. ROOM 2501，JIAFA MANSION, BEIJING WEST ROAD, SHANGHAI 210005，P.R.CHINA		B/L No. 中国外运江苏公司 SINOTRANS JIANGSU CO. **OCEAN BILL OF LADING**
Consignee or order TO ORDER OF THE ROYAL BANK OF CANADA		SHIPPED on board in apparent good order and condition (unless otherwise indicated)，the goods or packages specified herein and to be discharged at the mentioned port of discharge or as near thereto as the vessel may safely get and be always afloat.
Notify address NEO GENERAL TRADING CO. #362 JALAN STREET，VANCOUVER, CANADA		The weight，measure，marks and numbers，quality，contents and value，being particulars furnished by the Shipper，are not checked by the Carrier on loading.
Pre-carriage by	Port of loading SHANGHAI，CHINA	The Shipper，Consignee and the Holder of this Bill of Lading hereby expressly accept and agree to all printed,
Vessel JIN YOU	Port of transshipment HONGKONG	written or stamped provisions，exceptions and conditions of this Bill of Lading，including those on the back hereof.
Port of discharge VANCOUVER, CANADA	Final destination	IN WITNESS whereof the number of original Bills of Lading stated below have been signed，one of which being accomplished the other(s) to be void.

Container seal No. or marks and Nos.	Number and kind of package	Description of goods	Gross weight (kgs)	Measurement (m^3)
N/M	44 CTNS 30-PIECE DINNERWARE AND	1 260 KGS	19M^3	TEA SET
	800 CTNS 20-PIECE DINNERWARE	1 590 KGS	27.8M^3	SET
	443 CTNS 45-PIECE DINNERWARE	950 KGS	17.8M^3	SET
	245 CTNS 95-PIECE DINNERWARE	920 KGS	17.3M^3	SET
	--			
	TOTAL：1 532 CTNS	4 720 KGS	81.9 M^3	

Freight and Charges FREIGHT PREPAID			REGARDING TRANSHIPMENT INFORMATION PLEASE CONTACT
Ex. rate	Prepaid at	Freight payable at	Place and date of issue
	Total prepaid	Number of original Bs/L THREE	Signed for or on behalf of the Master As Agent

（三）

BILL OF EXCHANGE

No._____52589D41_____

For_____USD 35 229.00_____   MAY 05，2015 SHANGHAI，CHINA

        (amount in figure)   (place and date of issue)

At _____******_____ sight of this FIRST Bill of exchange (SECOND being unpaid)

pay to _____SHANGHA FINANCE CORPORATION___ or order the sum of

U.S. DOLLARS THIRTY-FIVE THOUSAND TWO HUNDRED AND TWENTY-NINE ONLY

        (amount in words)

Drawn under THE ROYAL BANK OF CANADA

L/C No._____01/0501-FTC__ dated_____APR. 8，2015_____

To：   For and on behalf of
THE ROYAL BANK OF CANADA
BRITISH COLUMBIA INTERNATION CENTRE   SHANGHAI FOREIGN TRADING CO.，
1055 WEST GEORGIA STREET，VANCOUVER，B.C. LTD.
V6E 3P3 CANADA   _____

                                    (Signature)

（四）

中国人民保险公司上海分公司

The People's Insurance Company of China SHANGHAI Branch

PICC　　　总公司设于北京　　　　　　一九四九年创立

　　　　　Head Office Beijing　　　　Established in 1949

货物运输保险单

CARGO TRANSPORTATION INSURANCE POLICY

发票号 (INVOICE NO.) 2003SDT007　　　　保单号次 (POLICY NO.) PICCSH034582

合同号 (CONTRACT NO.) HSDS03027

信用证号 (L/C NO.) 01/0501-FCT

被保险人 (Insured) SHANGHAI FOREIGN TRADING CO.，LTD.

中国人民保险公司 (以下简称本公司) 根据被保险人的要求，由被保险人向本公司缴付约定的保险费，按照本保险单承保险别和背面所载条款与下列条款承保下列货物运输保险，特立本保险单。

THIS POLICY OF INSURANCE WITNESSES THAT THE PEOPLE'S INSURANCE COMPANY OF CHINA (HEREINAFTER CALLED "THE COMPANY") AT THE REQUEST OF THE INSURED AND IN CONSIDERATION OF THE AGREED PREMIUM PAID TO THE COMPANY BYTHE INSURED, UNDERTAKES TO INSURE THE UNDERMENTIONED GOODS IN TRANSPORTATION SUBJECT TO THE CONDITIONS OF THIS POLICY AS PER THE CLAUSES PRINTED OVERLEAF AND OTHER SPECIL CLAUSES ATTACHED HEREON.

标记 MARKS&NOS	包装及数量 PACKING & QUANTITY	保险货物项目 DESCRIPTION OF GOODS	保险金额 AMOUNT INSURED
N/M	2 032 CARTONS	4 ITEMS OF CHINESE CERAMIC DINNERWARE	US$ 35 229.00

总保险金额 (TOTAL AMOUNT INSURED) SAY U.S. DOLLARS THIRTY-FIVE THOUSAND TWO HUNDRED AND TWENTY-NINE ONLY NINE.

保费 (PERMIUM) AS ARRANGED　　　启运日期 (DATE OF COMMENCEMENT) AS PER B/L

装载运输工具 (PER CONVEYANCE) JIN YOU

自 (FROM) SHANGHAI，CHINA　　经 (VIA) _____　　至 (TO) VANCOUVER，CANADA

承保险别 (CONDITIONS) INSURANCE CARGO CLAUSES (A) AS PER I.C.C. DATED 1/1/1982

ALL RISKS

所保货物，如发生保险单项下可能引起索赔的损失或损坏，应立即通知本公司下列代理人查勘。如有索赔，应向本公司提交保单正本 (本保险单共有__份正本) 及有关文件。如一份正本已用于索赔，其余正本自动失效。

IN THE EVENT OF LOSS OR DAMAGE WHICH MAY RESULT IN A CLAIM UNDER THIS POLICY, IMMEDIATE NOTICE MUST BE GIVEN TO THE COMPANY'S AGENT AS MENTIONED HEREUNDER. CLAIMS，IF ANY，ONE OF THE ORIGINAL POLICY WHICH HAS BEEN ISSUED IN ORIGINAL(S) TOGETHER WITH THE RELEVENT DOCUMENTS SHALL BE SURRENDERED TO THE COMPANY . IF ONE OF THE ORIGINAL POLICY HAS BEEN ACCOMPLISHED. THE OTHERS TO BE VOID.

赔款偿付地点

CLAIM PAYABLE AT VANCOUVER，CANADA

中国人民保险公司上海分公司

The People's Insurance Company of China Shanghai Branch

Authorized Signature

地址 (ADD)：中国上海石鼓路 225 号　　　　电话 (TEL)：(021)6521049

邮编 (POST CODE)：210029　　　　　　　　传真 (FAX)：(021)4404593

（五）

SHANGHAI FOREIGN TRADING CO.，LTD.

ROOM 2501，JIAFA MANSION，BEIJING WEST ROAD，

SHANGHAI 110005，P.R.CHINA

TEL：021-77009910 025-77008820 FAX：021-77009930

COMMERCIAL INVOICE

To:	NEO GENERAL TRADING CO. #362 JALAN STREET，VANCOUVER，CANADA	Invoice No.：	2003SDT007
		Invoice Date：	APR. 20，2015
		S/C No.：	HSDS02703
		S/C Date：	APR. 3，2015

From： SHANGHAI，CHINA	To：VANCOUVER，CANADA
Letter of Credit No.：01/0501-FCT	Issued By：APR. 8，2015

Marks and Numbers	Number and kind of package Description of goods	Quantity	Unit Price	Amount
				CFR VANCOUVER
N/M	ABOUT 544 CARTONS OF 30-PIECE DINNERWARE AND TEA SET	544 SETS	USD 17.50	USD 9 520.00
	ABOUT 800 CARTONS OF 20-PIECE DINNERWARE SET	800 SETS	USD 15.00	USD 12 000.00
	ABOUT 443 CARTONS OF 45-PIECE DINNERWARE SET	443 SETS	USD 19.00	USD 8 417.00
	ABOUT 245 CARTONS OF 95-PIECE DINNERWARE SET	245 SETS	USD 21.60	USD 5 292.00
	TOTAL:	2 032 SETS		USD 35 229.00

SAY TOTAL: U.S. DOLLARS THIRTY FIVE THOUSAND TWO HUNDRED AND TWENTY NINE ONLY.

（六）

SHANGHAI FOREIGN TRADING CO.，LTD.
ROOM 2501，JIAFA MANSION，BEIJING WEST ROAD，
SHANGHAI 110005，P. R. CHINA
TEL：021-77009910 025-77008820 FAX：021-77009930

PACKING LIST

To:

NEO GENERAL TRADING CO.
#362 JALAN STREET，VANCOUVER，CANADA

From：SHANGHAI，CHINA
Letter of Credit No.：01/0501-FCT

Invoice No.：　2003SDT009
Invoice Date：APR. 20，2015
S/C No.：　HSDS03027
S/C Date：　APR. 3，2015

To：VANCOUVER，CANADA
Date of Shipment：APR. 8，2015

Marks and Numbers	Number and kind of package Description of goods	Quantity	Package	G.W	N.W	Meas.
N/M	ABOUT 544 CARTONS OF 30-PIECE DINNERWARE AND TEA SET	800 SETS	544 CTNS	1 260 KGS	1 010 KGS	19M^3
	ABOUT 800 CARTONS OF 20-PIECE DINNERWARE SET	443 SETS	800 CTNS	1 590 KGS	1 320 KGS	27.8M^3
	ABOUT 443 CARTONS OF 45-PIECE DINNERWARE SET	245 SETS	443 CTNS	950 KGS	780 KGS	17.8M^3
	ABOUT 245 CARTONS OF 95-PIECE DINNERWARE SET	544 SETS	245 CTNS	920 KGS	790 KGS	17.3M^3
	TOTAL：	2 032 SETS	2 032 CTNS	4 740 KGS	3 900 KGS	81.3 M^3

SAY TOTAL：TWO THOUSAND AND THIRTY TWO CARTONS ONLY

（七）

单据审核结果

实训项目47

缮制托收项下全套议付单据

根据以下销售确认书、出货补充资料及空白单据模版缮制全套结汇单据向银行委托收汇。

一、销售确认书

<table>
<tr>
<td colspan="4" align="center">销售合同
SALES CONTRACT</td>
</tr>
<tr>
<td rowspan="3">卖方
SELLER:</td>
<td rowspan="3">HAINAN YUANYANG RED SEEDLESS LITCHI FARM CO.
136 LO NGKUN ROAD，HAIKOU，CHINA
TEL：089866708109</td>
<td>编号 NO.:</td>
<td>00056LY128010</td>
</tr>
<tr>
<td>日期 DATE：</td>
<td>JUN.10，2014</td>
</tr>
<tr>
<td>地点 SIGNED IN：</td>
<td>HAIKOU，HUAINAN</td>
</tr>
<tr>
<td>买方
BUYER：</td>
<td colspan="3">HONG KONG SUNRISE DEVELOPMENT (AGRICULTURE) CORPORATION
228COMMERCIAL STREET KOWLOON HONG KONG
TEL：00852-358975623</td>
</tr>
<tr>
<td colspan="4">买卖双方同意按以下条款达成交易：
This contract is made by and agreed between the BUYER and SELLER，in accordance with the terms and conditions stipulated below.</td>
</tr>
<tr>
<td align="center">1. 品名及规格
Commodity & Specification</td>
<td align="center">2. 数量
Quantity</td>
<td align="center">3. 单价及贸易条款
Unit Price & Trade Terms</td>
<td align="center">4. 金额
Amount</td>
</tr>
<tr>
<td></td>
<td></td>
<td></td>
<td>CIF SINGAPORE</td>
</tr>
<tr>
<td>SEEDLESS LITCHI
LONGAN</td>
<td>3 000 KGS
5 000 KGS</td>
<td>@HKD 30.00
@HKD 40.00</td>
<td>HKD 90 000.00
HKD 200 000.00</td>
</tr>
<tr>
<td align="right">Total:</td>
<td>8 000 KGS</td>
<td></td>
<td>HKD 290 000.00</td>
</tr>
<tr>
<td>允许
With</td>
<td colspan="3">溢短装，由卖方决定
More or less of shipment allowed at the sellers' option</td>
</tr>
<tr>
<td colspan="4">5. 总值
Total Value　SAY H.K.DOLLARS TWO HUNDRED AND NINTY THOUSAND ONLY</td>
</tr>
<tr>
<td colspan="4">6. 包装　STORAGE AND TRANSPORTATION CONDITIONS: SET TEMPERATURE AT +3° REFRiGERATED
Packing　CONTAINER TRANSPORT</td>
</tr>
<tr>
<td colspan="4">7. 唛头
Shipping Marks</td>
</tr>
<tr>
<td colspan="4">8. 装运期及运输方式
Time of Shipment & means of Transportation　ON OR BEFORE JUL 01，2014</td>
</tr>
<tr>
<td colspan="4">9. 装运港及目的地
Port of Loading & Destination　FROM HAIKOU，CHINA TO SINGAPORE VIA HK</td>
</tr>
<tr>
<td colspan="4">10. 保险
Insurance</td>
</tr>
<tr>
<td colspan="4">11. 付款方式
Terms of Payment　BY D/P AT SIGHT</td>
</tr>
</table>

（续表）

12. 备注 Remarks   DOCUMENTS REQUIRED: 1. SIGNED COMMERCIAL INVOICE IN TRIPLICATE AND L/C NO AND THE GOODS ARE OF CHINESE ORIGIN. 2. PACKING LIST IN DUPLICATE，INDICATING TOTAL QUANTITY，GROSS WEIGHT，NET WEIGHT AND MEASUREMENT. 3. FULL SET(3/3) CLEAN ON BOAD OCEAN BILL OF LADING MADE OUT TO ORDER BLANK ENDORSED NOTIFY THE BUYER AND SUNRISE FRUIT CO. LTD(SINGAPORE). 4. DRAFT AT SIGHT FOR 100 PERCENT OF THE INVOICE VALUE. 5. INSURANCE POLICY OR CERTIFICATE IN DUPLICATE FOR 120% OF THE INVOICE VALUE COVERING ALL RISKS AND WAR RISK AS PER CIC OF PICC DATED 09/18/2009 CLAIM PAYABLE AT SINGAPORE IN THE CURRENCY OF THIS SALES CONFIRMATION. 6. CHINA-SINGAPORE FREE TRADE AREA PREFERENTAL TARIFF CERTIFICATE OF ORIGIN IN DUPLICATE CONSIGNED TO SUNRISE FRUIT CO. LTD(SINGAPORE).
13. 仲裁 ARBITRATION   ANY DISPUTE ARISING FROM THE EXECUTION OF OR IN CONNECTION WITH THIS CONTRACT SHALL BE SETTLED AMICABLY THROUGH NEGOTIATION. IN CASE SHALL THEN BE SUBMITTED TO CHINA INTERNATIONA ECONOMIC & TRADE ARBITRATION COMMISSION IN BEIJING FOR ARBITRATION IN ACCORDANCE WITH ITS ARBITRATION RULES. THE ARBITRATION AWARD IS FINAL AND BINDING UPON BOTH PARTIES. THE FEE FOR ARBITRATION SHALL BE BORNE BY LOSING PARTY UNLESS OTHERWISE AWARDED.
The Buyer   The Seller HONG KONG SUNRISE DEVELOPMENT   HAINAN YUANYANG RED SEEDLESS LITCHI FARM (AGRICULTRUE) CORPORATION   CO. DAVID   林伟

二、补充资料

1. 发票号码：10UY03450；发票日期：2015 年 6 月 15 日；

2. 公司手签员：林伟（也是受益人公司其他单据的签字人）；Tel：089866708109

3. 公司账号：267502330009

4. 保险费率：一切险 3‰，战争险 5‰；Policy No：2145JU00045；签署人：张丽红

保险公司在新加坡的保险代理人（FUHUA INSURANCE COMPANY LTD）：No.1 jalan kilang timor #5-05 pacific tech centre Singapore

5. 运单信息：

VESSEL：BAODAO V.8745 / CHANGHE V.012E；在香港转船

B/L DATE：2015 年 6 月 18 日

B/L NO：30HGU627894

提单签署人为海南中远作为承运人 cosco 的代理人签署；王红

6. 产地证号码：X114601004520049

H. S. CODE：SEEDLESS LITCHI：0810902000

H. S. CODE：LONGAN：081090l00

产地证申请时间：2015 年 6 月 16 日签证机构授权签发人：吴强。

7. 货物信息：

ITEM	QUANTITY	N.W/ITEM	G.W/ITEM	M³
SEEDLESS LITCHI	150 CTNS	3 000 KGS	3 150 KGS	18
LONGAN	250 CTNS	5 000 KGS	5 250 KGS	30

8. 货物装在一个 40 英尺的高柜冷藏集装箱中，CY TO CY 的交接方式；运费 2 900 港元；CONTAINER NUMBER/TYPE/SEAL No：TRLU24607O1/40' RH/CO254168

9. SHIPPING MARK：SUNRISE

00056LYl28010

SINGAPORE

1-UP

10. 托收行：BANK 0F CHINA HAINAN BRANCH；　　代收行：HSBC K0WLO0N BRANCH

11. 收货方：SUNRISE FRUIT CO. LTD(SINGAPORE)

（一）

ISSUER:		商业发票 COMMERCIAL INVOICE		
To:				
		No.:	Date:	
TRANSPORT DETAILS		S/C No.:	L C No.:	
		TERMS OF PAYMENT D/P AT SIGHT		
Marks and Numbers	Number and kind of package Description of goods	Quantity	Unit Price	Amount
		TOTAL:		
SAY TOTAL:				

（二）

ISSUER	装箱单 PACKING LIST				
To					
	S/C No.:		L/C No.:		
Marks and Numbers	Description of goods	Number and kind of package	G. W	N. W	Meas
	TOTAL:				
SAY TOTAL :					

（三）

ORIGINAL	
1. Exporter 2. Consignee	Certificate No. ## CERTIFICATE OF ORIGIN ## OF ## THE PEOPLE'S REPUBLIC ## OF CHINA
3. Means of transport and route 4. Country / region of destination	5. For certifying authority use only

6. Marks and numbers	7. Number and kind of packages；description of goods	8. H.S.Code	9. Quantity	10. Number and date of invoices

SAY TOTAL：

11. Declaration by the exporter	12. Certification
The undersigned hereby declares that the above details and statements are correct，that all the goods were produced in China and that they comply with the Rules of Origin of the People's Republic of China. ------------------------------------ Place and date，signature and stamp of authorized signatory	It is hereby certified that the declaration by the exporter is correct. ------------------------------------ Place and date，signature and stamp of certifying authority

注：HS 编码一般只需写到前面 6 位，如果一定要写到 8 位或 10 位，必须是进口国的编码，如本例中的龙眼在中国的编码是 0810903000，在新加坡的编码是 0810901000。

（四）

中保财产保险有限公司
The People's Insurance (Property) Company of China，Ltd.

发票号码 Invoice No.	保险单号次 Policy No.

海洋货物运输保险单
MARINE CARGO TRANSPORTATION INSURANCE POLICY

被保险人：中保财产保险有限公司(以下简称本公司)根据被保险人的要求及其所缴付约定的保险费，按照本保险单承担险别和背面所载条款与下列特别条款承保下列货物运输保险，特签发本保险单。

Insured：This policy of Insurance witnesses that the People's Insurance (Property) Company of China，Ltd. (hereinafter called "The Company")，at the request of the Insured and in consideration of the agreed premium paid by the Insured，undertakes to insure the under mentioned goods in transportation subject to the conditions of the Policy as per the Clauses printed overleaf and other special clauses attached hereon.

保险货物项目 Descriptions of Goods	包装 Packing	单位 Unit	数量 Quantity	保险金额 Amount Insured

承保险别 Conditions	货物标记 Marks of Goods

总保险金额：
Total Amount Insured：_____

保费 Premium As arranged	装载运输工具 Per conveyance S.S. _____	开航日期 Slg. on or abt._____
起运港 From _____	目的港 To _____	

所保货物，如发生本保险单项下可能引起索赔的损失或损坏，应立即通知本公司下述代理人查勘。如有索赔，应向本公司提交保险单正本(本保险单共有　份正本)及有关文件。如一份正本已用于索赔，其余正本则自动失效

In the event of loss or damage which may result in a claim under this Policy，immediate notice must be given to the Company's Agent as mentioned hereunder.Claims，if any，one of the Original Policy which has been issued in____original (s) together with the relevant documents shall be surrendered to the Company. If one of the Original Policy has been accomplished，the others to be void.

赔款偿付地点
Claim payable at _

日期 Date _____	在 at _____

地址：
Address：

（五）

1. Shipper		B/L NO.
2. Consignee		中远集装箱运输有限公司 COSCO CONTAINER LINES ORIGINAL Port-to-Port or Combined Transport BILL OF LADING
3. Notify Party		RECEIVED in apparent good order and condition except as otherwise noted. The total number of packages or unites stuffed in the container. The description of the goods and the weights shown in this Bill of lading are furnished by the Merchants，and which the carrier has no reasonable means of checking and is not a part of this Bill of lading contract. The carrier has carrier has
4. Combined Transport* Pre-carriage by	5. Combined Transport* Place of Receipt	issued the number of Bill of lading stated below，all of this tenor and date，one of the original Bill of lading must be surrendered and endorsed or signed against
6. Ocean Vessel Voy. No.	7. Port of Loading	the deliver of the shipment and where upon any other original Bill of lading shall be void. the Merchants agree to be bound by the terms and conditions of this Bill of lading
8. Port of Discharge	9. Combined Transport* Place of Delivery	as if each had personally Bill of lading signed this Bill of lading. See clause 4 on the back of this Bill of lading (Terms continued on the back Hereof，please read carefully). *Applicable only when Document Used as a Combined Transport Bill of lading.
Marks & Nos Container/Seal No.	No. of Containers or Packages	Description of Goods (If Dangerous Goods, See Clause 20)	Gross Weight (Kgs)	Measurement (cu-metres)

10. Total Number of Containers/Packages (in words)

11. FREIGHT & CHARGES	Revenue Tons	Rate	Per		Prepaid	Collect
	Prepaid at	Payable at		Place and Date of Issue:		
Ex. Rate:	Total Prepaid	No. of Original B(s)/L		Signed for the Carrier，COSCO CONTAINER LINRS as agent of the Carrier		

LADEN ON BOAD THE VESSEL BAODAO V8745
DATE JUN 18，2014 HAINAN BY HAINAN COSCO CONTAINER SHIPPING CO. LTD
王红 as agent of the Carrier

（六）

BILL OF EXCHANGE (ON COLLECTION)

NO... ....Exchange for_____D/P At_____sight this

First of Exchange (**Second** being unpaid) Pay to the order of _____

_____. The sum of _____

Value received for_____of_____as per Invoice No. _____

       (quantity)   (name of commodity)

To.

实训项目48

缮制项下全套议付单据

一、信用证

2015 年 4 月 1 日，海南艺术品进出口公司与以色列的 HIJ LTD 公司签订了一份出口销售合同，不久，海南艺术品进出口公司收到了中国银行海南分行国际业务部的信用证通知，告知以色列的 HIJ LTD 公司已经通过开证行开来信用证，内容如下：

SENDER：CFG

BANK LEUMI LE ISRAEL B. M. (TEL-AVIV MAIN BRANCH)，TEL-AVIV，IL

RECEIVER：BANK OF CHINA HAINAN BRANCH CN

INPUT DATE & TIME：2011-04-09 08：03：00

<u>MT 700 ISSUE OF A DOCUMENTARY CREDIT</u>

27：SEQUENCE OF TOTAL：1/1

40A：FORM OF DOCUMENTARY CREDIT：IRREVOCABLE

20：DOCUMENTARY CREDIT NUMBER：333-01-0699806XH

31C：DATE OF ISSUE：150410

40E：APPLICABLE RULES：UCP LATEST VERSION

31D：DATE AND PLACE OF EXPIRY：150615 CHINA

50：APPLICANT：HIJ LTD.

543 ST. KIRYAT MALACHI ISRAEL

59：BENEFICIARY：HAINAN ART IMP AND EXP CO. LTD.

NO. 532 LANTIAN ROAD HAIKOU CHINA

32B：CURRENCY CODE，AMOUNT：USD 62 000.00

41D：AVAILABLE WITH...BY...：ANY BANK IN CHINA，BY NEGOTIATION

42C：DRAFTS AT SIGHT FOR 100 PCT INVOICE VALUE

42D：CFG BANK LEUMI LE ISRAEL B. M. (TEL-AVIV MAIN BRANCH)，TEL-AVIV，IL

43P：PARTIAL SHIPMENTS：ALLOWED

43T：TRANSHIPMENT：ALLOWED

44E：PORT OF LOADING/AIRPORT OF DEPARTURE：HAIKOU PORT，CHINA

44F：PORT OF DISCHARGE/AIRPORT OF DESTINATION：ASHDOD PORT

44C： LATEST DATE OF SHIPMENT： 150531

45A： DESCRIPTION OF GOODS AND /OR SERVICES

COCONUT ART

ART NO 3323 2000 PCS

ART NO 3324 3000 PCS

IN 250 CTNS USD12.40/PC CIF ASHDOD PORT， AS PER CONTRACT NO.LT07060 DATED APR 2015 GOODS OF CHINA ORIGIN

46A： DOCUMENTS REQUIRED

1) MARINE BILL OF LADING FULL SET(3/3) PLUS 3 NON-NEGOTIABLE COPIES CLEAN ON BOARD MADE OUT TO THE ORDER OF BANK LEUMI LE ISRAEL BM PRINCIPAL BR.TEL-AVIV NOTIFY APPLICANT MARKED FREIGHT PREPAID SPECIFYING THAT IN VIEW OF THE DANGER OF CONFISCATION WARRANTED VESSEL NOT TO CALL AT PORTS AND NOTTO ENTER TE TERRITRIAL WATERS OF ANY ARAB COUTNRIES BELLIGERENT TO THE STATE OF ISRAEL AND/ OR ACTIVEL SUPPORTING THE ARAB PRIOR T UNLOADING AT PORT OF DESTINATION UNLESS IN DESTRESS OR SUBJECT TO FORCE MAJEURE.

2) ORIGINAL INVOICE SIGNED BY BENEFICIARY IN 2 FOLD.

3) PACKINGLIST IN 2 FOLD.

4) ORIGINAL CERTIFICATE OF ORIGIN ISSUED BY ENTRY-EXIT INSPECTION AND QUARANTINE BUREAU， THE PEOPLES REPUBLIC OF CHINA STATING.THAT GOODS ARE OF CHINESE ORIGIN.

5) INSURANCE POLICY OR CERTIFICATE ENDORSED IN BLANK FOR 110 PCT OF CIF VALUE， COVERING ALL RISKS AND WAR RISK OF PICC INDICATING CLAIMS PAYABLE IN ASHDOD PORT.

6) SHIPPING ADVICES MUST BE SENT TO APPICANT IMMEDIATELY AFTER SHIPMENT， ADVISING THE INVOICE VALUE， NUMBER OF PACKAGES， VESSEL NAME， BILL OF LADING NO. AND DATE.

47A： ADDITIONAL CONDITIONS

1) ALL DOCUMENTS TO OUR L/C NUMBER.

2) GOODS ARE TO BE SHIPPED AS FULL 20 FOOT CONTAINER FCL.

3) ALL DOCS TO BE ISSUED IN ENGLISH.

4) A CHARGE OF USD100(OR ITS COUNTERVALUE) PLUS RELATED SWIFT COSTS WILL BE DEDUCTED FROM PAYMENTS OF DISCREPANT DOCUMENTS.

71B： CHARGES： ALL BANK CHAGES AND COMMISSIONS OUTSIDE ISRAEL ARE FOR BENEFICIARYS ACCOUNT.

48： PERIOD FOR PRESENTATION WITHIN 15 DAYS FROM DATE OF

TRANSPORT DOCUMENT(S).

49：CONFIRMATON INSTRUCTIONS：WITHOUT

78：INSTRUCTIONS TO THE PAYING/ACCEPTING /NEGOTIATING BANK：

AFTER RECEIPT OF DOCUMENTS BY US STRICTYLY CONFORMING WITH CREDIT

TERMS WE SHALL PAY AS INSTRUCTED. PLS ADVISE US BY TESTED TELEX/SWIFT AMOUNT INVOICED，NAME OF VESSEL，DATE AND NO. OF B/L ALTERNATIVELY，ADVISE CANCELLATION IF CREDIT UNUTILIZED.

FORWARD US DOCS BY SPECIAL COURIER TO OUR ADDRESS-19 HERZL STR. TEL AVIV 61000 ISRAEL FOR THE ATTENTIOEN OF INTERNATIONAL TRADE CTR.

72：SENDER TO RECEIVER INFORMATION：PLS. ACKNOWLEDGE RECEIPT

二、补充材料

1. POLICY NO.：HC45690；签发人：陈东

保险公司在以色列的代理人：

MATI INSURANCE COMPANY LTD.

125 ST. KIRYAT MALACHI ASHDOD ISRAEL

TEL：00972—25958698

2. CONTA1NER/SEAL NO.：TGHUl534190/C065450l；1×20 CONTAINER

3. VESSEL：YEXIANG PRINCESS V9437

B/L 的签发日期：20150525；B/L NO：21HE645

HAINAN COSCO CONTAINER SHIPPING AGENCY CO.，LTD 作为承运人中远的代理人签署了提单签署人为：王小红

4. SHIPPING MARK：ST

A5HDOD

NOSl—UP

5. INVOICE NO.：NHD789；发票签发日：2015 年 5 月 18 日；签发人：林强（也是受益人公司其他单据的签字人）；公司账号：366417458600；TEL：0898—36681980

6. G. W：5 500 KGS；N. W：5 000 KGS；MEAS：30×40×50CM/CTN

7. PACKING：20PCS/CTN

8. H.S CODE：96020090

9. 货物是用中国原料，全部工序在中国境内完成加工成品；产地证申请时间：2015 年 5 月 20 日；签证机构授权签发人：符小伟；CERTIFICATE OF ORIGIN NO.：C114618000780035。

（一）

ISSUER:	商业发票 COMMERCIAL INVOICE			
To:				
	No.:		Date:	
TRANSPORT DETAILS	S/C No.:		L C No.:	
	TERMS OF PAYMENT			
Marks and Numbers	Number and kind of package Description of goods	Quantity	Unit Price	Amount
	TOTAL:			
SAY TOTAL:				

（二）

ISSUER		装箱单 PACKING LIST			
To					
		S/C No.:	L/C No.:		
Marks and Numbers	Description of goods	Number and kind of package	G.W	N.W	Meas.
	TOTAL :				
SAY TOTAL:					

（三）

ORIGINAL				
1. Exporter	Certificate No. CERTIFICATE OF ORIGIN OF THE PEOPLE'S REPUBLIC OF CHINA			
2. Consignee				
3. Means of transport and route	5. For certifying authority use only			
4. Country / region of destination				
6. Marks and numbers	7. Number and kind of packages；description of goods	8. H.S.Code	9. Quantity	10. Number and date of invoices
SAY TOTAL：				
11. Declaration by the exporter The undersigned hereby declares that the above details and statements are correct，that all the goods were produced in China and that they comply with the Rules of Origin of the People's Republic of China. -- Place and date，signature and stamp of authorized signatory	12. Certification It is hereby certified that the declaration by the exporter is correct. -- Place and date，signature and stamp of certifying authority			

（四）

中保财产保险有限公司
The People's Insurance (Property) Company of China，Ltd.

发票号码 Invoice No.	保险单号次 Policy No.

海洋货物运输保险单
MARINE CARGO TRANSPORTATION INSURANCE POLICY

被保险人：中保财产保险有限公司(以下简称本公司)根据被保险人的要求及其所缴付约定的保险费，按照本保险单承担险别和背面所载条款与下列特别条款承保下列货物运输保险，特签发本保险单。

Insured：This policy of Insurance witnesses that the People's Insurance (Property) Company of China，Ltd. (hereinafter called "The Company")，at the request of the Insured and in consideration of the agreed premium paid by the Insured，undertakes to insure the under mentioned goods in transportation subject to the conditions of the Policy as per the Clauses printed overleaf and other special clauses attached hereon.

保险货物项目 Descriptions of Goods	包装 Packing	单位 Unit	数量 Quantity	保险金额 Amount Insured

承保险别 Conditions	货物标记 Marks of Goods

总保险金额：
Total Amount Insured: _____

保费 Premium **As arranged**	装载运输工具 Per conveyance S.S. _____	开航日期 Slg. on or abt. _____

起运港　　　　　　　　目的港
From _____　　　To _____

所保货物，如发生本保险单项下可能引起索赔的损失或损坏，应立即通知本公司下述代理人查勘。如有索赔，应向本公司提交保险单正本(本保险单共有　份正本)及有关文件。如一份正本已用于索赔，其余正本则自动失效

In the event of loss or damage which may result in a claim under this Policy，immediate notice must be given to the Company's Agent as mentioned hereunder.Claims，if any，one of the Original Policy which has been issued in_____ original (s) together with the relevant documents shall be surrendered to the Company. If one of the Original Policy has been accomplished，the others to be void.

赔款偿付地点
Claim payable at __

日期　　　　　　　　在
Date _____　　at _____

地址：
Address:

（五）

Shipper	B/L NO.
	COSCO **中远运输公司** **BILL OF LADING** **ORIGINAL**
Consignee	RECEIVED in apparent good order and condition except as otherwise noted. The total number of packages or unites stuffed in the container. The description of the goods and the weights shown in this Bill of lading are furnished by the Merchants，and which the carrier has no reasonable means of checking and is not a part of this Bill of lading contract. The carrier has carrier has issued the number of Bill of lading stated below，all of this tenor and date，one of the original Bill of lading must be surrendered and endorsed or signed against the deliver of the shipment and where upon any other original Bill of lading shall be void. the Merchants agree to be bound by the terms and conditions of this Bill of lading as if each had personally Bill of lading signed this Bill of lading. See clause 4 on the back of this Bill of lading (Terms continued on the back Hereof，please read carefully).
Notify Party	

Pre-carriage by	Place of Receipt	

Ocean Vessel	Voy. No.	Port of Loading

Port of Discharge	Place of Delivery	*Final Destination	No. of Original B(s)/L

Marks & Nos	No. of Kind of Packages	Description of Goods	Gross Weight	Measurement(M3)

10. Total Number of Containers/Packages (in Words)

11. FREIGHT & CHARGES	Revenue Tons	Rate	Per	Prepaid	Collect	Prepaid at	Payable at

Total Prepaid	Place and Date of Issue：

(TERMS PLEASE FIND ON BACK OF ORIGINAL B/L)	Signed for the Carrier，COSCO CONTAINER LINRS as agent of the Carrier

*Applicable only when document used as a through Bill of Lading

（六）

SHIPPING ADVICE		
TO:	ISSUE DATE：	
	L/C NO.：	
	S/C NO.：	

Dear Sir or Madam：

We are Pleased to Advice you that the following mentioned goods has been shipped out，Full details were shown as follows：

Invoice Number：	
Bill of Lading Number：	
Ocean Vessel：	
Port of Loading：	
Date of Shipment：	
Port of Destination：	
Estimated Date of Arrival：	
Containers/Seals Number：	
Description of Goods：	
Shipping Marks：	
Quantity：	
Gross Weight：	
Net Weight：	
Total Value：	

Thank you for your patronage. We look forward to the pleasure of receiving your valuable repeat orders.

Sincerely yours，

（七）

BILL OF EXCHANGE (ON L/C)

Drawn Under _____Irrevocable L/C No._____

Date_____Payable With interest @____%_____

No._____ Exchange for _____

At _____ Sight of THIS FIRST of Exchange (Second of Exchange Being unpaid)

Pay to the order of _____

the sum of _____

TO.

_____

附录1
信用证结算审单准则

一、按照《跟单信用证统一惯例》的规定审单

《跟单信用证统一惯例》(以下简称《统一惯例》) 是确保在世界范围内将信用证作为可靠支付手段的准则,已被大多数的国家与地区接受和使用。《统一惯例》所体现出来的国际标准银行惯例是各国银行处理结算业务必须遵循的基本准则。我们必须按照《统一惯例》的要求,合理谨慎地审核信用证要求的所有单据,以确定其(表面上)是否与信用证条款相符。

二、按照信用证所规定的条件、条款审单

信用证是根据买卖双方的贸易合同而开立的,它一旦为各有关当事人所接受,即成为各有关当事人必须遵守的契约性文件。在信用证结算业务中,各有关当事人必须受其约束,按照信用证所规定的条件、条款,逐条对照,以确定单据是否满足信用证的要求。当信用证的规定与《统一惯例》有抵触时,应遵循信用证优先于《统一惯例》的原则,按照信用证的要求审核单据。这其中又包括表面一致性和内容相符性两条原则。

1.遵循表面一致性原则

受益人提交的单据名称及其内容等表面上必须与信用证规定完全一致。例如,某信用证将货物描述为 ATTACHES SANITARY WARE(卫生洁具附件),而受益人具体的货为 EXPASION BOLT(膨胀螺栓)。虽然如此,有关单据中货物描述仍必须与信用证的规定相一致。可能有的单据因某种特殊作用如清关报税等需显示具体货名,此时,我们仍必须将信用证所规定的 ATTACHES SANITAIRE 显示在上面,而在其后加注具体货名 EXPASION BOLT。

2.遵循内容相符性原则

我们在审单时应注意避免照搬、照抄信用证的原话,只要内容相符即可。例如,信用证的有关人称指向、时态、语态等转到单据上时,即应作相应的调整,以避免不必要的误会。

三、按照银行的经营思想、操作规程审单

国际贸易结算作为银行经营的一项重要业务,在操作过程中,必须按照有关操作规程行事,尤其是向客户融资时,更应明确银行的观点和看法,对单据有关条目的处理作

出自己的选择和判断，以体现银行的经营方针和经营作风。

四、按照普遍联系观点，结合上下文内容审单

信用证是一个与商务合同分离的独立文件，其内容是完整的、互为联系的。其中要求的条件、单据等是相辅相成、前后一贯的。审单时必须遵循普遍联系的观点，结合上下文内容进行，避免片面、孤立地看待某一条款。例如，欧盟某国开来一信用证，要求提交的单据中有一项是 CERTIFICATE OF ORIGIN(原产地证)，而在后文中又要求受益人将正本 GSP CERTIFICATE OF ORIGIN FORM A(普惠制产地证) 寄交开证申请人。结合上下文内容，我们就能判断出信用证要求向银行提交的是副本 GSP CERTIFICATE OF ORIGIN(普惠制产地证)，而非一般的原产地证。

五、按照合情、合理、合法的原则审单

所谓合情、合理、合法，是指审单员应根据自己所掌握的国际贸易结算知识，对各种单据的完整性和准确性做出合乎情理的判断。例如，普惠制产地证是施惠国赋予受惠国出口货物减免进口关税的一种优惠凭证，其"收货人"一栏应填写最终买主。如信用证未作明确规定的，我们应根据提单的收货人、通知人及货至目的地对最终买主做出合理的选择。

六、按照商业功能和结算功能相统一的原则审单

单据的商业功能在商务流转及商品买卖过程中的作用是主要的，结算功能是次要的，审单时应着重考虑其商业功能。我们应该了解各类单据的作用及功能，按照其自身的功能及用途审单，避免将不必要的内容强加于单据。

集装箱种类和规格

一、集装箱种类

1. 普通集装箱，又称干货集装箱 (dry cargo container)

普通集装箱以装运件杂货为主，包括文化用品、日用百货、医药、纺织品、工艺品、化工制品、五金交电、电子机械、仪器及机器零件等。这种集装箱占集装箱总数的70% ～ 80%。

2. 冷冻集装箱 (reefer container)

冷冻集装箱分外置式和内置式两种，温度可在 -28℃ ～ 26℃ 之间调整。内置式集装箱在运输过程中可随时启动冷冻机，使集装箱保持指定温度；而外置式集装箱则必须依靠集装箱专用车、船和专用堆场、车站上配备的冷冻机来制冷。这种箱子适合在夏天运输黄油、巧克力、冷冻鱼肉、炼乳、人造奶油等物品。

3. 开顶集装箱 (open top container)

开顶集装箱没有箱顶，可用起重机从集装箱上面装卸货物，装运时用防水布覆盖顶部，其水密要求和干货箱一样。其适合于装载体积高大的物体，如玻璃板等。

4. 框架集装箱 (flat rack container)

框架集装箱没有箱顶和两侧，其特点是从集装箱侧面进行装卸。它以超重货物为主要运载对象，也便于装载牲畜以及钢材之类可以免除外包装的裸装货。

5. 牲畜集装箱 (pen container)

牲畜集装箱侧面有金属网，通风条件良好，而且便于喂食，是专为装运牛、马等活动物而制造的特殊集装箱。

6. 罐式集装箱 (tank container)

罐式集装箱又称液体集装箱，是为运输食品、药品、化工品等液体货物而制造的特殊集装箱。其结构是在一个金属框架内固定上一个液罐。

7. 平台集装箱 (platform container)

平台集装箱的形状类似铁路平板车，适宜装超重、超长货物，长度可达 6 米以上，宽 4 米以上，高 4.5 米左右，重量可达 40 吨，且两台平台集装箱可以连接起来，装 80 吨的货，用这种箱子装运汽车极为方便。

8. 通风集装箱 (ventilated container)

通风集装箱的箱壁有通风孔，内壁涂塑料层，适宜装新鲜蔬菜和水果等怕热、怕闷的货物。

9. 保温集装箱 (insulated container)

保温集装箱的箱内有隔热层，箱顶又有能调节角度的进出风口，可利用外界空气和风向来调节箱内温度，紧闭时能在一定时间内不受外界气温影响。其适宜装运对温湿度敏感的货物。

10. 散装货集装箱 (bulk cargo container)

散装货集装箱一般在顶部设有 2～3 个小舱口，以便装货。底部有升降架，可升高成 40° 的倾斜角，以便卸货。其适宜装粮食、水泥等散货。如要进行植物检疫，还可在箱内熏舱蒸洗。

11. 散装粉状货集装箱 (free flowing bulk material container)

散装粉状货集装箱与散装货集装箱基本相同，但装卸时使用喷管和吸管。

二、集装箱规格

	L	W	H	CU ft^3	CU m^3
CONTAINER SPC.	20"	8"	8"6"		
CONTAINER	19"4 1/4	7"8" 5/8	7"10"	1 170×1 000	
	5.899m	2.352m	2.386m		33.1×28
CONTAINER SPC.	40"	8"	8"6"		
CONTAINER	39.5" 3/8	7"8" 5/8	7"10"	2 283×2 000	
	12.02m	2.35m	2.38m		67.5×57

附录3

币制符号代码表

币制代码	币制符号	币制名称
110	HKD	港币
113	IRR	伊朗里亚尔
116	JPY	日本元
118	KWD	科威特第纳尔
121	MOP	澳门元
122	MYR	马来西亚林吉特
127	PKR	巴基斯坦卢比
129	PHP	菲律宾比索
132	SGD	新加坡元
136	THB	泰国铢
142	CNY	人民币
143	TWD	台币
201	DZD	阿尔及利亚第纳尔
300	EUR	欧元
301	BEF	欧元
302	DKK	欧元
303	GBP	英镑
305	FRF	欧元
309	NLG	欧元
312	ESP	欧元
326	NOK	挪威克朗
330	SEK	瑞典克朗
331	CHF	瑞士法郎
332	SUR	俄罗斯卢布
398	ASF	清算瑞士法郎

附录4

报关条件代码表

报关条件	报关证件名称
1	进口许可证(包括商务部、特派员、省级商务厅发证)
4	商务部出口许可证
5	特派员出口许可证
6	省级商务厅出口许可证
7	特定商品进出口登记证明
8	商务部禁止出口的商品
9	机电产品进口配额证明
A	进口商检证明
B	出口商检证明
C	动植物检疫放行证
D	医药检验合格证
E	食品进口检验证
F	濒危物种进出口允许证
G	被动出口配额证
H	文物出口证书
I	精神药物进(出)口准许证
J	金银产品出口准许证
K	非军事枪药进(出)口批件
L	无委办无线电设备进关审查批件
M	保密机进口许可证
N	机电产品进口证明
O	机电产品进口登记表
P	进口废物批准证书
R	兽药进口批准证书
S	统一经营的进口商品
T	全国经营管理出口港澳果菜放行证
U	广东经营管理出口港澳果菜放行证
V	有毒化学品进出口放行通知单
W	麻醉药品进出口准许证
X	有毒化学品环境管理放行通知单
Z	音像制品进口管理许可证明
0110	一般贸易
0130	易货贸易
0214	来料加工
0243	来料以产顶进

贸易方式代码表

贸易方式代码	贸易方式代码简称	贸易方式代码全称
0245	来料料件内销	来料加工料件转内销
0255	来料深加工	来料深加工结转货物
0258	来料余料结转	来料加工余料结转
0265	来料料件复出	来料加工复运出境的原进口料件
0300	来料料件退换	来料加工料件退换
0345	来料成品内销	来料加工成品转内销
0420	加工贸易设备	加工贸易项下外商提供的进口设备
0446	加工设备内销	加工贸易免税进口设备转内销
0456	加工设备结转	加工贸易免税进口设备结转
0466	加工设备退运	加工贸易免税进口设备退运出境
0513	补偿贸易	补偿贸易
0642	进料以产顶进	进料加工成品以产顶进
0644	进料料件内销	进料加工料件转内销
0654	进料深加工	进料深加工结转货物
0657	进料余料结转	进料加工余料结转
0664	进料料件复出	进料加工复运出境的原进口料件
0700	进料料件退换	进料加工料件退换
0715	进料非对口	进料加工（非对口合同）
0744	进料成品内销	进料加工成品转内销
0844	进料边角料内销	进料加工项下边角料转内销
0845	来料边角料内销	来料加工项下边角料内销
0864	进料边角料复出	进料加工项下边角料复出口
0865	来料边角料复出	来料加工项下边角料复出口
1110	对台贸易	对台直接贸易
1139	国轮油物料	中国籍运输工具境内添加的保税油料、物料
1215	保税工厂	保税工厂
1233	保税仓库货物	保税仓库进出境货物
1234	保税区仓储转口	保税区进出境仓储转口货物
1300	修理物品	进出境修理物品
1427	出料加工	出料加工
1500	租赁不满一年	租期不满一年的租赁贸易货物
1523	租赁贸易	租期在一年及以上的租赁贸易货物
1616	寄售代销	寄售、代销贸易
1741	免税品	免税品
1831	外汇商品	免税外汇商品

（续表）

贸易方式代码	贸易方式代码简称	贸易方式代码全称
2025	合资合作设备	合资合作企业作为投资进口的设备物品
2215	三资进料加工	三资企业为履行出口合同进口料件和出口成品
2225	外资设备物品	外资企业作为投资进口的设备物品
2439	常驻机构公用	外国常驻机构进口办公用品
2600	暂时进出货物	暂时进出口货物
2700	展览品	进出境展览品
2939	陈列样品	驻华商业机构不复运出口的进口陈列样品
3010	货样广告品 A	有经营权单位进出口的货样广告品
3039	货样广告品 B	无经营权单位进出口的货样广告品
3100	无代价抵偿	无代价抵偿货物
3339	其他进口免费	其他进口免费提供货物
3410	承包工程进口	对外承包工程进口物资
3422	对外承包出口	对外承包工程出口物资
3511	援助物资	国家和国际组织无偿援助物资
3611	无偿军援	无偿军援
3612	捐赠物资	华侨、港澳、台同胞、外籍华人捐赠物资
3910	有权军事装备	直接军事装备（有经营权）
3939	无权军事装备	直接军事装备（无经营权）
4019	边境小额	边境小额贸易（边民互市贸易除外）
4039	对台小额	对台小额贸易
4200	驻外机构运回	我驻外机构运回旧公用物品
4239	驻外机构购进	我驻外机构境外购买运回国的公务用品
4400	来料成品退换	来料加工成品退换
4539	进口溢误卸	进口溢卸、误卸货物
4561	退运货物	因质量不符、延误交货等原因退运进出境货物
4600	进料成品退换	进料成品退换
9639	海关处理货物	海关变卖处理的超期未报货物、走私违规货物
9700	后续退补税	无原始报关单的后续退、补税
9739	其他贸易	其他贸易
9800	租赁征税	租赁期一年及以上的租赁贸易货物的租金
9839	留赠转卖物品	外交机构转售境内或国际活动留赠放弃特批货
9900	其他	其他

附录6

运输方式代码表

运输方式代码	运输方式名称
0	非保税区
1	监管仓库
2	江海运输
3	铁路运输
4	汽车运输
5	航空运输
6	邮件运输
7	保税区
8	保税仓库
9	其他运输
Z	出口加工

附录7

成交方式代码表

代码	名称
1	CIF
2	C&F
3	FOB
4	C&I
5	市场价
6	垫仓

附录8

各类商品投保险别参考表

商品名称	包装	投保险别名称
土、畜产类，废棉、麻类：	麻布包	平安险或水渍险，附加偷窃提货不着险、淡水雨淋险、污染险、战争险
烟叶	箱装	平安险或水渍险，附加淡水雨淋险、污染险、发霉险、发酵险、战争险
核桃仁、山桃仁	箱装	平安险或水渍险、淡水雨淋险、变潮变热险、发霉险、生虫险、战争险
松子仁、核桃等	袋装	变潮变热险、发霉险、生虫险、战争险。注：5—10月间出运必须利用冷藏设备，保险单上应附贴冷藏条款，负责因冷藏机器损坏所致的损失
苦杏仁、黑白瓜子及其他干果	箱装	平安险或水渍险，附加淡水雨淋险、变潮变热险、战争险
淀粉	袋装	平安险或水渍险、包装破裂险、短量险、淡水雨淋险、受潮受热险、污染险、战争险
香料油	桶装	平安险或水渍险、渗漏险、短量险、战争险
木材	无包装	平安险、偷窃提货不着险、战争险
陶瓷器	箱装	平安险或水渍险、偷窃提货不着险、碰损、破碎险、战争险
土纸、神纸	捆扎	平安险或水渍险、淡水雨淋险、污染险、钩损险、战争险
药材	箱装或捆装	平安险或水渍险、淡水雨淋险、受潮受热险、包装破裂险、战争险
袋装成药	箱装	平安险或水渍险、破碎险、渗漏险、战争险
湿肠衣	桶装	平安险或水渍险、渗漏险、短量险、战争险
活家禽		牲畜运输死亡险、战争险
羽毛，鬃类：	箱装	平安险或水渍险、淡水雨淋险、受潮受热险、包装破裂险、战争险
地毯	箱装	平安险或水渍险、偷窃提货不着险、钩损险、污染险、战争险
各种毛皮及毛皮制品		平安险或水渍险、偷窃提货不着险、受潮受热险、钩损险、战争险
纺织、服装类棉布	麻布装	平安险或水渍险、偷窃提货不着险、淡水雨淋险、污染险、战争险
针棉织品	箱装	平安险或水渍险、偷窃提货不着险、淡水雨淋险、污染险，战争险
生丝	包装	平安险或水渍险、偷窃提货不着险、淡水雨淋险、污染险、战争险（包装：加钩损险）
生丝复制品	箱装	平安险或水渍险、偷窃提货不着险、淡水雨淋险、污染险、战争险（包装：加钩损险）

（续表）

商品名称	包装	投保险别名称
绸缎	包装	平安险或水渍险、偷窃提货不着险、淡水雨淋险、污染险、战争险（包装：加钩损险）
服装	箱装	平安险或水渍险、偷窃提货不着险、淡水雨淋险、污染险、战争险
手工艺品类珠宝、翠钻、木刻、牙刻、料器、陶瓷器、珐琉器等	箱装	平安险或水渍险、偷窃提货不着险、碰损破碎险、战争险。如系邮包寄递应按邮包险投保
泥人、石膏像、宫灯	箱装	平安险或水渍险、偷窃提货不着险、淡水雨淋险、碰损破碎险、战争险
草帽辫、草制品	箱装	平安险或水渍险、偷窃提货不着险、淡水雨淋险、污染险、战争险
台布、枕袋、印花餐巾	箱装	平安险或水渍险、偷窃提货不着险、淡水雨淋险、包装破裂险、战争险
纸制品、绒绢制品、香料及其他手工艺品	箱装	平安险或水渍险、偷窃提货不着险、淡水雨淋险、污染险、战争险
茶叶类：		
茶叶	箱装	平安险或水渍险、偷窃提货不着险、淡水雨淋险、污染险、受潮受热险、包装破裂险、变味险、战争险
茶砖	篓装	平安险、战争险
食品类：		
盐黄，蜜黄	木桶装	平安险或水渍险、渗漏险、战争险
鲜蛋	箱装	平安险或水渍险、偷窃提货不着险、淡水雨淋险、污染险、战争险。如使用冷藏设备应附加冷藏条款，负责冷藏机器损坏所致的损失
皮蛋、咸蛋	篓装、坛装	平安险或水渍险、破碎险、战争险
冰冻鲜肉、鱼虾家禽和蛋品等	箱装	平安险或水渍险、偷窃提货不着险、淡水雨淋险、污染险、战争险，附加冷藏条款
新鲜水果	筐、箱装	平安险、偷窃提货不着险、受潮受热险、战争险
新鲜蔬菜	篓装、散装	平安险或水渍险、战争险。注：自然变坏和自然短量均不避免保险责任，应附加易腐货物条款
感腌腊食品	各种包装	平安险或水渍险、偷窃提货不着险、淡水雨淋险、战争险
酱油、醋、冬菜	桶装、瓶装、坛装	平安险或水渍险、破碎险、渗漏险、战争险，如装舱面应加保舱面险
酒	坛装、箱装	平安险或水渍险、偷窃提货不着险、破碎险、渗漏险、战争险
各种类罐头	箱装	平安险或水渍险、偷窃提货不着险、包装破裂险、破碎险、战争险

（续表）

商品名称	包装	投保险别名称
各种果脯、糖果、饼干	箱装	平安险或水渍险、偷窃提货不着险、淡水雨淋险、受潮受热险、战争险
粮油类：		
生仁、生果	袋装	平安险或水渍险、偷窃提货不着险、淡水雨淋险、受潮受热险、短量险、发霉险、生虫险、战争险
大豆、大米、其他豆类	散装	平安险或水渍险、偷窃提货不着险、淡水雨淋险、受潮受热险、短量险、自然险、战争险
大麻籽	袋装、散装	平安险或水渍险、短量险、战争险
甜菜子	袋装	平安险或水渍险、受潮受热险、发霉险、战争险
谷类		平安险或水渍险、受潮受热险、战争险
油类	桶装、散装	平安险或水渍险、短量险、污染险、战争险
桐油	桶装、散装	平安险或水渍险、短量险、污染险、掺杂险(另有散装桐油险)、战争险
食盐	袋装	平安险或水渍险、战争险
轻工业品类：		
窗玻璃、玻璃器皿、热水瓶胆、搪瓷、瓷砖、陶瓷制品		平安险或水渍险、偷窃提货不着险、碰损破碎险、战争险
家用金属制品	箱装	平安险或水渍险、偷窃提货不着险、淡水雨淋险、生锈险、战争险
自行车、缝纫机	箱装	平安险或水渍险、偷窃提货不着险、淡水雨淋险、生锈险、战争险
无线电	箱装	平安险或水渍险、偷窃提货不着险、淡水雨淋险、受潮受热险、碰损破碎险、生锈险、战争险
乐器	箱装	平安险或水渍险、偷窃提货不着险、碰损险、战争险
纸张	卷筒、箱装	平安险或水渍险、淡水雨淋险、污染险、钩损险、战争险
墨水	瓶装外加木箱	平安险或水渍险、偷窃提货不着险、碰碎险、渗漏险、战争险
其他文教用品	箱装	平安险或水渍险、偷窃提货不着险、战争险
五金类：		
小五金	箱装	平安险或水渍险、偷窃提货不着险、淡水雨淋险、生锈险、战争险
大五金	捆装或无包装	平安险或水渍险、偷窃提货不着险、战争险。注：大五金容易生锈，但不影响使用，可不保生锈险，但铝片应加保白锈险 White Rusting
矿产类：		
滑石粉	袋装	平安险或水渍险、包装破裂险、短量险、战争险

（续表）

商品名称	包装	投保险别名称
各种矿砂	散装	平安险、短量险、战争险
各种矿砂、矿石	散装	平安险、偷窃提货不着险、战争险
煤	散装	平安险、短量险、自燃险、战争险
化医类：		
粉状化工原料	袋装	平安险或水渍险、偷窃提货不着险、包装破裂险、短量险、淡水雨淋险、受潮受热险、战争险
医疗器械	箱装	平安险或水渍险、偷窃提货不着险、碰损险
液体化工原料	玻璃瓶装，陶瓷器、木、铁桶装	平安险或水渍险、偷窃提货不着险、破碎险、战争险。装舱面时加保舱面险
仪器类：		
各种仪器、仪表、无线电、真空管	箱装	平安险或水渍险、偷窃提货不着险、碰损破碎险、淡水雨淋险、战争险
机械类：		
机械配件	箱装	平安险、偷窃提货不着险、战争险
船舶		船舶险、战争险
铁路车辆、其他各种车辆		车辆损失险
汽车	箱装	一切险
	裸装	平安险、偷窃提货不着险、碰损破碎险、战争险

附录9

运输税方式代码表

运输税方式代码	运输税方式代码
0	非保税区
1	监管仓库
2	江海运输
3	铁路运输
4	汽车运输
5	航空运输
6	邮件运输
7	保税区
8	保税仓库
9	其他运输

附录10

征免税方式代码表

征免税方式代码	征免税方式全称
1	照章征税
2	折半征税
3	全免
4	特案
5	随征免性
6	保证金
7	保函
8	折半补税
9	全额退税

报关代码表

备案号的标记码

首位代码	备案审批文件	首位代码	备案审批文件
B ★	加工贸易手册（来料加工）	RZ	减免税进口货物结转联系函
C ★	加工贸易手册（进料加工）	H	出口加工区电子账册
D	加工贸易不作价设备登记手册	J	保税仓库记账式电子账册
E ★	加工贸易电子账册	K	保税仓库备案式电子账册
F	加工贸易异地报关分册	Y ★	原产地证书
G	加工贸易深加工结转异地报关分册	Z ★	征免税证明
RT	减免税进口货物同意退运证明	RB	减免税货物补税通知

经济区划代码

"1"表示经济特区；

"2"表示经济技术开发区和上海浦东新区，海南洋浦经济开发区两个特殊开放地区；

"3"表示高新技术开发区；

"4"表示保税区；

"9"表示其他。

企业性质代码

"1"表示国有企业，包括外贸专业公司、工贸公司及其他有进出口经营权的国有企业；

"2"表示中外合作企业；

"3"表示中外合资企业；

"4"表示外商独资企业；

"5"表示有进出口经营权的集体企业；

"6"表示有进出口经营权的私营企业；

"8"表示有报关权而无进出口经营权的企业；

"9"表示其他，包括外商企业驻华机构，外国驻华使、领馆和临时有进出口经营权的企业。

贸易方式代码表

贸易方式代码	贸易方式代码简称	贸易方式代码全称
0110 ★	一般贸易	一般贸易
0130	易货贸易	易货贸易
0139	旅游购物商品	用于旅游者5万美元以下的出口小批量订单货
0200	料件放弃	主动放弃交由海关处理的来料或进料加工料件

（续表）

贸易方式代码	贸易方式代码简称	贸易方式代码全称
0214 ★	来料加工	来料加工 装配贸易进口料件及加工出口货物
0245	来料料件内销	来料加工料件转内销
0255 ★	来料 深加工	来料 深加工 结转货物
0258	来料余料结转	来料加工余料结转
0265	来料料件复出	来料加工复运出境的原进口料件
0300	来料料件退换	来料加工料件退换
0314	加工专用油	国家贸易企业代理来料加工企业进口柴油
0320	不作价设备	加工贸易外商提供的进口设备
0345	来料成品内销	来料加工成品转内销
0400	成品放弃	主动放弃交由海关处理的来料或进料加工成品
0420	加工贸易 设备	加工贸易 项下外商提供的进口设备
0444	保区来进料成品	按成品征税的保税区进料加工成品转内销货物
0445	保区来料成品	按成品征税的保税区来料加工成品转内销货物
0446	加工设备内销	加工贸易免税进口设备转内销
0456	加工设备结转	加工贸易免税进口设备结转
0466	加工设备退运	加工贸易免税进口设备退运出境
0500	减免设备结转	用于监管年限内减免设备的结转
0513	补偿贸易	补偿贸易
0544	保区进料料件	按料件征税的保税区进料加工转内销货物
0545	保区来料料件	按料件征税的保税区来料加工转内销货物
0615 ★	进料对口	进料加工（对口合同）
0642	进料以产顶进	进料加工 成品以产顶进
0644	进料料件内销	进料加工料件转内销
0654 ★	进料深加工	进料深加工结转货物
0657	进料余料结转	进料加工余料结转
0664	进料料件复出	进料加工复运出境的原进口料件
0700	进料料件退换	进料加工料件退换
0744	进料成品内销	进料加工成品转内销
0815	低值辅料	低值辅料
0844	进料边角料内销	进料加工项下边角料转内销
0845	来料边角料内销	来料加工项下边角料内销
0864	进料边角料复出	进料加工项下边角料复出口
0865	来料边角料复出	来料加工项下边角料复出口
1139	国轮油物料	中国籍运输工具境内添加的保税油料、物料
1200	保税间货物	海关保税场所及保税区域之间往来的货物
1233	保税仓库货物	保税仓库进出境货物
1234	保税区仓储转口	保税区进出境仓储转口货物

贸易方式代码	贸易方式代码简称	贸易方式代码全称
1300	修理物品	进出境修理物品
1427	出料加工	出料加工
1500	租赁 不满一年	租期不满一年的 租赁 贸易货物
1523	租赁贸易	租期在一年及以上的 租赁贸易 货物
1616	寄售 代销	寄售、代销贸易
1741	免税品	免税品
1831	外汇商品	免税外汇商品
2025 ★	合资合作设备	合资合作企业作为投资进口设备物品
2225 ★	外资设备物品	外资企业作为投资进口的设备物品
2439	常驻机构公用	常驻机构公用
2600 ★	暂时进出货物	暂时 进出口 货物
2700	展览品	进出境展览品
2939	陈列样品	驻华商业机构不复运出口的进口陈列样品
3010 ★	货样广告品 A	有经营权单位 进出口 的货样广告品
3039	货样广告品 B	无经营权单位进出口的货样广告品
3100 ★	无代价抵偿	无代价抵偿货物
3339	其他进口免费	其他进口免费提供货物
3410	承包工程进口	对外承包工程进口物资
3422	对外承包出口	对外承包工程出口物资
3511	援助物资	国家和国际组织无偿援助物资
3612	捐赠物资	华侨、港澳、台同胞、外籍华人捐赠物资
4019	边境小额	边境 小额贸易 (边民互市贸易除外)
4039	对台小额	对台 小额贸易
4200	驻外机构运回	我驻外机构运回旧公用物品
4239	驻外机构购进	我驻外机构境外购买运回国的公务用品
4400	来料成品退换	来料加工成品退换
4500 ★	直接退运	直接退运
4539	进口溢误卸	进口溢卸、误卸货物
4561 ★	退运货物	因质量不符、延误交货等原因退运进出境货物
4600	进料成品退换	进料成品退换
9639	海关 处理货物	海关 变卖处理的超期未报货物，走私违规货物
9700	后续退补税	无原始 报关单 的后续退、补税
9739	其他贸易	其他贸易
9800	租赁征税	租赁期一年及以上的租赁贸易货物的租金
9839	留赠转卖物品	外交机构转售境内或国际活动留赠放弃特批货
9900	其他	其他

征免性质代码表

代码	简称	全称	代码	简称	全称
101 ★	一般征税	一般征税进出口货物	502 ★	来料加工	来料加工装配和补偿贸易进口料件及出口成品
201	无偿援助	无偿援助进出口物资	503 ★	进料加工	进料加工贸易进口料件及出口成品
299 ★	其他法定	其他法定减免税进出口货物	506	边境小额	边境小额贸易进口货物
301	特定区域	特定区域进口自用物资及出口货物	510	港澳 OP A	港澳在内地加工的纺织品获证出口
307	保税区	保税区进口自用物资	601 ★	中外合资	中外合资经营企业进出口货物
399	其他地区	其他执行特殊政策地区出口货物	602 ★	中外合作	中外合作经营企业进出口货物
401 ★	科教用品	大专院校及科研机构进口科教用品	603 ★	外资企业	外商独资企业进出口货物
403	技术改造	企业技术改造进口货物	605	勘探开发	勘探开发煤层气
406	重大项目	国家重大项目进口货物	606	海洋石油	勘探、开发海洋石油进口货物
412	基础设施	通信、港口、铁路、公路、机场建设进口设备	608	陆上石油	勘探、开发陆上石油进口货物
413	残疾人	残疾人组织和企业进出口货物	609	贷款项目	利用贷款进口货物
417	远洋渔业	远洋渔业自捕水产品	611	贷款中标	国际金融组织贷款、外国政府贷款中标机电设备零部件
418	国产化	国家定点生产小轿车和摄录机企业进口散件	789 ★	鼓励项目	国家鼓励发展的内外资项目进口设备
419	整车特	征构成整车特征的汽车零部件进口	799 ★	自有资金	外商投资额度外利用自有资金进口设备、备件、配件
420	远洋船舶	远洋船舶及设备部件	801	救灾捐	赠救灾捐赠进口物资
421	内销设备	内销远洋船用设备及关键部件	802	扶贫慈善	境外向我境内无偿捐赠用于扶贫慈善的免税进口物资
422	集成电路	集成电路生产企业进口货物	888	航材减免	经核准的航空公司进口维修用航空器材
423	膜晶显	"膜晶显"生产企业进口货物	898	国批减	免国务院特准减免税的进出口货物
499	ITA 产品	非全税号信息技术产品	998	内部暂	定享受内部暂定税率的进出口货物
501 ★	加工设备	备加工贸易外商提供的不作价进口设备	999	例外减	免例外减免税进出口货物

监管证件代码表

许可证或批文代码	许可证或批文名称	许可证或批文代码	许可证或批文名称
1★	进口许可证	L	药品进出口准许证
2	两用物项和技术进口许可证	O★	自动进口许可证（新旧机电产品）
3	两用物项和技术出口许可证	P★	固体废物进口许可证
4★	出口许可证	Q	进口药品通关单
5	纺织品临时出口许可证	S	进出口农药登记证明
6	旧机电产品禁止进口	T	银行调运现钞进出境许可证
7★	自动进口许可证	W	麻醉药品进出口准许证
8	禁止出口商品	X	有毒化学品环境管理放行通知单
9	禁止进口商品	Y★	原产地证明
A★	入境货物通关单	Z	进口音像制品批准单或节目提取单
B★	出境货物通关单	a	请审查预核签章
D	出/入境货物通关单（毛坯钻石用）	c	内销征税联系单
E★	濒危物种允许出口证明书	e	关税配额外优惠税率进口棉花配额
F★	濒危物种允许进口证明书	s	适用ITA税率的商品用途认定证明
G	两用物项和技术出口许可证（定向）	t	关税配额证明
H	港澳OPA纺织品证明	v★	自动进口许可证（加工贸易）
I	精神药物进（出）口准许证	x	出口许可证（加工贸易）
J	金产品出口证或人总行进口批件	y	出口许可证（边境小额贸易）
K	深加工结转申请表		

用途代码表

用途代码	用途	用途代码	用途
1★	外贸自营内销	7	收保证金
2	特区内销	8	免费提供
3★	其它内销	9	作价提供
4★	企业自用	10	货样，广告品
5★	加工返销	11	其它
6	借用	13	以产顶进

常用货币代码表

货币代码	货币符号	货币名称	货币代码	货币符号	货币名称
110.★	HKD.	港币.	113.	IRR.	伊朗里亚尔.
116.★	JPY.	日本元.	118.	KWD.	科威特第纳尔.
121.	MOP.	澳门元.	122.	MYR.	马来西亚林吉特.
127.	PKR.	巴基斯坦卢比.	129.	PHP.	菲律宾比索.
132.	SGD.	新加坡元.	136.	THB.	泰国铢.

（续表）

货币代码	货币符号	货币名称	货币代码	货币符号	货币名称
142. ★	CNY.	人民币.	143.	TWD.	台币.
201.	DZD.	阿尔及利亚第纳尔.	300. ★	ECU.	欧洲货币单位.
301.	BEF.	比利时法郎.	302.	DKK.	丹麦克朗.
303. ★	GBP.	英镑.	304.	DEM.	德国马克.
305.	FRF.	法国法郎.	306.	IEP.	爱尔兰镑.
307.	ITL.	意大利里拉.	309.	NLG.	荷兰盾.
312.	ESP.	西班牙比赛塔.	315.	ATS.	奥地利先令.
318.	FIM.	芬兰马克.	326.	NOK.	挪威克朗.
330.	SEK.	瑞典克朗.	331.	CHF.	瑞士法郎.
332.	SUR.	俄罗斯卢布.	398.	ASF.	清算瑞士法郎.
501.	CAD.	加拿大元.	502. ★	USD.	美元.
601.	AUD.	澳大利亚元.	609.	NZD.	新西兰元.

结汇方式代码表

结汇方式代码	结汇方式名称	英文缩写	英文名称
1 ★	信汇	M/T	Mail Transfer
2 ★	电汇	T/T	Telegraphic Transfer
3 ★	票汇	D/D	Remittance by Banker's Demand Draft
4 ★	付款交单	D/P	Documents against Payment
5 ★	承兑交单	D/A	Documents against Acceptance
6 ★	信用证	L/C	Letter of Credit
7	先出后结		
8	先结后出		
9	其他		

主要国别代码

代码	中文名称	代码	中文名称
110 ★	中国香港	307	意大利
116 ★	日本	331	瑞士
121	中国澳门	344 ★	俄罗斯联邦
132	新加坡	501	加拿大
133 ★	韩国	502 ★	美国
142 ★	中国	601 ★	澳大利亚
143 ★	台澎金马关税区	609	新西兰
303 ★	英国	701	国（地）别不详的
304 ★	德国	702	联合国及机构和国际组织
305 ★	法国	999	中性包装原产国别

附录12

收结汇方式代码表

收结汇方式代码	收结汇方式名称	收结汇方式英文名称
1	信汇	M/T
2	电汇	T/T
3	票汇	D/D
4	付款交单	D/P
5	承兑交单	D/A
6	信用证	L/C
7	先出后结	
8	先结后出	
9	其他	other

2014 年全国国际商务单证专业考试 国际商务单证基础理论与知识试题

一、单项选择题 (80 小题，每小题 0.5 分，共 40 分。单项选择题的答案只能选择一个，多选不得分，请在答题卡上将相应的选项涂黑)

1. 根据《UCP 600》将信用证项下的单据所做的分类，不包括 (　　)。

A. 包装单据
B. 保险单据
C. 运输单据
D. 商业发票

2. 按照单据形式，国际贸易单证分为 (　　)。

A. 金融单据和商业单据
B. 纸面单证和电子单证
C. 基本单据和附属单据
D. 保险单据和包装单据

3. 根据《INCOTERMS 2010》，以下适用于任何运输方式的术语是 (　　)。

A. FOB
B. FAS
C. FCA
D. CFR

4. 海运提单日期应理解为 (　　)。

A. 签订运输合同的日期
B. 货物开始装船的日期
C. 货物装船过程中任何一天
D. 货物装船完毕的日期

5. 根据《INCOTERMS 2010》，下列贸易术语中，进口清关由卖方完成的是 (　　)。

A. EXW
B. DAT
C. FOB
D. DDP

6. 海运提单的抬头是指提单的 (　　)。

A. Shipper
B. Consignee
C. Notify Party
D. Voyage No.

7. 下列不属于 T/T 的基本当事人的是 (　　)。

A. 汇款人
B. 代收行
C. 汇入行
D. 收款人

8. 某开证行 7 月 2 日 (周一) 收到来自 H 公司寄来的单据，根据《UCP 600》规定，最迟的审单日期应当截止到 (　　)。

A. 7 月 6 日
B. 7 月 7 日
C. 7 月 8 日
D. 7 月 9 日

9. 受益人审核信用证的依据是 (　　)。

A. 开证申请书
B. 一整套单据
C. 合同
D. 商业发票

10. 如商业汇票见票日为 3 月 17 日，见票后 30 天付款，则到期日为 (　　)。

A. 4 月 14 日
B. 4 月 15 日
C. 4 月 16 日
D. 4 月 17 日

11. 承兑是 (　　) 对远期汇票表示承担到期付款责任的行为。

A. 付款人
B. 收款人
C. 出口人
D. 开证银行

12. 信用证的第一付款人是 ( )。

　　A. 进口人　　　　　B. 开证行　　　　　C. 议付行　　　　　D. 通知行

13. 某公司以 CIF 贸易术语进口一批货物，国外卖方提交的海运提单上有关 "运费支付" 一项应写成 ( )。

　　A. Freight Prepaid　　　　　　　　　B. Freight as Arranged

　　C. Freight Collect　　　　　　　　　D. Freight Payable at Destination

14. 航空运单 ( )。

　　A. 代表物权，经背书可转让

　　B. 代表物权，但不能转让

　　C. 不代表物权，也不能凭以向承运人提货

　　D. 不代表物权，但可以作为提货凭证

15. 某合同以 CIF C5 成交，总价为 100 000 美元，则佣金为 ( ) 美元。

　　A. 50 000　　　　　B. 5 000　　　　　C. 10 000　　　　　D. 1 000

16. 在《INCOTERMS 2010》中，卖方承担的责任、费用最小的贸易术语是 ( )。

　　A. EXW　　　　　B. DAT　　　　　C. CIF　　　　　D. FCA

17. 某公司从日本进口一套设备，合同价格 1 000 万日元。支付日银行牌价 100 日元 =6.12-6.18 元人民币，该公司购汇需用 ( ) 人民币。

　　A. 61.8 万　　　　　B. 61.2 万　　　　　C. 61.6 万人民币　　　　D. 60 万

18. 普惠制原产地证明书 (FORM A) 中的原产地标准栏目，如果出口商品为完全原产品，不含有任何进口成分，出口到所有给惠国，正确填写代码是 ( )。

　　A. "P"　　　　　B. "F"　　　　　C. "Y"　　　　　D. "W"

19. 托收业务中不会涉及的当事人是 ( )。

　　A. 委托人　　　　　B. 付款人　　　　　C. 开证行　　　　　D. 代收行

20. 我某公司 3 月 5 日对外发盘，规定 7 月份装运，国外客户回电："接受你方 3 月 5 日发盘，立即装运。" 此回电是对原发盘的 ( )。

　　A. 有效接受　　　　　　　　　　B. 实质性变更

　　C. 非实质性变更　　　　　　　　D. 只是添加未作变更

21. 由出口商签发的、作为结算货款和报关纳税依据的核心单据是 ( )。

　　A. 海运提单　　　　　B. 商业汇票　　　　　C. 商业发票　　　　　D. 海关发票

22. 某公司按 CIF London USD 120 Per M/T 向英国出口数量为 10 000 M/T 的散装货，国外开立信用证金额为 120 万美元且不能增减，则卖方发货 ( )。

　　A. 数量和金额不能增减

　　B. 数量和金额可在 5% 以内增减

　　C. 数量和金额可在 10% 以内增减

　　D. 数量在 9 500 ～ 10 000 吨之间，金额不得超过 120 万美元

23. 根据《UCP 600》，信用证中货物的数量规定有 "约" "大约" "近似" 或类似意

义的词语时，应理解为其有关数量增减幅度不超过（　　）。

　　A. 3%　　　　　　　B. 5%　　　　　　　C. 10%　　　　　　　D. 15%

24. 属于银行信用的国际贸易支付方式是（　　）。

　　A. 汇付　　　　　　　B. 托收　　　　　　　C. 信用证　　　　　　　D. 票汇

25. 在国际商务单据的分类中，根据《URC 522》，商业单据通常是指（　　）。

　　A. 商业发票、装箱单和 GSP 产地证明书等

　　B. 商业汇票、重量单和保险单等

　　C. 商业发票、装箱单和商业汇票等

　　D. 商业发票、重量单和装箱单等

26. 根据《UCP 600》，受益人超过提单签发日期后 21 天才交到银行议付的提单称为（　　）。

　　A. 过期提单　　　　　B. 倒签提单　　　　　C. 预借提单　　　　　D. 转船提单

27. 出口人得到托运确认后，应填制（　　）连同发票等相关单据向海关申报出口货物。

　　A. 汇票　　　　　　　　　　　　　　B. 入境货物报检单

　　C. 出口货物报关单　　　　　　　　　D. 装货单

28. 我方报价 CIP 纽约 USD 2 000/MT，对方要求 5% 佣金，改报后的含佣价为（　　）。

　　A. USD 1 904.76　　　　　　　　　　B. USD 2 105.26

　　C. USD 1 900.00　　　　　　　　　　D. USD 2 100.00

请根据以下内容回答 29-31 题。

　　买卖双方按 CIF 条件和信用证支付方式达成一项买卖粮食的大宗交易，合同规定"1—5 月份分批装运，每月装运 1 万吨"。买方按合同规定开出信用证，卖方在 1—2 月，每月装运 1 万吨并提交了符合信用证要求的单据。3 月份卖方因故未按时装运，而延至 4 月 20 日才装运出口。

29. 卖方 1—2 月的交货能否安全收回货款（　　）。

　　A. 能　　　　　　　　　　　　　　　B. 不能

　　C. 不一定　　　　　　　　　　　　　D. 卖方必须出具保函

30. 根据《UCP 600》规定，关于卖方 4 月的交货说法正确的是（　　）。

　　A. 只要在 4 月底前再发出 1 万吨，就可以算作 3、4 月均按时交货了

　　B. 无须继续交货，因为已经无法按时结汇

　　C. 能否收汇不一定

　　D. 只要单据合格银行无权拒付

31. 根据《UCP 600》规定，以下说法正确的是（　　）。

　　A. 3、4、5 月均为交货失败

　　B. 只有 4、5 月交货失败

　　C. 4、5 月仍可交货

　　D. 4、5 月交货后，只要单据合格，银行就无权拒付

32. 海洋运输的船舶按照运营方式一般分为租船运输和 ( )。

A. 不定期运输　　　　B. 专线运输　　　　C. 内河运输　　　　D. 班轮运输

33. 信用证的汇票条款注明"drawn on us"，则汇票的付款人是 ( )。

A. 开证申请人　　　　B. 开证行　　　　C. 议付行　　　　D. 受益人

34. 在集装箱运输中，能够实现"门到门"运输的集装箱货物交接方式是 ( )。

A. LCL/LCL　　　　B. FCL/FCL　　　　C. LCL/FCL　　　　D. FCL/FCL

35. 如信用证规定"shipment on or about 15th Oct. 2013"，那么装运期应为 ( )。

A. 9天　　　　B. 10天　　　　C. 11天　　　　D. 12天

36. 当空运货物为重货时，一般按照货物的 ( ) 作为计费重量。

A. 实际净重　　　　　　　　　　B. 体积重量

C. 实际毛重　　　　　　　　　　D. 较高重量较低运价的分界点重量

37. 根据《URC 522》的分类，( ) 不属于进口国官方要求的单据。

A. 原产地证明　　　　B. 船龄证明　　　　C. 领事发票　　　　D. 海关发票

38. CEPA原产地证书是指 ( )。

A. 中国—东盟自贸区优惠原产地证书

B. 中国—巴基斯坦自贸区原产地证书

C. 中国—智利自贸区原产地证书

D. 大陆—港澳更紧密经贸关系原产地证书

39. 下列货币代码中，分别代表了欧元、港币、英镑的是 ( )。

A. EUR、SEK、GBP　　　　　　　B. GBP、CHF、SEK

C. EUR、HKD、GBP　　　　　　　D. CHF、EUR、GBP

40. 受开证行的指示或授权，对有关代付行或议付行的索偿予以照付的银行是 ( )。

A. 保兑行　　　　B. 偿付行　　　　C. 承兑行　　　　D. 转让行

41. 出口商最迟于货物装运前 ( ) 天向出入境检验检疫局申请办理普惠制原产地证书。

A. 3　　　　B. 5　　　　C. 7　　　　D. 10

42. 我某进出口公司于2014年3月15日用特快专递向美国ABC公司发盘，限2014年3月29日复到。3月25日下午3时同时收到ABC公司的表示接受的特快专递和撤回接受的邮件。根据《联合国国际货物销售合同公约》，对此项接受 ( )。

A. 可以撤回　　　　　　　　　　B. 不得撤回，合同成立

C. 在我方同意的情况下，可以撤回　　　　D. 以上答案都不对

43. 按照《联合国国际货物销售合同公约》，一项发盘在尚未送达受盘人之前，是可以阻止其生效的，这叫发盘的 ( )。

A. 撤销　　　　B. 撤回　　　　C. 还盘　　　　D. 接受

44. 以下抬头的汇票中，可以经过背书转让的是 ( )。

A. Pay to bearer

B. Pay to the holder

C. Pay to the order of ×××company

D. Pay to ×××company only

45. 我方 6 月 10 日向国外某客商发盘，限 6 月 15 日复到，6 月 13 日接到对方复电称，"你 10 日电接受，需提供船龄证明。"该接受（　　）。

A. 属还盘

B. 在我方缄默的情况下，则视为有效接受

C. 属有效的接受

D. 属询盘

46. 下列术语中，（　　）术语卖方在指定港口或目的地的指定运输终端将货物从抵达的载货运输工具上卸下，交给买方处置时，即为交货。

A. DAT　　　　　　B. DAP　　　　　　C. DDP　　　　　　D. CIF

47. 我国甲公司与加拿大乙公司签订出口服装销售合同，拟采取空运方式，甲公司承担将货物运至目的地的运费但不负责保险，根据《INCOTERMS 2010》，应采用的贸易术语是（　　）。

A. CPT　　　　　　B. CFR　　　　　　C. FOB　　　　　　D. FAS

48. A 商与 B 商签订一出口合同，合同中规定 B 商应于 4 月底之前开来信用证，A 商应于 5 月 20 日之前装运。B 商在 4 月 28 日将信用证开到，但信用证的有效期为 5 月 15 日。A 商已无法在 15 日前完成装运，遂电请对方展延信用证的有效期至 5 月 25 日，B 商电报同意延期，但未能通过开证行开来修改书。A 商于 5 月 20 日完成装运并向银行议付。A 商能否从银行收回货款（　　）。

A. 可以，因为交单时间没有超过信用证规定有效期

B. 不可以，因为超过了信用证有效期交单

C. 具体要看进口商对开证行的指示

D. 可以，因为没有超过规定的装运期装运

49. 以下有关信用证修改程序描述，正确的是（　　）。

A. 信用证的修改要由受益人通知开证行修改

B. 信用证的修改要由通知行通知开证行修改

C. 只要开证申请人与受益人达成一致，就可以，不用通知其他当事人

D. 要由受益人通知申请人，申请人向开证行提出申请修改

50. 信用证修改通知书的内容在两项以上者，受益人（　　）。

A. 要么全部接受，要么全部拒绝

B. 只能全部接受

C. 只能全部拒绝

D. 只能部分接受

51. 使用 L/C、D/P、D/A 三种支付方式结算贷款，就卖方的收汇风险而言，从小到

大依次排序为（　　　）。

 A. D/P、D/A 和 L/C   B. D/A、D/P 和 L/C

 C. L/C、D/P 和 D/A   D. L/C、D/A 和 D/P

52. 某公司出口电冰箱共 1 000 台，合同和信用证都规定不准分批装运。运输时有 30 台被撞，包装破裂，冰箱外观变形，不能出口。根据《UCP 600》规定，只要货款不超过信用证总金额，交货数量允许有 5% 的增减。据此，发货时可以装运（　　　）。

 A. 1 000 台   B. 970 台   C. 950 台   D. 1 050 台

53. 卖方自负费用、自担风险把货物运到进口国指定地点，但不负责卸货，不负担办理进口海关手续，也不支付进口关税及其他税费，应选择以下（　　　）术语。

 A. DAT   B. DAP   C. DDP   D. CIP

54. 出口商委托货代向船公司办理租船订舱，出口商须填写（　　　）。

 A. 海运货物运输合同   B. 海运货物委托书

 C. 海运单   D. 装货单 .

55. 根据海关规定，进口货物的进口日期是指（　　　）。

 A. 载货的运输工具申报的日期   B. 货物进口报关的日期

 C. 申报货物准予提取的日期   D. 申报货物进入海关监管仓库的日期

56. 2012 年 4 月 10 日，卖方以电子邮件形式发盘限 4 月 16 日复到有效，15 日下午收到买方电子邮件要求提前 1 个月交货，次日上午又收到买方电子邮件表示完全接受原发盘。这说明（　　　）。

 A. 已按卖方发盘条件达成合同   B. 合同尚未达成

 C. 已按买方提出条件达成合同   D. 无法判断

57. 根据《INCOTERMS 2010》，一笔 DDP 贸易术语成交的合同，以下（　　　）选项不是卖方应承担的义务。

 A. 卖方应按合同的规定将货物置于买方的控制之下

 B. 承担一切出口应付的税费

 C. 按照合同规定提供有关的货物凭证，并代买方销售货物

 D. 承担运输过程中的风险和费用

58. 一张商业汇票见票日为 1 月 31 日，见票后 1 个月付款，则到期日为（　　　）。

 A. 2 月 28 日   B. 3 月 1 日   C. 3 月 2 日   D. 3 月 3 日

59. 某合同价格条款规定为每吨 CIFC 5 新加坡 100 美元，这种价格是（　　　）。

 A. 净价   B. 含佣价   C. 离岸价   D. 折扣价

60. 进口商填写开证申请书的主要依据是（　　　）。

 A. 发票   B. 贸易合同   C. 订单   D. 进口许可证

61. 按《UCP 600》规定，若信用证中对是否分批装运与转运未予规定，则受益人（　　　）。

 A. 可以分批装运，也可转运   B. 不得分批装运，也不得转运

 C. 可分批装运，但不得转运   D. 不得分批装运，但可转运

62. FOB 与 FCA 的主要区别是 (   )。

    A. 适合的运输方式不同   B. 办理出口手续的责任方不同

    C. 负责订立运输合同的责任方不同   D. 风险和费用是否同时转移不同

63. 出口单证中最重要的单据，能让有关当事人了解一笔交易的全貌，其他单据都是以其为依据的单据是 (   )。

    A. 装箱单   B. 产地证书   C. 发票   D. 提单

64. 保兑行的责任是 (   )。

    A. 在开证行不履行付款义务时履行付款义务

    B. 在开证申请人不履行付款义务时履行付款义务

    C. 承担第一性的付款义务

    D. 开证行承担第一性的付款责任，保兑行承担第二性的付款责任

65. 一张有效的信用证必须规定一个 (   )。

    A. 装运期   B. 有效期   C. 交单期   D. 开证日期

66. 信用证注明：10 000 pcs Shirts CIFC4 Oslo at EUR 5.00/pce.，出口商在一次全部出运后，提交的发票最终金额应写 (   )。

    A. EUR 50 000.00   B. EUR 48 000.00

    C. USD 50 000.00   D. USD 48 000.00

67. 某出口公司对外以 CFR 报价，如果该公司采用多式联运，应采用 (   ) 术语为宜。

    A. FCA   B. CIP   C. DDP   D. CPT

68. 出票人签发支票的金额高于其银行存款的金额，这种支票称为 (   )。

    A. 空头支票   B. 划线支票   C. 现金支票   D. 转账支票

69. 进口商在货物到达目的港后，应在运输工具进境之日起 (   ) 天内向海关申报。

    A. 3   B. 7   C. 14   D. 15

71. 渣打银行东京分行开立一份 L/C，开证申请人是 ABC LTD. CO., TOKYO, JAPAN，L/C 规定 Invoice must made out to XYZ LTD. CO., TOKYO JAPAN，出口商发票的抬头人应该做成 (   )。

    A. ABC LTD. CO., TOKYO, JAPAN

    B. XYZ LTD. CO., TOKYO JAPAN

    C. ABC LTD. CO., TOKYO, JAPAN AND XYZ LTD. CO., TOKYO JAPAN

    D. 渣打银行东京分行

72. D/D 是 (   )。

    A. 信汇   B. 电汇   C. 票汇   D. 汇票

73. 就出口商的收汇时间来说，假远期信用证相当于 (   )。

    A. 循环信用证   B. 远期信用证

    C. 备用信用证   D. 即期信用证

74. 根据《UCP 600》规定，如果信用证使用诸如：in duplicate, in two fold, in two

copies 等用语要求提交多份单据，则至少 (　　) 正本，其余使用副本即可。

A. 三份　　　　　　B. 两份　　　　　　C. 十份　　　　　　D. 一份

75.《出境货物报检单》中的起运地栏目，根据规定应填报 (　　)。

A. 货物最后离境的口岸　　　　　　　B. 货物存放地

C. 装货地　　　　　　　　　　　　　D. 原产地

76. 进口商向银行买入外汇时使用 (　　)。

A. 银行买入价　　　　　　　　　　　B. 银行卖出价

C. 中间价　　　　　　　　　　　　　D. 以往汇率的平均值

77. 检验证书的作用不包括 (　　)。

A. 作为证明买方所交货物的品质、重量 (数量)、包装以及卫生条件等是否符合合同规定及索赔、理赔依据

B. 确定检验标准和检验方法的依据

C. 作为卖方向银行议付货款的单据之一

D. 作为海关验关放行的凭证

78. 计算航空运费时，体积重量 (KGS)= 货物体积 (m³)÷(　　)。

A. 0.006　　　　　B. 0.06　　　　　C. 0.005　　　　　D. 0.05

79. 关于不可撤销信用证的修改，下列说法正确的是 (　　)。

A. 不容许任何形式的修改

B. 只能在一定范围内修改

C. 在信用证有效期内，任何一方的任何修改，都必须经过买卖双方协商一致同意后，由申请人通过开证行办理修改

D. 买卖双方都可直接要求开证行修改

80. 朝鲜某公司需以管道运输方式从我国进口石油，可采用 (　　)。

A. FAS　　　　　　B. CIP　　　　　　C. FOB　　　　　　D. CIF

二、多项选择题 (30 小题，每小题 1 分，共 30 分。多项选择题的答案多选、少选、错选均不给分，请在答题卡上将相应的选项涂黑)

1. 国际贸易单证通常用于处理进出口货物的 (　　)。

A. 交付　　　　　B. 运输与保险　　　　C. 检验检疫

D. 报关　　　　　E. 结汇

2. 贸易术语在国际贸易中的主要作用有 (　　)。

A. 简化交易手续　　　B. 明确交易双方责任

C. 缩短磋商时间　　　D. 节省费用开支　　　E. 明确风险划分界限

3. 根据《联合国国际货物销售合同公约》，构成一项有效接受的条件是 (　　)。

A. 须由特定的受盘人做出

B. 以用口头、书面的方式做出

C. 必须与发盘条件相符

D. 必须在发盘规定的有效期内送达发盘人

E. 可以用行为的方式做出

4. 一方对另一方的发盘表示接受可以采取的方式有（　　）。

A. 书面　　　　　　B. 行动　　　　　　C. 口头

D. 缄默　　　　　　E. 不行动

5. 下列贸易术语中，风险转移的界限在进口国的有（　　）。

A. FCA　　　　　　B. DAP　　　　　　C. DDP

D. CIP　　　　　　E. CPT

6. 信用证支付方式的特点（　　）。

A. 信用证是一种银行信用

B. 信用证是一种商业信用

C. 信用证是一种自足文件

D. 信用证是一种单据的买卖

E. 以上都对

7. 按《UCP 600》规定，海运提单中货物的描述（　　）。

A. 只要不与信用证的描述相抵触

B. 必须使用货物的全称

C. 必须与商业发票的货物描述完全一致

D. 符合信用证或合同，与实际货物的名称、规格、型号、成分、品牌等相一致

E. 可使用货物的统称

8. 按照《联合国国际货物销售合同公约》的规定，受盘人对（　　）内容提出更改或添加，应被视为实质性变更发盘条件。

A. 价格　　　　　　B. 付款　　　　　　C. 质量和数量

D. 交货时间和地点　E. 单据份数

9. 报关程序按时间先后分为三个阶段：前期阶段、进出境阶段、后续阶段。其中对进出口收发货人而言，在进出境阶段包括（　　）等环节。

A. 进出口申报　　　B. 缴纳税费　　　　C. 备案

D. 配合查验　　　　E. 销案

10. CPT 与 CFR 的区别有（　　）。

A. 交货地点　　　　B. 适用的运输方式　C. 风险划分界限

D. 出口结关手续　　E. 进口结关手续

11. 进口人审核提单时，应注意的要点是（　　）。

A. 提单应具备全套可转让提单并注明承运人具体名称

B. 提单上的文字如有更改时，应有提单签署人的签字或签章

C. 提单日期不得迟于信用证上规定的最迟装运期

D. 提单向指定银行提示的日期原则上不得迟于提单签发日后21天

E. 提单日期可以早于信用证的开证日期

12. 进出口商品单价包括（　　）。

A. 计量单位　　　　　B. 计算重量的方法　C. 单位价格金额

D. 计价货币　　　　　E. 贸易术语

13. 国际贸易单证中的"标准运输标志"包括下列（　　）。

A. 目的地　　　　　B. 件数编号　　　　　C. 收货人

D. 货物数量　　　　E. 参考号（合同号、订单号等）

14. 多式联运应该具备以下（　　）条件。

A. 必须一个多式联运合同

B. 必须两种或两种以上不同运输方式

C. 必须包括海运

D. 必须使用一份包括全程的多式联运单据

E. 必须是跨国运输

15. 下列关于海关发票的说法正确是（　　）。

A. 进口商凭以报关，进口海关估价完税的凭证

B. 进口国海关核定货物原产地

C. 作为进口国海关编制统计资料之用

D. 海关发票与商业发票的填制方法有差异

E. 海关发票采用的是进口国海关制定的格式

16. 国际贸易单证工作的基本环节包括（　　）。

A. 审单　　　　　B. 制单　　　　　C. 审证

D. 交单　　　　　E. 归档

17. 下列（　　）抬头的汇票可以转让。

A. PAY TO XXX CO.ONLY

B. PAY TO HOLDER

C. PAY TO BEARER

D. PAY TO XXX CO.OR ORDER

E. PAY TO XXX CO.，NOT TRANSFERBLE

18. 银行审单的内容包括（　　）。

A. 信用证规定的单证种类、份数是否齐全

B. 单证、单单是否相符

C. 单据上的装运港、目的港、装运日期等是否与信用证规定相符

D. 单据上的商品规格、品质、金额等是否与信用证规定相符

E. 付款方式、日期、运费是否与信用证相符

19. 一项有效的发盘，应该是（   ）。

A. 向一个特定的人发出

B. 向一个或一个以上特定的人发出

C. 内容完整且明确肯定

D. 表明受盘人一旦接受发盘的内容，发盘人当立即受到约束

E. 发盘必须送达受盘人

20. 用于议付信用证项下的汇票可以是（   ）。

A. 即期汇票   B. 远期汇票   C. 商业汇票

D. 银行汇票   E. 以上都对

21. 按《联合国国际货物销售合同公约》的规定，发盘中至少应包括（   ）。

A. 货物名称   B. 货物价格   C. 交易数量

D. 支付方式   E. 交货时间

22. 常见的原产地证明有（   ）。

A. S/C   B. C/O   C. GSP   D. B/L   E. S/O

23. 在出口货物装运前的（   ）环节要使用商业发票。

A. 托运订舱   B. 商品报检   C. 出口报关

D. 海关查验   E. 办理投保

24. 出口货物托运人缮制《国际货物托运委托书》的依据是（   ）。

A. 外销出仓单   B. 销售合同   C. 信用证

D. 配舱回单   E. 海运提单

25. 根据《INCOTERMS 2010》规定，下列贸易术语中，适用于各种运输方式的有
（   ）。

A. EXW   B. FOB   C. CFR

D. CPT   E. FCA

26. 采用 FOB 术语出口时，信用证项下单据至少包括（   ）。

A. 装箱单   B. 汇票   C. 海运提单

D. 保险单   E. 商业发票

27. 进口商申请开立信用证的程序包括（   ）。

A. 递交有关合同副本及附件   B. 填写开证申请书   C. 缴付保证金

D. 支付开证手续费   E. 在开证申请书背面签字

28. 以下单据中对发票起补充说明作用的有（   ）。

A. 保险单   B. 尺码单   C. 重量单

D. 装箱单   E. 提单

29. 下列（   ）单证属于报关基本单证。

A. 商业发票   B. 贸易合同   C. 装箱单

D. 保险单   E. 海运提单

30. 根据《票据法》，汇票上必须记载的事项包括(　　)等内容。

A. 确定的金额　　　B. 汇票日期　　　C. 付款人名称

D. 汇票编号　　　　E. 付款期限

三、判断题 (60 小题，每题 0.5 分，共 30 分。答案为"是"的，请在答题卡上涂 A，答案为"否"的，请在答题卡上涂 B)

(　　)1. 运输包装上的标志就是运输标志，也就是通常所说的唛头。

(　　)2. 在出口业务中，采用 FOB 上海成交，卖方只需将货物交至上海港买方指定的船上。

(　　)3. FCA、CPT 和 CIP 三种贸易术语不仅适用于各种单一的运输方式，而且适用于多式联运。

(　　)4. 出口商采用 D/A30 天比采用 D/P60 天承担的风险要大。

(　　)5. 必须经过背书方可转让的提单是指示提单。

(　　)6. 根据我国海洋运输货物保险条款的规定，如投保一切险，保险公司对被保险货物在海运途中由于任何外来原因造成的损坏灭失，均应负责赔偿。

(　　)7. 由生产制造厂商提供的货物出厂装箱单中显示的货物具体规格、型号、数量、毛重、净重、尺码等是缮制装箱单的基本依据。

(　　)8. 票汇业务和托收业务都是商业信用，使用的都是商业汇票。

(　　)9. 根据《UCP 600》，除非信用证另有规定，商业发票应由开证申请人签发，必须做成受益人的抬头。

(　　)10. 我公司对外发盘，其中规定"限 8 月 15 日复到"。外商接受通知于 8 月 17 日上午到达我方。根据《联合国国际货物销售合同公约》，如我公司同意接受并立即予以确认，合同仍可成立。

(　　)11. 根据《联合国国际货物销售合同公约》的规定，买卖合同成立的一般程序是询盘、发盘、还盘、接受和签订书面合同。

(　　)12. 凡是逾期送达要约人的承诺，只要要约人缄默，合同即告成立。

(　　)13. 按我国有关规定，对于需要法定检验的商品，必须在报关前完成商检手续。

(　　)14. 货物外包装上的运输标志须在有关的托运单、商业发票、装箱单、提单上显示，但是指示性标志、警告性标志无须在上述单据上显示。

(　　)15. 一张纸质报关单上最多可打印 5 项商品；一张电子报关单最多允许打印 15 项商品。

(　　)16. 以 CIF 出口时，如合同和信用证中无特别规定，保险单中"INSURED"一栏应填写进口商名称。

(　　)17. 银行对于信用证未规定的单据将不予审核。

(　　)18. 单证工作能及时反映货、船、证等业务的管理情况，为了杜绝差错事故的发生，避免带来不必要的经济损失，单证员必须加强工作责任心。

（　　　）19. 还盘在形式上不同于拒绝，但还盘和拒绝都可导致原发盘的失效。

（　　　）20. 汇票、本票、支票都可以分为即期和远期。

（　　　）21. 第二受益人将可转让信用证再转让回给第一受益人是不允许的。

（　　　）22. 一张未记载付款日期的汇票，按惯例可理解为见票后 21 天付款。

（　　　）23. 空白抬头、空白背书的提单是指提单收货人一栏内空白而不需要背书的提单。

（　　　）24. 如果汇票上加注"货物到达后支付"，根据我国《票据法》，该汇票无效。

（　　　）25. 卖方发盘，限买方在 6 月 10 日复到。8 日下午，卖方收到买方复电，要求减价并修改交货期，次日上午又收到买方来电，接受发盘。卖方对此未做任何表示。此时，合同按卖方发盘条件已达成。

（　　　）26. 我某公司对外签发一张汇票，上面注明"AT 45 DAYS AFTER SIGHT"，这张汇票是远期汇票。

（　　　）27. 交单是指在合同、信用证规定的时间，以正确的方式，将符合合同要求的单证交给正确的当事人。

（　　　）28. 某公司出口一批货物，合同规定 2013 年 5 月份装船。信用证规定："shipment after April 10th till 30th"。该公司于 5 月 7 日装船，并取得提单。交单时遭到拒付，银行拒付是无理的。

（　　　）29. 出口商品检验证书的出证日期和保险单的出单日期均不得迟于提单日期。

（　　　）30. 如信用证要求提供 SIGNED INVOICE，则受益人必须在发票上进行签署。

（　　　）31. 信用证规定：FROM CHINA PORT TO LONDON 发票上应严格按照信用证要求填上"FROM CHINA PORT TO LONDON"。

（　　　）32. 不可撤销议付信用证列有"议付到期日"，而未列有"最迟装运日"，则应被理解为"双到期"，即最迟装运日与到期日为同一天。

（　　　）33. 不使用海关发票或领事发票的国家，通常要求出口商提供原产地证明书，以确定对货物征税的税率。

（　　　）34. 信用证规定的装运期是 6 月 30 日，有效期是 7 月 15 日，交单期是提单日期后 21 天。若实际装船日是 6 月 25，受益人可以于 7 月 16 日交单。

（　　　）35. 保险单据的签发日期应迟于提单签发日期。

（　　　）36. 发盘人在其提出的订约建议中加注诸如"仅供参考""须以发盘人的最后确认为准"或其他类似的保留条件，这样的订约建议就不是发盘，而只是发盘的邀请。

（　　　）37. 汇票经背书后，汇票的收款权利就转让给了被背书人，被背书人若日后遭拒付可向其前手行使追索权。

（　　　）38. 如果合同和信用证中均未规定具体唛头，货物为大宗散装货物，则发票的唛头栏可以留空不填。

（　　　）39. 按《UCP 600》若信用证没有明确禁止，商业发票的出票日期可以早于信用证的开证日期。

（　　）40. 信用证只规定了货物总称，发票除了要照样显示外，还可以加列详细的货名，可以与总称不一致。

（　　）41. 根据《INCOTERMS 2010》的规定，FOB 条件下，货物风险转移界限为装运港船上，但若因买方的原因无法按期装运，风险可以提前转移。

（　　）42. 在我国所有的进出口企业都必须亲自向海关办理报关手续。

（　　）43. 根据《联合国国际货物销售合同公约》规定，采用口头发盘时，除非发盘人另有声明，受盘人应立即表示接受方为有效。

（　　）44. 按 FOB、CFR、CIF 术语成交，货物在装运港装上船后，风险即告转移。因此，货到目的港后，买方如发现货物品质、数量、包装等与合同规定不符，卖方概不负责。

（　　）45. 信用证是一种银行开立的无条件承诺付款的书面文件。

（　　）46. 象征性交货的特点是卖方凭单交货，买方凭单付款。

（　　）47.《INCOTERMS 2010》中，买方责任最大的术语是 EXW，最小的是DDP。

（　　）48. 询盘对发盘人是没有约束力的。

（　　）49. 不同运输方式下的运输单据都是承运人签发给托运人的货物收据，都是物权凭证，都可凭此向目的地承运人提货。

（　　）50. 根据《INCOTERMS 2010》，在 FOB 术语条件下，如合同未规定"装船通知"条款，卖方将货物装船后可不发装船通知。

（　　）51. 信用证支付方式中，议付行若遭开证行拒绝，不得对受益人进行追索。

（　　）52. 不含佣金和折扣的价格称净价。

（　　）53. 填写开证申请书，必须按合同条款的具体规定，写明对信用证的各项要求，内容要明确完整、无词义不清的记载。

（　　）54. 根据《UCP 600》，凡信用证上未注明"可转让"字样的，就是不可转让信用证。

（　　）55. 货物装船后，托运人凭船公司的装货单换取已装船提单。

（　　）56. Drawee 是指汇票的出票人，一般情况下是开证行。

（　　）57. 某商品每箱体积为 30cm×40cm×50cm，毛重为 62kgs，如果班轮运费计收标准为 W/M，则船公司应按尺码吨计收运费。

（　　）58. 活牲畜、汽车等商品出口按重量计算运费。

（　　）59."你方 2 月 9 日电悉，所提出的各项条件接受，另在外包装左侧刷唛头。"这则传真属于接受。

（　　）60. 出票就是出票人在汇票上写明有关内容并签名的行为。

2014年全国国际商务单证专业考试
国际商务单证缮制与操作试题

一、根据下述合同内容审核信用证，指出不符之处，并提出修改意见。(36 分)

SHANGHAI ANDYS TRADING CO., LTD.

SALES CONTRACT

THE SELLER: SHANGHAI ANDYS TRADING CO., LTD.   NO. AD13007

NO. 126 Wenhua Road, Shanghai, China   DATE: MAR. 16, 2013

SIGNED AT: SHANGHAI, CHINA

THE BUYER: HAZZE AB HOLDING

BOX 1237, S-111 21 HUDDINGE, SWEDEN

This contract is made by and between the Seller and Buyer, whereby the Seller agree to sell and the Buyer agree to buy the under-mentioned commodity according to the terms and conditions stipulated below:

Commodity & specification	Quan.	Unit price	Amount
Gas Detectors		FOB SHANGHAI	
ART NO.BX616	50 pcs	USD 380.00/pc	USD 19 000.00
ART NO.BX319	50 pcs	USD 170.00/pc	USD 8 500.00
Total	100 pcs		USD 27 500.00
Total Amount: SAY U.S. DOLLARS TWENTY SEVEN THOUSAND AND FIVE HUNDRED ONLY			

PACKING: In Carton.

TIME OF SHIPMENT: During July, 2013.

PLACE OF LOADING AND DESTINATION:

From Shanghai, China to Stockholm, Sweden

Partial shipment and transshipment are allowed.

INSURANCE: To be effected by the Buyer.

SHIPPING MARKS:

HAZZE

AD2013007

STOCKHOLM, SWEDEN

NOS.1- UP

TERMS OF PAYMENT: By irrevocable L/C at sight which should be issued before May 31, 2013, valid for negotiation in China for further 15 days after time of shipment.

INSPECTION：In the factory.

This contract is made in two original copies and become valid after signature，one copy to be held by each party.

Signed by：

THE SELLER　　　　　　THE BUYER

SHANGHAI ANDYS TRADING CO.，LTD.　　HAZZE AB HOLDING

Andynar　　　　　　　　　　　　Hazze

信用证：

MT 700		ISSUE OF A DOCUMENTARY CREDIT
SENDER		SWEDBANK
RECEIVER		BANK OF CHINA，SHANGHAI，CHINA
SEQUENCE OF TOTAL	27	1 / 1
FORM OF DOC.CREDIT	40A	IRREVOCABLE
DOC. CREDIT NUMBER	20	BCN1008675
DATE OF ISSUE	31C	130612
APPLICABLE RULES	40E	UCP LATEST VERSION
DATE AND PLACE OF EXPIRY.	31D	DATE 130630 PLACE IN SWEDEN
APPLICANT	50	HAZZE ABC HOLDING BOX 1237，S-111 21 HUDDINGE，SWEDEN
BENEFICIARY	59	SHANGHAI ANDY TRADING CO.，LTD. NO. 126 WENHUAROAD，SHANGHAI，CHINA.
AMOUNT	32B	CURRENCY EUR AMOUNT 27，000.00
AVAILABLE WITH/BY	41D	ANY BANK IN CHINA， BY NEGOTIATION
DRAFTS AT ...	42C	30 DAYS AFTER SIGHT
DRAWEE	42A	HAZZE AB HOLDING
PARTIAL SHIPMTS	44P	NOT ALLOWED
TRANSSHIPMENT	44T	NOT ALLOWED
PORT OF LOADING	44E	TIANJIN，CHINA
PORT OF DISCHARGE	44F	STOCKHOLM，SWEDEN
LATEST SHIPMENT	44C	130615
DESCRIPTION OF GOODS	45A	1000 PCS OF GAS DETECTORS AS PER S/C NO.AD13007 CIF STOCKHOLM PACKED IN CARTONS
DOCUMENTS REQUIRED	46A	+COMMERCIAL INVOICE SIGNED MANUALLY IN TRIPLICATE. + PACKING LIST IN TRIPLICATE. + CERTIFICATE OF CHINESE ORIGIN CERTIFIED BY CHAMBER OF COMMERCE.

（续表）

MT 700		ISSUE OF A DOCUMENTARY CREDIT
		+ INSURANCE POLICY/CERTIFICATE IN DUPLICATE ENDORSED IN BLANK FOR 110% INVOICE VALUE, COVERING ALL RISKS AND WAR RISK OF CIC OF PICC (1/1/1981).
		+ FULL SET OF CLEAN 'ON BOARD' OCEAN BILLS OF LADING MADE OUT TO ORDER MARKED FREIGHT PREPAID AND NOTIFY APPLICANT.
ADDITIONAL CONDITION	47A	+ ALL PRESENTATIONS CONTAINING DISCREPANCIES WILL ATTRACT A DISCREPANCY FEE OF USD50.00. THIS CHARGE WILL BE DEDUCTED FROM THE BILL AMOUNT WHETHER OR NOT WE ELECT TO CONSULT THE APPLICANT FOR A WAIVER.
CHARGES	71B	ALL CHARGES AND COMMISSIONS ARE FOR ACCOUNT OF BENEFICIARY.
CONFIRMATION INSTRUCTION	49	WITHOUT

二、根据下面相关资料指出下列进口单据中错误的地方，并改正。(24 分)

相关资料：

卖方：La GUYENNOISE GROUP

      3 RUE DES ANCIENS COMBATTANTS 33460 SOUSSANS FRANCE

授权签字人：MAITY

买方：TIANJIN LINBEICHEN COMMERCE AND TRADE CO.，LTD.

      NO. 81 JINGSAN ROAD，TIANJIN，CHINA

授权签字人：林晓婉

货物描述：12 000 PCS OF BOTTLED WINE

包装：2 000 WOODEN CASES

W.G：21 000 KGS

N.W：15 000 KGS

MEAS.：31 CBM

开证行：BANK OF CHINA，TIANJIN BRANCH

信用证号：LC14231679

开证日期：May. 15 2014

汇票金额：EUR 83 340.00

付款期限：即期

出票日期：MAY. 1，2014

议付行：BANQUE NATIONALE PARIS

合同号：LBC14005

发票号：LBC2014015

贸易术语：FOB

装运港：FOS

目的港：TIANJIN

1. 汇票（每错1分，共12分）

BILL OF EXCHANGE

Drawn under：<u>BANQUE NATIONALE PARIS</u> L/C N0. <u>LC14231670</u> Dated：<u>May. 15，2013</u>

No. <u>LBC2013015</u> Exchange for <u>€ 83，430.00 Paris</u>　　　　Date：MAY 1，2013

At <u>30 days after</u> sight of this FIRST of Exchange(Second of Exchange being unpaid)

pay to the order of<u>　BANK OF CHINA，TIANJIN BRANCH　　　　　　</u>

the sum of <u>SAY EURO EIGHTY THREE THOUSAND FOUR HUNDRED AND THIRTY ONLY.</u>

To：BANQUE NATIONALE PARIS

　　　　　　　　TIANJIN LINBEICHEN COMMERCE AND TRADE CO.，LTD.

　　　　　　　　　　　　　Laura

2. 订舱委托书（每错1分，共12分）

WO 万侨物流		海运进口货物订舱委托书			
装运港： TIANJIN	目的港： FOS	合同号： LBC13005	出口国： FRANCE	委托单位编号： LBC2014016	
唛头标记及号码	包装件数	货物描述	重量（公斤）	尺码（立方米）	
N/M	12 000 WOODEN CASES	BOTTLED RED WINE	W.G: 20 000 KGS N.W: 16 000 KGS	30 CBM	
				价格条件： CFR	
托运人 (Shipper)： TIANJIN LINBEICHEN COMMERCE AND TRADE CO.，LTD. NO. 81 JINGSAN ROAD，TIANJIN CHINA				需要提单正本 3 份；副本 3 份	
收货人 (Consignee)： TO ORDER				信用证号： LC14231679	
				装期：140430 效期：140515	
				可否分批：NO 可否转运：NO	
被通知人 (Notify Party)： LA GUYENNOISE GROUP 3 RUE DES ANCIENS COMBATTANTS 33460 SOUSSANS FRANCE				运费支付： FREIGHT 　COLLECT	
特约事项：					
委托单位名称：TIANJIN LINBEICHEN COMMERCE AND TRADE CO.，LTD. 联系人：林晓婉　电话：0086-022-86759221　传真：0086-022-86759229					

三、根据第一大题的合同和下面资料缮制下列单据。请在答题纸上作答。（共 40 分）

制单资料：

发票号：AD2013011　　　　发票日期：2013 年 7 月 5 日

贸易方式：一般贸易

装船日期：2013 年 7 月 20 日　　船名、航次号："HAIHE" V. 917

提单号：TA5019E

包装：纸箱装，每箱装 10PCS

毛重：260KGS　　　　　　体积：15.8cbm

HS 编码：90271000

授权签署人：ANDYS

参考文献

I. 常用资源类网站

1. 中华人民共和国商务部，http://www.mofcom.gov.cn/

2. 中华人民共和国海关总署，http://www.customs.gov.cn/

3. 阿里巴巴，http://china.alibaba.com/

4. 中国企业在线，http://www.71ab.com/

5. 中华大黄页，http://www.chinabig.net/

6. 中国进出口商品网，http://www.cantonfairtrading.org.cn/

7. World Trade Organization，http://www.wto.org/

8. 中国展览网，http://www.sino-expo.com.cn/

9. 中国国际展览中心集团公司，http://www.ciec-expo.com/ciecnew/index.html

10. 中国展览交易网，http://marketccnf.xiaomi001.com/

11. 中国反倾销反补贴保障措施网上图书馆，http://www.zftec.gov.cn/gpmy/yqlj/gnyq/T161119.shtml

12. 中国国际货运代理协会，http://www.cifa.org.cn/

13. 东方海外货柜航运有限公司，http://www.oocl.com/schi/Pages/default.aspx

14. A. P. MOLLER 马士基集团，http://www.maersk.com/

15. P & O NEDLOY 铁行渣华，http://www.ponl.com/

16. 中国国家税务总局，http://www.chinatax.gov.cn/

II. 参考书目

1. 谢娟娟. 国际贸易单证实务与操作 [M]. 北京：清华大学出版社，2007

2. 郑椒援，邹建华. 实用进出口单证 [M]. 北京：电子工业出版社，2005

3. 耿伟. 出口贸易单证实务 [M]. 北京：首都经济贸易大学出版社，2003

4. 余世明. 国际商务单证 [M]. 广州：暨南大学出版社，2001

5. 周端赎，王小欧，徐月芳. 国际贸易实务 [M]. 北京：对外经济贸易大学出版社，2008

6. 姚大伟. 国际贸易单证实务 [M]. 北京：中国对外经济贸易出版社，2002

7. 刘启萍，周树玲. 外贸英文制单 [M]. 北京：对外经济贸易大学出版社，2006

8. 黎孝先. 国际贸易实务 [M]. 北京：对外经济贸易大学出版社，2007

9. 郑淑媛，邹建华. 外贸单证模拟实训 [M]. 海口：南海出版公司，2003

10. 全国国际商务单证专业培训考试办公室 . 国际商务单证理论与实务 (2008 版)[M]. 北京：中国商务出版社，2007

11. 易露霞 . 国际贸易实务双语教程 [M]. 北京：清华大学出版社出版，2010

12. [美] 布朗奇 . 国际贸易实务 (第 5 版)[M]. 北京：清华大学出版社，2008

13. Edward G. Hinkelman. International Trade Documentation，3_{rd} edition[M]. Novato：World Trade Press，2008

14. Thomas E. Johnson. Export/Import Procedures and Documentation，4_{th} edition[M]. New York：Ama.com，2002